THE GUINNESS BOOK OF
BRITISH
ROYALTY

(i)

(ii)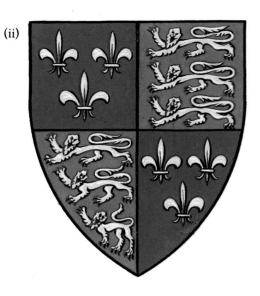

(iii)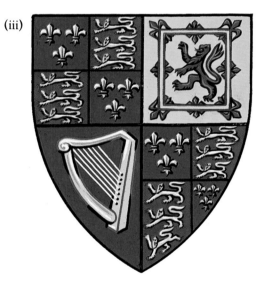

(iv)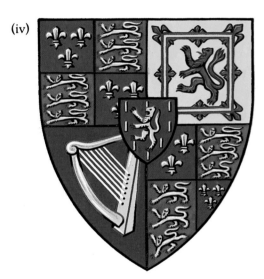

(v)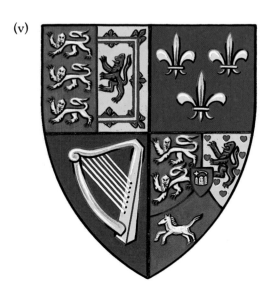

(vi)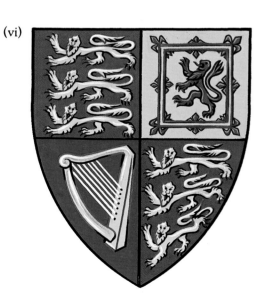

THE GUINNESS BOOK OF
BRITISH
ROYALTY

by Geoffrey Hindley

GUINNESS BOOKS

Editor: Beatrice Frei
Design and Layout: Eric Drewery
Picture Editor: Alex Goldberg

© Geoffrey Hindley 1989

Published in Great Britain by Guinness Publishing Ltd,
33 London Road, Enfield, Middlesex

Typeset in Itek Goudy by
Ace Filmsetting Ltd, Frome, Somerset
Printed and bound in Italy by
New Interlitho SpA, Milan

'Guinness' is a registered trade mark of Guinness Superlatives Ltd

British Library Cataloguing in Publication Data
Hindley, Geoffrey, 1935–
    The Guinness book of British royalty
    1. Great Britain. Royal families.
    I. Title.
    941'. 009'92

    ISBN 0-85112-383-x

Frontispiece: The six shields are a sketch history of the British monarchy over the past 800 years. The idea of a personal coat of arms did not come into fashion before the 12th century—neither William the Conqueror nor his Anglo-Saxon predecessors King Edward the Confessor and Harold II had their own personal devices. However, in 1189, King Richard I adopted the symbol of a single lion rampant and then, on his second great seal of 1198, displayed the three lions which have remained the arms of England ever since. (i) In the terms of 'blazon', the language of heraldry, the coat is described as gules (i.e. red), 'three lions passant guardant or' (i.e. gold). This remained the royal arms until 1340 when King Edward put forward his claim to the French crown and adopted the 'quartered' French royal arms along with England's (ii). Then, in 1603, King James VI of Scotland succeeded Queen Elizabeth I to the throne of England. The royal arms of England were put in the first and fourth quarters of the shield, the arms of Scotland ('or, a lion rampant within a double tressure flory counterflory gules') in the second quarter and those of Ireland ('azure (i.e. blue) a harp or stringed argent (i.e. silver)) in the third (King Henry VIII had been granted the hereditary title King of Ireland in 1541).

These Stuart arms (iii) remained the royal arms of England until 1689 when William III (of Nassau Orange) and his wife Mary II displaced James II. Control of England was an important part of the Dutch king's European policy against France. His shield shows four realms under the house of Nassau whose lion is superimposed on its own 'escutcheon', or inner shield (iv). When the German family of Brunswick Luneberg, the Electors (i.e. rulers) of Hanover, came to the throne in the person of George I in 1714, Britain's royal arms changed yet again, the arms of Hanover being placed in the fourth quarter (v). In 1801, the French claim being finally abandoned, the French fleur de lys were also dropped from the coat of arms. Then, in 1837, the death of King William IV who was also ruler of Hanover, and the succession of his niece Victoria, meant the end of the Hanover connection, since by Hanoverian law a woman could not succeed. So, in 1837, the royal arms of the United Kingdom took the form we know today (vi).

Title page: Her Majesty Queen Elizabeth II.

Over page: The scene outside St Paul's for Queen Victoria's Diamond Jubilee.

CONTENTS

PICTURE CREDITS

Front Cover
Camera Press, Photograph by Albert Watson

Back Cover
All Sport
Keystone
Royal Collection

Special thanks to:
Marcus Bishop M.V.O., Registrar of the Royal Collection
Rob and Rhoda Burns (maps)
Charles Heath-Saunders (artwork)
Siobhan Hewitt
Anne Jones
O'Reilly Clark (genealogical tables)
Judith Prendergast
Ronald Sheridan
Peter Spurrier, Portcullis, Pursuivant of Arms

Other Illustrations
All Sport
Ancient Art & Architecture Collection
Anwar Hussein
Ashmolean Museum
Bridgeman Art Library
British Library
British Rail
Buckingham Palace
Fotomas
Guildhall Library
Her Majesty's Stationery Office
The Hulton Picture Company
The Irish Tourist Board
Keystone Collection (Hulton Picture Company)
The Mansell Collection
Mary Evans Picture Library
The National Gallery of Scotland
The National Maritime Museum
The National Portrait Gallery
The Photo Source
Popperfoto
Rex Features
The Royal Academy of Arts
The Royal Collection
Spectrum Colour Library
The Victoria & Albert Museum
Wales Tourist Board
Weidenfeld (Publishers) Ltd
Westminster Cathedral Library

INTRODUCTION

The Guinness Book of British Royalty has been written and designed so as to offer both a narrative and analytical account of its subject. The text is set in a pageant of brilliant pictures, both colour and black and white whose captions are an essential part of the text presentation. A glance at the contents page will guide the reader to that aspect of monarchy and its story that he or she may wish to begin with, from the facts, figures and theories of monarchy's chronicles to the dangers and hazards which have beset royalty through the ages. Alternatively, the text can be read as a developing sequence, from the Queen's title which describes her unique position in the world, to the working life and grand occasions of a very special life style. Each section is prefaced by a brief introduction which expands the information on the contents page and in every section the monarchs of the past are referred to, to illustrate or highlight aspects of the theme being discussed. Where readers want to follow up a special personality mentioned in the section they are reading, they should refer to the comprehensive and detailed index.

A few conventions are followed. The essay sections begin with the modern examples before tracing the history of their aspect of royalty. In references to events in a king's life before he came to the throne, his regnal number is sometimes included in square brackets after his name to facilitate identification.

There have been times when the future of the British monarchy may have seemed in jeopardy. Today it appears to be secure. King Farouk of Egypt once famously quipped, 'there will soon be only five kings left—the King of Spades, Hearts, Diamonds, Clubs and of England'. Certainly the succession to the throne is well secured.

THE ORDER OF SUCCESSION

The first 10 in line to the British throne are as follows:

1 HRH The Prince of Wales, then follows his son
2 HRH Prince William of Wales, then his brother
3 HRH Prince Henry of Wales, then their uncle
4 HRH The Duke of York, then his daughter
5 HRH Princess Beatrice of York, then her uncle
6 HRH The Prince Edward, then his sister
7 HRH The Princess Royal, then her son
8 Peter Phillips, Esq., then his sister
9 Zara Phillips, then her great aunt
10 HRH The Princess Margaret, Countess of Snowdon

CHRONICLE OF ROYALTY

To set the scene for the pageant of royalty which is the book's theme, this section opens up the story by investigating the meaning and historical background to the title of the present Queen. This leads naturally to a discussion of the origins and history of the various territorial divisions of the United Kingdom of Great Britain and Northern Ireland and an exploration of their Celtic and Saxon royal antecedents. From the title of the monarch herself and its background the text moves on to the heir to the crown and his traditional title 'Prince of Wales'. Next follows the listings of the kings and queens who have ruled in Scotland and England over the past thousand years. The chronicles of the royals are followed by a picture spread describing some of the friends, favourites and mistresses of monarchy in the past. The section concludes with a discussion of just what makes a monarch by examining the idea of the 'pretender' through the centuries, and by showing how the laws which now govern the succession to the throne have taken generations to evolve and how that evolution was broken more than once by rulers who, nowadays, would be considered to have had very poor hereditary claims to the crown. The links in the chain, as it was actually forged over history, are made clear by a group of family trees.

Right: A 13th-century view of four earlier English kings. From the top left they are William I the Conqueror, William II 'Rufus', Henry I and Stephen. The artist was the 13th-century churchman and chronicler Matthew Paris.

Left: As Head of the Commonwealth, a title she greatly values, Elizabeth II is also Queen of numerous territories overseas. Here her subjects of Tuvalu in the Pacific proudly bear their monarch ashore on the ceremonial canoe barge in which they have rowed her to the island from the royal yacht *Britannia*. Her ancestor, the 10th-century King Edgar of England, was once rowed by eight lesser British kings on the River Dee.

ORIGINS, TITLES AND TERRITORIES

Origins

In 1989, the bicentenary year of the French Revolution which upturned one of Europe's oldest monarchies and opened the way to the founding of a great republic, books on Britain's royalty might seem quaint or old fashioned. Not so. In France herself the British Royal Family is constantly in the media. More significant and interesting is the fact that in the European Community, of which both France and England are members, of the 12 member states six are monarchies. The ancient institution of government is still very much alive.

The British monarchy has its roots in ancient Germanic and Celtic traditions. At first in both of them kings were essentially war leaders heading small tribal groups but in the Germanic tradition the office of king came to be associated with rule over territory as well. From an early time kings in the Germanic tradition were thought to have divine ancestry. Early in the 400s Britain, until that time part of the Roman empire, was deserted by the Roman legions and raiders from the Continent, among them Angles and Saxons from Germany, began to occupy the country. These tribal groupings were headed by leaders who claimed descent from the Germanic god Woden, patron both of harvest and war. To this day, adventurous genealogists claim the same descent for Queen Elizabeth II. If medieval churchmen were right, her descent would reach back still further for they provided the pagan Woden himself with a set of ancestors which took his descent back to Adam.

Whether or not she is the lineal descendant of the founder of the human race, Her Majesty Queen Elizabeth II has a venerable lineage reaching back at least to King Egbert of Wessex in the early 800s. But where Egbert was praised by contemporaries because his authority was recognized throughout the midlands and south of England, Her Majesty is recognized as Queen by nations far beyond the confines of the British Isles. In addition to the United Kingdom, she is also the sovereign of: Antigua and Barbuda, Australia, Bahamas, Barbados, Belize, Canada, Grenada, Jamaica, Mauritius, New Zealand, Papua New Guinea, Saint Christopher and Nevis, Saint Lucia, Saint Vincent and the Grenadines, Solomon Islands, and Tuvalu.

Variations in the royal title

Over the centuries, variations in the royal title have indicated changes in the reality and perception of royal powers. The Queen's title in the United Kingdom is: 'Elizabeth the Second, by the Grace of God of the United Kingdom of Great Britain and Northern Ireland and of her other Realms and Territories Queen. Head

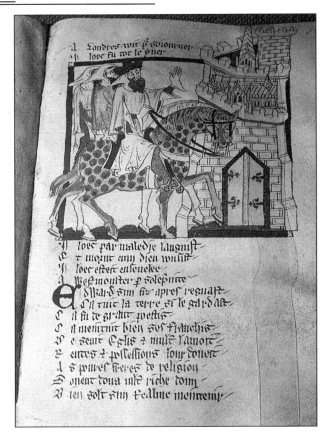

According to a medieval legend, Britain was so called because its first ruler had been the Trojan Brutus, who had established his rule at Totnes in Devon even before the coming of the Romans. For this reason early histories and chronicles of Britain were sometimes called 'Chronicles of Brut'. This page, from a 1340s example, depicts King Edward I (d. 1307) who was regarded as a hero because of his victories over the Scots and Welsh.

of the Commonwealth, Defender of the Faith.' There is history in almost every word. It was not until the reign of King Henry VIII that sovereigns began to number themselves. (It was in his reign, too, that the term Majesty first became the standard mode of address; until that time 'Your Grace' was often heard.) From Henry, too, comes the title 'Defender of the Faith' awarded to him by the Pope for a treatise Henry wrote against the teachings of Luther. It was also Henry who assumed the title 'King of Ireland'. Another pope had conferred the 'lordship' of Ireland on Henry II, back in the 12th century.

The fact that the Queen is described in her title as ruler of 'territories' seems obvious enough today. However, her earliest predecessors called themselves kings, not of England or Wessex, but of the English or the West Saxons. The term King of Scots continued the usual style in Scotland until the union of the crowns in the person of King James VI and I in 1603. The Old English king Athelstan proudly called himself king of all Britain, but this was more a hopeful assertion of overlordship over other kings than a truly territorial designation. This first appears in the royal title of Henry I in 1100, who called himself 'King of England'.

Four hundred years earlier the historian Bede had used a strange term which seems to have had some feeling of territorial meaning behind it. Writing in the 730s he applied the term 'Bretwalda' to seven early regional kings of England: Aelle of Sussex (d. *c.* 500), Ceawlin of Wessex (d. 593), Æthelberht of Kent (d. 616), Redwald of East Anglia (d. *c.* 627); Edwin of Northumbria (d. 632); Oswald of Northumbria (d. 641); and Oswiu of Northumbria (d. 670). Later the Anglo Saxon Chronicle added the name of Egbert of Wessex (d. 839). Historians still debate what significance the term had for people at the time. It seems to have been rather an academic word, for no king ever used it of himself. Certainly, it was ancient even when Bede used it. It may merely have meant extensive rule, the 'bret' being related to the word 'broad', or it may have recalled a dim memory of a time when all Britain acknowledged one authority (in this interpretation the 'Bret' relates to Britain). Perhaps the word echoed distant memories of Roman times when Britain had recognized the single rule of Rome.

Of all the Anglo Saxon ruling houses who boasted descent from the continental god Woden, only the kings of Mercia could actually trace a known historical ancestor from their continental past. The name Mercia probably meant 'marchlands' (i.e. border country) and recalls the long decades of Germanic encroachment into British territories as frontiersmen pushed westward, leaving the safety of the conquered territories of the East Angles behind them. By the mid-eighth century, these Angles of the March dominated their neighbours. King Æthelbald of Mercia (716–57) styled himself king of the Southern English and even king of Britain.

With Æthelbald's successor, Offa of Mercia (757–96), we come to the first great figure in early English history. With the massive earthwork, Offa's Dyke (between England and Wales), he left his name on the landscape of the country and demonstrated his great wealth and power with England's first silver coinage. In the year 787, hoping to ensure the succession, Offa had his son Egfrith 'hallowed' as king, probably the first such religious consecration in the history of English royalty.

Before this time rulers had occasionally used the words *gratia dei*, 'by the grace of God'. Offa (who in fact outlived his son) employed the intriguing formula 'by the divine controlling grace king of the Mercians' and also called himself 'king of the whole land of the Eng-

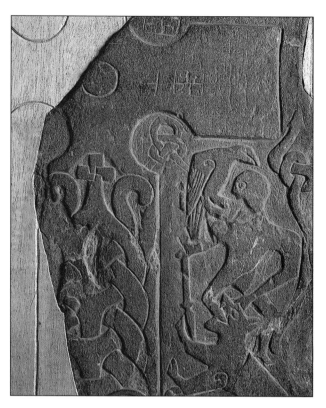

The early English kings of the diverse Anglo Saxon kingdoms of the early Middle Ages boasted their descent from a Norse god known to the Vikings as Odin but to other northern Germanic peoples as Wotan or, as in England, Woden. His attributes were almost as numerous as the different tribal kingdoms who worshipped him but in all traditions he was considered to be the patron of war. The raven was one of his symbols. This ninth-century carving depicts Odin of the Vikings, at that time busily making war on their distant English royal cousins.

One of the greatest rulers of early medieval England was King Offa the Great of Mercia (in the English Midlands). He forced homage from all neighbouring kings and established a fine silver coinage. This depiction of the great King, on one of his coins, shows him with the long hair considered an attribute of kingship among certain Germanic peoples.

lish'. In fact Mercia seemed poised to conquer the whole country. But then in 825 King Egbert of the West Saxons defeated Beornwulf of Mercia. Following this victory, Egbert was acknowledged as king in Kent, Sussex, East Anglia and Essex and later even the Northumbrians 'offered him submission and peace'. Egbert's descendant Alfred, the only ruler in England ever to have been honoured with the designation the Great, appears on his coins as both 'king of the English' and 'king of the Saxons'. His grandson Athelstan occasionally used 'Basileus', the official title of the East Roman emperor, while Edgar the Peaceful (959–75) was called by an admiring monkish chronicler 'Edgar

the Glorious, by the Grace of Christ illustrious king of the English and of the other peoples within the bounds of the island of Britain'.

It was no idle boast. At Chester, in the year 973, Edgar received the homage of the kings of Strathclyde and the Scots and of five Welsh kings. According to a well founded tradition they symbolized their homage by rowing the King in his state barge down the River Dee at Chester. Edgar also bore the traditional title of *rex anglorum* as did his son Æthelred II. With Cnut the royal title changed yet again for he was not only king of the English but also of Denmark and Norway. Edward the Confessor (son of Æthelred II) used the style

Left: King James VI and I of Scotland and England. King James, who through his mother Mary Queen of Scots was descended from Henry VII of England, succeeded the childless Elizabeth I of England on her death in 1603. The full union of the two Crowns did not take place until 1707.

Right: The ring of King Æthelwulf of Wessex, father of Alfred the Great. Its shape, reminiscent of a bishop's mitre, may be no coincidence since in Old English the word used to describe the ritual consecration of a king was the same as that used for the consecration of a bishop.

Below: The famous depiction of King Harold II of the English shown at his coronation, on the Bayeux Tapestry. Archbishop Stigand of Canterbury is shown in the act of presenting the new king to the people—a vital part of the coronation ritual. In fact, the Pope regarded Stigand as schismatic and accordingly gave his blessing to the campaign of conquest launched by William of Normandy in 1066. Only seven years before, William himself had been an excommunicate on a technicality concerning his marriage.

'*Anglorum Basileus*'. His successor for nine months, Harold II, is shown proudly enthroned as '*rex anglorum*' on the Bayeux tapestry. Slain at Hastings, he was followed by 'William, Duke of the Normans and King of the English'. William's son Henry I adopted the style 'King of England' as did his successor Stephen. Henry's daughter Matilda, on the other hand, was never crowned and instead of 'Queen' bore the title 'Lady of the English'.

Over the centuries, then, Her Majesty's predecessors have boasted an array of titles from Dukes of Normandy (still the title by which she is known in the Channel Islands) and Dukes of Aquitaine, to Counts of Anjou and Electors of Hanover (1714–1815). When the Congress of Vienna raised Hanover to the status of a kingdom (in June 1815) George III, George IV and William IV enjoyed an additional royal title. However, the law of succession in Hanover did not permit women to rule. So Hanover missed out on a Victorian age and had Ernst August, Duke of Cumberland and George III's fifth son as king instead (reigned 1837–51). For close on 500 years England's rulers claimed to be rulers of France.

The story began in 1340 with King Edward III who claimed to have inherited the French crown through his mother, the French Princess Isabel. Edward and his descendants did conquer large areas of France—the nine-year-old Henry VI was even crowned King of France in 1431. When Mary I lost Calais in 1558 it must have seemed the adventure was over but 100 years later Cromwell took Dunkirk. The town was sold back to Louis XIV by his client Charles II who nevertheless retained the anachronistic claim to the French crown.

In May 1707 England and Scotland had become one and Queen Anne became the first sovereign of Great Britain and Ireland. In 1801, with a second act of union, King George III became King of the United Kingdom and Ireland. In this year, too, the title 'King of France' was finally abandoned. Compared with it the imperial title of India, proclaimed by Parliament for Victoria on 1 May 1876, would prove a short-lived affair. In December 1937 the Irish Free State adopted a republican constitution and George VI became King of the United Kingdom of Great Britain and Northern Ireland and on 15 August 1947 he ceased to be emperor of India. The reality was symbolized by a small change to the royal signature. Since Victoria, Britain's sovereigns had signed themselves with their name followed by the initials 'R.I.' for *Rex* or *Regina* ('king' or 'queen') *Imperator* (Emperor). Later that August, the King wrote to his mother Queen Mary and signed himself George R. She noted in her diary, 'the first time Bertie [for 'Albert', always his name to the family] wrote me a letter with the I for Emperor of India left out, very sad'.

THE EARLY CELTIC MONARCHIES

As Queen of the United Kingdom of Great Britain and Northern Ireland, Elizabeth II symbolizes some 1500 years of history shared by the people of the British Isles in which monarchy has played a central role. It is centuries since high kings ruled in Ireland or Celtic kings and princes in Wales; even the crowns of England and Scotland were united nearly 300 years ago. Yet memory runs deep. Close on a millennium has passed since British kings held sway from Dumbarton in the western Lowland counties of Scotland but the name of their kingdom is commemorated in the name of the modern university of Strathclyde. Over the centuries Saxon, Celt and Norman French have alternately contended and cooperated in the history of the British Isles and the Celtic monarchies are an essential part of that story.

Left: George III, the first King of England not to bear the arms of France on the royal coat for 460 years but also the first King of Hanover, is shown in this friendly cartoon as a benevolent King of Brobdignag examining Napoleon-Gulliver with amused contempt.

Below left: From 1871 when, with the permission of Parliament in London Queen Victoria assumed the title, until 1947 when King George VI formally relinquished it, the monarchs of Britain dubbed themselves Emperors of India. Here, the King Emperor George V and his wife the Queen Empress Mary are seen at the Imperial Durbar (or grand congress) in Delhi in December 1911.

Right: This fantasy on the theme of the legendary King Arthur dates from the later 1480s, just after the Battle of Bosworth when the Tudor Henry, Earl of Richmond overthrew King Richard III to make himself King as Henry VII. Henry, who had a Welsh grandfather among his largely English ancestry, made a great thing of being Welsh and called his first-born son Arthur.

CELT AND SAXON

The idea that monarchy was some kind of system of government, took time to develop. Early kings might be credited with semi-divine qualities but above all a king was expected to deliver largesse and successful war to his followers. Geoffrey of Monmouth, who in his famous book *The History of the Kings of Britain* created the legend of King Arthur, the most famous Celtic king of them all, tells us by way of introduction to his hero that: 'Once invested with the royal insignia, Arthur followed the custom of giving gifts freely to everyone.' When the supply ran out, Arthur, in whom 'courage was closely linked with generosity', quickly found the solution to his problem—he raided the Saxons so that he could use their wealth to reward his loyal retainers.

The concept of king as tribal warleader survived much longer among those peoples of the old Celtic traditions than in those kingdoms established by the Anglo Saxon newcomers to the British Isles.

Geoffrey has much to say about the court and courtiers of Arthur whose kingdom, according to tradition, embraced the whole of Britain. This was a powerful legend but the reality was different. Celtic kingships were personal lordships, like that of Arthur, but they were small in territorial extent. The system remained small scale because it was customary for a dead king's domain to be divided between his successors or for the rule to be exercised jointly between them.

In Ireland, where the system lasted longest, it was not so damaging nor so dangerous as one might think. Here, wealth was counted in horned beasts rather than acres and since land counted for less, the fragmentation of authority among a score of petty kings was less important, while the fact that there were many small power centres to overcome, perhaps made conquest of the whole country more difficult. The Viking invaders of Ireland remained confined to their ports of Wexford, Waterford and Dublin. Like their cousins in the Isle of Man and at York, those at Dublin set themselves up as kings, yet their authority never stretched far inland. In the rest of the country, Irish provincial, or 'under', kings held sway under the nominal, and sometimes effective, rule of a high king.

IRELAND'S HIGH KINGS

From about the year 400 when, according to tradition, the first high king (Irish 'ard ri') Niáll of the Nine Hostages held sway, the various provinces of Ireland fluctuated in their boundaries and relative importance. However, the principal ones were: Munster, Leinster, Meath, Connaught (or Connacht), and Ulster.

Principal attributes of an Irish high king were: to be inaugurated at the Hill of Tara (the famous Neolithic site in County Meath); to 'make the circuit of the high king', i.e. march with his armies overcoming any opposition on a traditionally recognized route round the country; to have his summons as ard ri answered by a number of provincial or under kings; and to summon and preside over the Aonach of Tailten, a great national assembly—part fair, part court of justice, part parliament, and part festival of poetry and music. A standard way of securing the allegiance of under kings was the taking of hostages.

Long before the death of Niáll (c. 415), it was believed, Ireland had been divided (along an imaginary line from Dublin to Galway) into the Leth Mogha (the southern half) and the Leth Cuinn (northern half). From the time of Niáll until the year 1002 with only one brief interruption, the high kingship alternated between two lines of his decendants, the Northern and the Southern Ui Néill (O'Neil).

The Hill of Tara, County Meath, Ireland. The ring forts dating from the early Iron Age (more than 3000 years old) are on a site long known as the royal enclosure. It was the site for the installation of Ireland's ancient kings and for the great assemblies held by the high kings.

Niáll's immediate successor, Loegaire, is famed for a legendary encounter with St Patrick; Aed Findlaith, high king in the late ninth century, fought valiantly against the Norsemen, though one of his successors, Niáll Glundubh, was slain at the Battle of Dublin in 919. But the most celebrated man to hold the office of high king was Brian Boru (d. 1014) who displaced Maelsechlainn II, the last king of the Ui Néill line in 1002.

FROM BRIAN BORU TO RORY O'CONNOR (1002–1175)

From a minor royal house of Munster, Boru seemed an upstart in the high kingship after six centuries of Ui Néill tradition. But his was a notable reign ended in heroic fashion when he led his allies to a crushing victory over the Norsemen at the Battle of Clontarff in 1014. After a brief restoration of his predecessor, the Ui Néill high kingship came to an end to be followed by a period known as the 'kings with opposition', many of them Brian's descendants. Turloch O'Brien (d. 1086), called 'king of Ireland' in the annals of Ulster, was addressed as 'magnificent king of Ireland' by the archbishop of Canterbury. No doubt there was an element of ecclesiastical flattery. At this time the popes at Rome were mounting a massive reform campaign in the Church. It was partly to spread the reforming movement that the Pope had blessed William of Normandy's conquest of England as a crusade. Ireland, still further from the centre of Church government, was looked to as the next zone for reform and Canterbury, now headed by an Italian archbishop, was the natural 'recruiting centre'.

Murchertach, who made the circuit of Ireland as high king in 1101 and the following year marched north making a rich offering of gold on the high altar of Armagh Cathedral, was similarly flattered by Canterbury. He brought the Irish Church into line with the Roman reforms, though it meant the bishops of Dublin being ordained from Canterbury for the next half century. After a crushing defeat at the hands of a rival near Newry in 1103, Murchertach's power waned. He died in 1119.

The next challenge for the high kingship came two years later from Connacht whose king, the 30-year old Turloch More O'Connor, eventually made his power felt throughout Ireland. But the idea of the high kingship was fading. When he died in 1156 the records of the various chroniclers reflect the difficulty of establishing claims to a kingship in Ireland. One called him 'the Augustus of the west of Europe', another dubbed him merely 'archking of Connacht', while a third recognized him as 'King of all Ireland with opposition'.

Five years later, the Norsemen of Dublin recognized the king of Tyrone as high king and he in turn recognized Dermot MacMurrough as king of Leinster and Dublin. Dermot 'of the foreigners', as he came to be known, would be a fateful figure in the history of Ireland. In 1166 Rory O'Connor, another king of Connacht, seized the high kingship from Dermot's patron and Dermot, now well hated for his oppressions, was forced to flee overseas.

Thirsting for vengeance, Dermot petitioned King Henry II for help. He received royal letters authorizing him to recruit supporters among Henry's barons—the most important was the powerful Norman-Welsh lord Richard de Clare, Earl of Pembroke and Strigil, known to history as 'Strongbow'. In 1170 Dermot and his Norman abettors, aided by other Norman settlers already in Ireland, seized Dublin. The moment of triumph for Dermot turned into a time of disaster for Ireland when, in 1171, he died and, under the terms of their agreement 'Strongbow', his son-in-law, took over his position.

Fearful that a Norman 'king' in Ireland would prove too much of a threat, King Henry crossed the Irish Sea and, having firmly asserted his authority, made the treaty of Windsor with High King Rory O'Connor. By its terms Rory agreed to recognize Henry as his suzerain and to pay tribute, while Henry recognized Rory's absolute authority outside the Anglo-Norman sphere of influence.

For many Irishmen, of course, Windsor was a dead letter from the start. Various under kings had refused Rory recognition as high king even before the treaty and were certainly not prepared to recognize the subjection of Ireland on his terms. After many years spent in pious and obscure retreat at his abbey of Cong, Rory died in 1199. With him, too, died the pretensions of Ireland's high kings to anything but nominal authority. Attempts by England's medieval monarchs to enforce their claims as rulers of Ireland would meet with little better success. Equally, however, the centuries-long tradition of independence among rival provincial rulers made it next to impossible for Ireland's kings to force out the aliens.

Where Celtic Scotland was able to maintain independence of England despite a fluctuating land frontier, Celtic Ireland was unable even to capitalize on its island status. In both instances the development of the institution of monarchy may have had a part to play in the development of history. From an early stage, Scotland recognized a single king, even though powerful nobles often contested his power. In Ireland those contestants were themselves accounted kings. In such a state of affairs, although the concept of national identity (to use modern terms) developed earlier in Ireland than perhaps in any other part of Britain, the concept of national unity had little chance.

SCOTLAND IN THE AGE OF THE PICTS AND THE SCOTS

The people known as the Scots in fact arrived on the coast of Kintyre from the kingdom of Dalriada in Antrim, northern Ireland, in the early sixth century. The land they settled became known as Argyll, 'the land of the Gael', a significant place name because at that time the country was occupied by a non-Celtic people. The Irish called them 'Cruithni' or 'Pritani'; the Romans called them 'Picti', painted men. Little survives of their culture but such well known Scottish names as Kenneth and Angus are Pictish in origin. The Pictish royal succession seems to have been through the female line and the early Scottish kings continued the tradition.

The first Scots may have been invited to Pictland, or Alba as it was also known, as mercenaries by the Pictish kings. However, the men from Ireland were to bring something yet more potent than their military prowess—the Christian religion. Sometime in the 570s a churchman and member of the Irish royal house, known to us as St Columba (from the Latin for 'dove'), arrived with a band of followers on the coast of Argyll. It was said he had left Ireland, rather than permit his supporters to fight in defence of his good name, when he was accused of the theft of a valuable psalter.

In 574 he performed the first known ceremony of consecration in Britain when he laid his hands upon Aidan in the lordship of Dalriada to anoint him king. Some ten years later Columba converted King Bridei of the Picts to Christianity. (The first English king to become a Christian was Æthelberht of Kent, converted by St Augustine from Rome in 597.)

Columba established a monastery on the island of Iona and this remained the principal burial place of the kings, whether Scottish or Pictish, down to Macbeth in the 11th century. By the 630s, Dalriada had completely broken with the Irish home country and its kings devoted themselves to warfare—principally against their Pictish neighbours, then the principal power in North Britain. In 685 King Nechtan of Pictland defeated the armies of English Northumbria and shortly after received what seemed like divine blessing when a pilgrim brought him bones said to be those of St Andrew the Apostle. A shrine was built on the coast of Fife at modern St Andrews and thus the land received the relics of its patron saint. In the 720s, Pictland seemed poised to destroy Dalriada once and for all. But the king turned instead on his southern British neighbours in Strathclyde only to be defeated. A century later the way at last lay open for the Scots of Dalriada to dominate the country which was to bear their name. In 839 King Eogham of the Picts defeated and slew Alpin of Dalriada, only to have the triumph snatched from

him on the very same day by an army of Viking raiders who arrived fresh on the battlefield, Eogham and his exhausted men surveyed their victory. The Vikings destroyed the Pictish army and killed King Eogham.

The Vikings took to sea with their booty, while the son of Alpin, Kenneth Macalpin, looted the Pictish stronghold of Fortriu or Forteviot in Perthshire. In 843 he went to his inauguration at Scone which from this time forth was the coronation place of Scotland's kings. Soon he established his religious capital at Dunkeld, haven for relics sent from Iona for safety against the Vikings.

Yet despite the honour attaching to his grand title, ard ri of Albainn, high king of Alba, Macalpin's reign lasted but 15 years and his kingdom was beset by unrest of the Picts and enemies on many hands—British, English and Norse.

The kingdom of Alba over which Macalpin ruled was, effectively, modern Scotland north of the Forth: Angus, Atholl, Strathearn, Fife, Mar, Moray, Caithness. His successors followed the Celtic system—each senior surviving male taking the throne in turn, whether brother, cousin or son. Our knowledge of their history is scanty—the earliest king list for the Scots royal

Left: Scotland in the early 800s.

Right: The holy island of Iona, long the burial place of Scotland's kings.

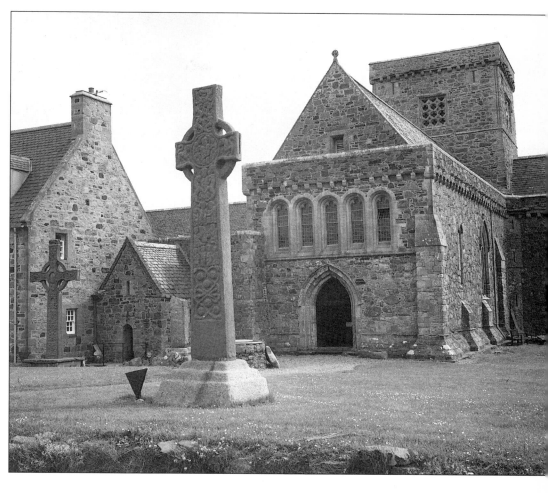

house dates from the 13th century but in essence it appears to have been a story of treachery, usurpation and murder interspersed with moments of achievement. Twice in the 10th century Scottish kings made formal submission to kings of England. In 921 at Bakewell in Derbyshire, Constantine II accepted Edward the Elder as 'father and lord'. On Edward's death he withdrew his allegiance, to be crushed, along with his allies from Strathclyde, Ireland and Northumbria, by King Athelstan at the battle of Brunanburh. In 973 Kenneth II joined many lesser kings of Britain in doing homage to Edgar of England, having been bought with the lordship of Lothian. In the next century Malcolm II, having achieved the throne by the murder of Kenneth III, ruled for 29 years. Honours between England and Scotland were about equal until Malcolm presumed to designate one of his grandsons, Duncan, king of All Cumbria. Cnut, the Danish king of England, won considerable popularity at home by leading an expedition to the banks of the Tay and forcing submission from yet another Scottish king. But Malcolm seems to have been murdered by his own men because he planned to end the old system of inheritance in favour of his grandson Duncan. The new king

ruled for six years before being defeated and killed by Macbeth, his second cousin, and the Earl of Orkney at the battle of Elgin. It was also a gesture against the growing anglicization at court and a last victory for the old ways. Duncan's sons Malcolm and Donald Bane harassed him from Strathclyde but he ruled successfully for 17 years. In 1050 he was sufficiently confident to make the pilgrimage to Rome. Eventually Malcolm, with help from south of the border, brought him to battle at Lumphanan in Aberdeenshire.

The idea that Macbeth murdered Duncan first appeared in the history written by Andrew Wyntoun of Loch Leven in Fife about the year 1400. But it was Hector Boece of Aberdeen University in his Latin history of Scotland, published in Paris in 1527, who added details like the weird sisters, Banquo, the murder of Lady Macduff and an evil and ambitious Lady Macbeth. The story was accepted by the distinguished historian George Buchanan and then used by Ralph Holinshed in his *Chronicles of England, Scotland and Ireland*, which began publication in London in 1577. Unfortunately for the historical Macbeth, the world's most famous playwright was destined to choose his story for one of his greatest works.

WALES

The early history of Wales and its rulers is rich in legend. Up to the early seventh century the Celts of Wales were joined to the territories of the Celts of Strathclyde and Cumbria (Welsh 'Cymry'). The victory of the Northumbrian king Oswy at Winwaed Field in 645 broke the link. For the next two centuries the country was divided between the rule of small chieftains. With the reign of Rhodri Mawr, 'the Great' (r. 844–78), most of it was brought under the rule of one man. Son of the king of Gwynedd and a princess of the royal house of Powys, Rhodri repulsed Viking incursions and married Angharad, daughter to the king of Seisyllwg (roughly Ceredigion and the valley of the Twyi). But in 876 Rhodri was driven from his lands by renewed Viking attacks and two years later he died in battle with a Mercian army. Seisyllwg regained its independence, while Gwynedd and Powys later acknowledged the overlordship of Alfred the Great of Wessex (d. 899). The attempt by Idwal Foel ('Idwal the Bald') of Gwynedd and Powys (r. 916–42) to regain full independence ended with his death in battle.

In the 940s a greater Welsh state emerged briefly with Hywel Dda, ruler of Dyfed (from 904) and Seisyllwg (from 920 sole ruler) and of Gwynedd (from 942). Until his death in 950, for some seven or eight years the whole of Wales, excluding only the petty kingdoms of Glamorgan and Gwent, acknowledged one lord.

Faced with continuing threat from the Vikings, Hywel acknowledged English overlordship. But two centuries after his death, his standing was so high that he received the sobriquet 'Dda', 'the Good' by which he is still known. In the 13th century the first written code of Welsh law was attributed to him, and parts of it probably derive from an oral tradition stretching back to his days.

Hywel's domains before his venture into Gwynedd, henceforward collectively known as Deheubarth, developed a certain coherence during the 40-odd years of his reign and were ruled jointly by his three sons Rhodri, Edwin and Owain. In 985, Owain, the last to die, left Deheubarth to his son Maredudd who two years before had re-established his family on the throne of Gwynedd. For the last decade of the 10th century Wales was once again under a single ruler.

Surprisingly, the pattern held. Maredudd was succeeded by his son-in-law Llywelyn ap Seisyll. On his death in 1023, Llywelyn's young son Gruffydd was easily shouldered aside for a time by a usurper. But in the late 1030s, having recovered his father's lordship of Gwynedd and Deheubarth, Gruffydd ap Llywelyn (r. 1039–63) turned his attention to England. This proved a mistake. Earl Harold Godwinsson (later King Harold

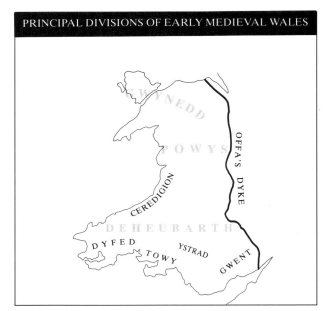

PRINCIPAL DIVISIONS OF EARLY MEDIEVAL WALES

II), leading the armies of King Edward the Confessor, marched on Rhuddlan where Gruffydd had his palace and sacked it. From an English point of view it was timely. Known to the Welsh as defender of the Britons and in England as 'king of all the Welsh', Gruffydd had become a menace. The following year the Welsh murdered Gruffydd and delivered his head to the English.

The old divisions between Gwynedd and Deheubarth now reopened and the old kingdom of Powys was briefly re-established. With the end of the English kingdom at Hastings in 1066, the Welsh faced a more fearsome enemy in the Franco-Norman adventurers who had come over with William the Conqueror. French lords and French castles began to appear in the lands once ruled by Welsh kings and homage began to be demanded more systematically from Welsh rulers, whose subjects were increasingly attracted eastward by the new continental contacts.

Intermarriage between the new Norman lords and the old royal families also increased contacts between the peoples. Giraldus Cambrensis or Gerald of Wales, one of the finest writers of his period whose travel journals for Wales and Ireland both survive, was the child of such a match. Proud of his descent from a free Welsh princess and the Norman Constable of Pembroke Castle, he contemptuously dismissed the defeated English as slaves.

But time was on the march. In the 1080s and 90s Gruffydd ap Cynan (r. 1081–1137) of Gwynedd languished in a Norman donjon. His second son Owain Gwynedd (r. 1137–70) encroached into Ceredigion but, though praised by the bards, perforce did homage to Henry II. Welsh rulers less and less boasted the name of king 'brenin' among their titles.

The last great lord of the south was the lord Rhys, king of Deheubarth, who ruled from 1155 to 1197 and who was eulogized in the Welsh *Chronicle of the Princes* as the 'unconquered head of Wales'. He had forced

Above left: The principal divisions of early medieval Wales.

Left: A modern idealized portrayal of Llywelyn the Last (d. 1282) grandson of Llywelyn ap Iorwerth, the Great. With his defeat by King Edward I of England in 1282 Welsh medieval independence was effectively over.

Right: The harp, the common courtly instrument of the later Middle Ages and very much favoured by English aristocratic households, came to be particularly associated with Wales. Here, King Henry VIII is depicted playing the instrument—to the ill-concealed dismay of his court jester Will Somers.

Norman lords to withdraw from his country, occupied castles in the Norman fashion, held a great Eisteddfod at Ceredigion, and was buried in St David's Cathedral. After him, Deheubarth was divided among squabbling princes, until, like most other Welsh rulers, they did homage to Llywelyn I ap Iorwerth of Gwynedd, called 'the Great' (r. 1194–1240). Marriage to John of England's illegitimate daughter Joan was a respectable coup and Llywelyn was able to exploit the barons' struggle with the King over Magna Carta. He proclaimed himself Lord of Powys and styled himself Prince of Aberffraw and Lord of Snowdon, though doing homage to Henry III. Llywelyn excluded his bastard son Gruffydd from the succession which passed to the legitimate but childless Dafydd II (b. 1208). He assumed the style of Prince of Wales with papal approval. But his death in 1246 left the field open to Gruffydd's sons. They had to concede humiliating terms to Henry III and cede the four Welsh provinces or cantreds lying between the rivers Dee and Conwy. In 1254 these were granted to the king's eldest son Edward who provocatively set about anglicizing the language and law of the cantreds and integrating them into the lordship of Chester. Llywelyn, Gruffydd's son, supporting the resulting rebellion, made a series of quicksilver conquests and over the next 20 years his towering ambition and ability brought him to a position matching anything achieved by his greatest predecessors. Taking the title of Prince of Wales, he allied with Scottish nobles and the English baronial opposition to Henry III. But his success provoked hostility in Wales and his own brother, Dafydd, deserted to Edward. In the late 1270s Edward I of England embarked on a series of campaigns which stripped Llywelyn of virtually all his lands. Forced back into Snowdonia, Llywelyn attempted a break out in November 1282—he ended a notable career in an obscure scuffle at Builth. His daughter was sent to a nunnery and his brother Dafydd, once the agent of the English King, hunted down and executed as a traitor the following June (1283). Early in the next century, Edward I, builder of Carnarvon Castle, created his own son, Edward of Caernarfon, the first English Prince of Wales.

It seemed that the Welsh were coming to accept English rule until the rising of Owain Glyndwr (1359?–1416?; English Owen Glendower), who in 1400 proclaimed himself 'Prince of Wales'. Glyndwr (who could trace his descent from a 13th-century Lord of North Powys) began his revolt not as a hero but as a disgruntled country gentleman. When his English neighbour, Lord Grey, seized part of his state and the new King Henry IV took no action, Owain raised the country. To make good his title he looked for alliance with the English. Owain recruited help from the Scots and began to look like a real threat. However, an English victory in 1405 broke the back of the resistance. A last ditch defence of Harlech castle became the stuff of legend but by 1410 the insurgency was all but over.

THE ENGLISH PRINCES OF WALES

By tradition the title of Prince of Wales is borne by male heirs to the English throne, though this is not automatic. From the moment of his birth the eldest son of an English monarch enjoys the status, and considerable revenues, of 'Duke of Cornwall' but the titles Earl of Chester and Prince of Wales are conferred by the monarch, usually when the boy is in his teens. The 'creation' of a Prince of Wales consists of the formal conferring of the title by royal proclamation. As from that moment the young man is Prince of Wales (the earldom of Chester is conferred at the same time). The creation may or may not be followed by a solemn ceremony of investiture.

The story of the native Welsh rulers of Wales is outlined on pages 22–24 while on page 31 a full list of the English princes to have borne the title will be found. For the Prince of Wales's coat of arms see page 26. With his coat of arms and his title, each Prince of Wales acquires the motto '*Ich Dien*', German for 'I serve', intended as a guide for life. Few holders of the title have so fully lived up to its motto as the present holder.

This section describes the creation and investiture of the present Prince of Wales, Prince Charles, the origins of the title and some of the more interesting or colourful episodes in the story of his predecessors. Most of them succeeded to the crown and are shown with their regnal number in brackets, thus, Edward [II].

> *Two views of the 'job specification':*
> 'I know what becomes a Prince; it is not necessary for me to be a professor, but a soldier and a man of the world.' Henry Frederick, Prince of Wales, eldest son of King James I, born 1594, created Prince of Wales 1610, died 1612.
>
> 'It's one of those things you grow up in.' HRH Prince Charles, The Prince of Wales (creation 1958).

Charles Philip Arthur George, Prince of the United Kingdom of Great Britain and Northern Ireland, Prince of Wales and Earl of Chester, Duke of Cornwall and Rothesay, Earl of Carrick, Baron of Renfrew, Lord of the Isles and Great Steward of Scotland.

In July 1958 HRH Prince Charles was created Prince of Wales by royal proclamation, the announcement being made in a message recorded by the Queen and played to a crowded stadium at the opening of the Commonwealth Games in Cardiff. On 1 July 1969 he was invested at Caernarfon Castle, the first English Prince of Wales to be able to speak at least some Welsh, having studied the language during a term in the University College of Wales at Aberystwyth.

Preparations for the ceremony had been supervised by the Duke of Norfolk, Earl Marshal of England,

Left: The courts of the ancient Welsh princes and kings were noted for their cultivation of the arts of poetry and music. The modern revival of the Eisteddfod looked back to those days. Here the Duke and Duchess of York (later King George VI and Queen Elizabeth) are shown in robes of honour at the 1926 National Eisteddfod, at Swansea.

Right: Three generations of Wales's. A photograph taken in the last years of his reign, showing King Edward VII (Prince of Wales from birth until the death of his mother Queen Victoria in 1901) with his son, the future King George V and his grandson, the future Edward VIII.

THE ARMORIAL BEARINGS OF HRH THE PRINCE OF WALES

When a person's full armorial bearings are all shown together, the result is called 'an achievement'. In the centre is the shield with the coat of arms; either side are 'the supporters'—here the lion for England and unicorn for Scotland; above is the helm—here the seven barred golden royal helm; it supports a crown or coronet—in this case the coronet of the heir apparent; atop that is the crest—here the lion of England; either side of the helm flows the 'mantling'—here the royal gold and ermine. Below the shield are grouped the badges of the Feathers of the Princes of Wales and the Red Dragon of Wales, either side of the shield of the Duchy of Cornwall. A scroll bears the Princes' motto *Ich Dien* (German, 'I serve') while round the main shield is the Garter with its motto to denote the Prince of Wales's membership of that noble order of chivalry. The actual arms of the Princes of Wales comprise the royal arms with the original gold and red lions of the princes of Gwynedd The white, three-tabbed 'label' shown on the animals and the royal arms is a sign that the arms are being worn by the eldest son of the chief holder.

The Investiture of Prince Charles as Prince of Wales on 1 July 1969.

assisted by Lord Snowdon, photographer and designer, husband to Princess Margaret and appointed Constable of Caernarfon Castle in anticipation of the event. The whole occasion was geared to the requirements of the 81 television cameras posted around the ancient castle and its approaches. As a precaution against rain the investiture itself took place under a Plexiglass canopy bearing a gilt emblem of the Feathers of the Prince of Wales. The walls were draped with banners bearing the Dragon of Wales, the heraldic device of a three pointed label to denote an eldest son around its neck. Wearing the regimental dress uniform of the Welsh Guards, Charles knelt as his mother invested him '. . . by girding him with a sword, by putting a coronet upon his head and a gold ring upon his finger and also by delivering a gold rod into his hand'. Charles was only the second English Prince of Wales to be invested in the principality (his great-uncle Edward [VIII] being the first, in 1911, see below); the gold coronet was 1960s 'contemporary' design and the formula of investiture not a great deal older, though the English crown has owned territories in Wales since the mid-1200s.

THE STORY OF A TITLE

By the middle of the 13th century the kings of England had acquired sizeable territories in Wales by conquest; in 1253 Henry III endowed his eldest son Edward I with these possessions and their revenues. He soon came into conflict with the native Welsh princes and when he became king continued to war against them. By 1285 it seemed Welsh resistance was broken. According to an old legend Edward promised to give the Welsh a prince of their own who was born in Wales and who could speak no English; he presented them with his baby son Edward II of Caernarfon, born on 25 April 1284. The story first appeared in the 16th century and historians now dismiss it as fiction. However, the young Edward was born in Wales and his first wet nurse was a Welsh woman, Mary Mawnsel. (She remained a member of his household when he, in turn, became king.)

1301 Edward II of Caernarfon, the first English Prince of Wales, was in fact invested with the title at Lincoln on 7 February in the presence of the Parliament which had been convened there. Pleased with his son's conduct while on campaign in Scotland the previous summer, King Edward created him Prince of Wales and Earl of Chester and gave him the revenues both of the earldom and those lands in Wales owned directly by the crown. (Today the title is purely honorific.)

1343 12 May, investiture at the Westminster Parliament of Edward the Black Prince, eldest son of Edward III, by his father with 'circlet, gold ring and silver rod'; the first detailed record of an investiture. Earl of Chester since 1333 and Duke of Cornwall since 1337, Edward won his spurs in his father's victory over the French king and his allies at the battle of Crécy in August 1346. After the battle the three ostrich feathers of the crest of the dead King John of Bohemia, an ally of France, were brought to the prince who adopted them as a badge; and also the king's motto 'Ich dien', 'I serve'.

1376 20 November, Richard [II], the eight-year-old son of Edward the Black Prince and grandson of Edward III was created Prince of Wales, Duke of Cornwall and Earl of Chester shortly after his father's early death, at the request of Parliament.

1483 7 September, investiture of Edward of Middleham, Earl of Salisbury, the 10-year-old son of King Richard III at York. For the usurper king the investiture was valuable propaganda. His post-coronation progress brought him to York on Friday 29 August; a week of banquets, speeches and pageants culminated on the Sunday with a great ceremony in the Minster. The Master of the King's Wardrobe had bought in stocks of velvet, satin and silk and lengths of cloth of gold; 13 000 badges with Richard's device of the silver boar were provided for spectators and royal retainers while the king ordered coats of arms beaten with fine gold 'for our own person'. A fanfare of 40 trumpets (the royal trumpeters being supplemented with players recruited from various noble households) greeted the arrival of the royal party. The prince was invested with a simple gold coronet and a golden rod of office and the senior foreign diplomat present, the Spanish ambassador, received a knighthood. It was, wrote an Italian commentator, 'a great day of state for York'—were there not present 'three princes wearing crowns, the King, the Queen and the Prince of Wales'?

1489 November, the creation of the three-year-old Arthur Tudor, son of Henry VII. Born on 20 September 1486, the year following publication of Malory's *Morte D'Arthur*, the boy was named 'in honour of the British race' by a father very fond of vaunting his Welsh connections. After his marriage to Catherine of Aragon in November 1501, Arthur moved his household to set up court at Ludlow Castle. He died just four months later.

1511 On 12 February, a tournament was held to celebrate the birth of a son (1 January) to King Henry VIII and Catherine of Aragon. Christened Henry and named Prince of Wales, the boy prompted great celebrations and a jubilant King Henry jousted before his queen in a coat embellished with the motto 'coure loyall', 'true heart'. Tragically, the child died three weeks later.

1610 February, the investiture of Henry Frederick, eldest son of James I on his 16th birthday, was celebrated with a masque in Whitehall designed by Inigo Jones, in which the prince jousted. Sadly, he too died before his father (1612).

1714 The 31-year-old George [II] was created Prince of Wales in the year his father, George I, came to the English throne. Father and son disliked one another cordially and a furious family quarrel broke out in 1717 over the choice of godfather for the Wales's second son. King George expelled Prince George and Princess Caroline from St James's Palace. For the next three years Leicester House, Leicester Square, which the Wales's chose as their new home, became a rival court and focus for opposition politicians. Among them was Sir Robert Walpole who, thanks to the Princess, was to be England's first Prime Minister when George became king.

1729 Two years after George II came to the throne his son Frederick Lewis was duly created Prince of Wales and the Hanoverian feuding continued. His father considered Frederick 'the greatest villain ever born'. Frederick and his wife Augusta lived virtual prisoners in St James's Palace until, early in the summer of 1738, they 'eloped' to Norfolk House, St James's Square. Shortly after, Frederick rented Leicester House, which once again became the centre for an 'opposition' court.

1762 On 17 August, George [IV], son of King George III was created Prince of Wales at St James's Palace just five days after his birth. In due course he, like his Hanoverian predecessors in the title, became focus for opposition to his father and his ministers. The Prince's home at Carlton House provided the meeting place for politicians, led by Charles James Fox, out of office and opposed to the government of William Pitt.

1841 On 4 December Albert Edward (later King Edward VII) was created Prince of Wales. (He had been born on 9 November and would not be christened until 25 January 1842.) Good natured, but idle as a boy, he was a disappointment to his parents Victoria and Albert. After Albert's death Victoria was even more cool to his son and when he married, secretly envied the social success of the Wales's at their London home of Marlborough House.

1910 On 23 June, Edward [VIII] was created Prince of Wales at Windsor. In July on his 16th birthday he was invested at Caernarfon. The first investiture there in the history of the title, this was the idea of the Welsh Prime Minister Lloyd George who played a large part in devising the ceremony. When he saw the ruched breeches and silk stockings he would be required to wear, the boy prince recoiled in horror at 'this preposterous rig'. Queen Mary attempted to pacify him with the words: 'Your friends will understand that as a prince you are obliged to do certain things that may seem a little silly.'

Above: The Investiture of Edward VIII at Caernarfon in 1911.

Right: Edward VIII when Prince of Wales, visiting a South Wales pit in 1919. He won much popularity as prince both through his charm and the widespread belief that when king he would put his influence behind changing the unjust conditions of British society.

Princes of Wales

Check list showing date of creation and, in brackets, dates of birth and death. Where the Princes succeeded as king their regnal number is shown in square brackets after their name.

Edward [II], 1301 (1284–1327)
Edward Black Prince, 1346 (1330–76)
Richard [II], 1376 (1369–99)
Henry [V], 1399 (1386–1422)
Edward 'of Westminster', son of Henry VI, 1454 (1453–71)
Edward [V], son of Edward IV, 1471 (1470–83?)
Edward of Middleham, son of Richard III, 1483 (1473–84)
Arthur, 1489 (1486–1502) 1st son of Henry VII
Henry [VIII], 1504 (?) (1491–1547)

Henry, 1511 (January–March 1511) first son of Henry VIII
Henry Frederick, 1610 (1594–1612) first son of James I
Charles [I], 1616 (1600–49)
Charles [II], 1638 (1630–85)
James Francis Edward Stuart, 1688 (1688–1766) the Old Pretender
George [II], 1714 (1683–1760)
Frederick Lewis, 1729 (1707–51) son of George II
George [III], 1751 (1738–1820]
George [IV], 1762 (1762–1820)
Edward [VII], 1841 (1841–1910]
George [V], 1901 (1862–1935)
Edward [VIII], 1910 (1894–1972)
Charles, 1958 (b. 1948)

Above: In his student years Prince Charles was something of a cellist.

Left: Frederick Lewis, Prince of Wales (1707–51), son of King George II and father of King George III. The picture, by his household painter Philip le Mercier, depicts the Prince—a noted amateur musician—with his sisters Anne, Caroline and Amelie.

Far left: Edward the Black Prince, Prince of Wales and England's hero in the early Hundred Years' War, celebrating victory at the Battle of Crécy with his father Edward III (1346).

KINGS AND QUEENS OF ENGLAND AND SCOTLAND

THE EARLY KINGDOMS OF ENGLAND

By the late 600s England, as we know it today, was divided among a number of kingdoms, sub-kingdoms and tribal units, both Germanic and British. The principal ones were the northern Angle kingdoms of Bernicia (chief royal residence, at Bamburgh), Deira (York) which merged as Northumbria in 654; Lindsey (Lincoln) with a shadowy history from the 550s to the early 700s; Mercia in the midlands (Tamworth); East Anglia (Elmham and Rendelsham); Essex (London, until this became a Mercian city about 730); Kent (Canterbury); Sussex (Chichester) and Wessex (Winchester). For each kingdom we give the first and the more interesting or important kings. Some of the early names may be legendary. Dates indicate the years of a reign.

Kent

Hengist (c. 455–c. 488), Germanic warleader recruited with his brother Horsa as a mercenary against Saxon marauders by the British King Vortigern but settled in Britain and founded the Kingdom of Kent.

Oisc or Oeric (d. c. 512), son or grandson of Hengist.

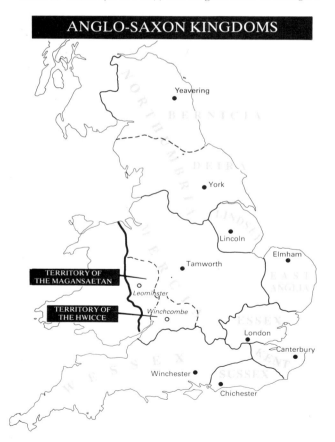

ANGLO-SAXON KINGDOMS

The Anglo-Saxon kingdoms of early medieval England.

Eormenric (d. c. 560).

Æthelberht (560–616), the first Christian English king, was converted by St Augustine in 597. He was already familiar with the religion, having married the Christian Frankish princess Bertha of Paris in the 580s and allowed her to practise her faith at his court. He issued the earliest known code of English laws.

Eadbald (616–40), Æthelberht's son, restored paganism.

Earconbert (640–64), married St Seaxburgha and restored Christianity.

Whitred (690–725), author of one of the earliest law codes.

From the 740s Kent fell under the domination first of Mercia, then Wessex. In 825 Baldred, the last king of Kent, was expelled by Egbert of Wessex.

Sussex

The Kingdom of the South Saxons, with its sub-kingdom of Haestingas.

Aelle (477–91), traditionally known as the first Bretwalda, though his power never extended much beyond West Sussex.

The shadowy kingdom came to an end in the eighth century when it fell under the domination of Mercia.

Essex

The kingdom of the East Saxons comprised the modern county of Essex, together with (up to the 730s) Middlesex and Hertfordshire.

Saeberht (c. 604–16/17), baptized by Mellitus, first bishop of London. In 825 Essex submitted to King Egbert of Wessex.

East Anglia

Raedwald (d. before 627), the fourth Bretwalda is a shadowy figure; he converted to Christianity under the influence of the king of Kent but reverted to paganism. The fabulous Sutton Hoo ship burial has been associated with his name.

Sigebert (d. 630/1), promoted Christianity, retired to a monastery but died in battle against Penda of Mercia.

Ethelhere (645–54), an ally of Penda of Mercia, he was killed with him at the battle of Winwaed.

During the eighth century East Anglia, like most of southern Britain, felt the weight of Mercian dominance. In the year 794 her king, Ethelbert, was beheaded on the orders of Offa of Mercia. He came to be revered as a saint and is the patron of Hereford Cathedral.

Edmund Saint (855–70), one of the most famous of all the old English kings. Edmund of East Anglia—defeated attempting to repulse an army of invading Danes—was taken prisoner. Refusing, it is said, to share his kingdom with the pagans, he was roped to a tree and shot to death. The great abbey of Bury St Edmund's was built on the site where his body was interred.

Northumbria

Bernicia (Bamburgh) and *Deira* (York) arose in the early sixth century. Over the next 100 years rival kings briefly united the realms or suffered defeat at the hands of their powerful southern neighbours, pagan Mercia.

St Oswald (604–41), of Bernicia restored Christianity in Northumbria and briefly made it a major power until he, too, fell to Penda of Mercia. At the battle of Winwaed in 654 **Oswiu** (612–70, also called Osary) of Bernicia killed Penda and firmly established a united Northumbria. In 664 Oswiu presided over the historic Synod of Whitby which determined that the English church would give allegiance to Rome rather than the Celtic church of Ireland. He is reckoned the seventh Bretwalda of Britain.

In the eighth century Northumbria produced the great historian Bede, and the scholar Alcuin who was principal adviser to Charlemagne's cultural renaissance. But there was a decline of the royal house and in 867 Danish invaders defeated and killed the last two kings of any consequence. On the death of Egbert II in 878 Northumbria was absorbed by the Danish kings of York.

Viking or Danish kings of York

Halfdan I (d. *c.* 880).

Ethelwald (899–902), exiled son of Edward the Elder of Wessex, accepted by Danes of York as their king.

Halfdan II (902–10), defeated and killed with two other joint kings by a Saxon army at Tettenhall near Wolverhampton.

Sihtric (921–7), married a sister of Athelstan of Wessex.

Ragnald Guthfrithson (d. 944), brought to an end a period when York had been in contact friendly and otherwise with the Vikings of Dublin. In 948 **Eric Bloodaxe** attempted to refound the kingdom but in 954 finally submitted to **King Edred**, of the house of Wessex.

Mercia

For most of the eighth century the most powerful of the English kingdoms, Mercia (the name means 'march', i.e. margin or border territories), arose in the early 600s as the invading Germanic peoples pressed westwards across Britain. The first great king was the pagan Penda.

Penda (*c.* 630–54), his victorious campaigns to the north defeated the newly Christian kingdom of Northumbria, whose kings Edwin (632) and Oswald (641) both fell to Penda. However, he himself was defeated and killed by Oswiu of Northumbria at the battle of Winwaed in November 654.

Wulfhere (657–74), son of Penda; by 660 he had thrown off Northumbrian occupation. Wulfhere accepted Christianity and established such an ascendancy in central England that he was able, in 661, to invade the Isle of Wight. He was succeeded by his brother **Æthelred** who in 704 abdicated to become a monk. Wulfhere's son **Coenred** (abdicated 709) died on pilgrimage to Rome.

Æthelbald (716–57), self-styled King of Britain and the most powerful ruler of his day, he dominated Northumbria, harassed Wessex and contained the Welsh. He was assassinated.

Offa (757–96), styling himself king of all the land of the English, he was second only to Charlemagne among the European rulers of his day. The great earthwork 'Offa's Dyke' is a lasting testimony to his greatness.

After Offa, the Mercian dynasty went into decline. In 825 King **Beornwulf** was defeated at the Battle of Elendun by Egbert of Wessex. Under **Wiglaf**, deposed by Egbert but restored for a 10-year reign, 830–40, Mercia seemed poised for revival but the defeat of Beorhtwulf by the Danes in 852 spelt the end. Puppet kings followed and in 883 Mercia submitted to Alfred of Wessex.

Wessex

The future kingdom of the West Saxons began as the kingdom of the Gewissae. It was founded by **Cerdic** (519–34) who, despite a name of Celtic origin, apparently claimed descent from Woden, the Germanic god, considered the common ancestor of all the English royal houses.

Cynric (d. 560), son or grandson of Cerdic.

Ceawlin (560–91), he defeated Æthelberht of Kent at Wimbledon in 568 and extended the frontiers of the Gewissae in the southern Midlands.

Cynegils (611–43), accepted Christianity.

Cenwalh (643–72), a pagan, he was temporarily ousted by Penda of Mercia and converted to Christianity. Cenwalh founded St Peter's, Winchester. He campaigned successfully against the Welsh and Wulfhere of Mercia and was succeeded by his widow.

Seaxburgh, Queen regnant (672–3[?]).

Centwine (or Kenten) (676–85), conquered areas of Somerset from the British and was a benefactor of Glastonbury Abbey.

Left and above: In the 1930s and 1940s excavations at Sutton Hoo, Suffolk, revealed a remarkable ship burial of the early seventh century. Since the greatest man of the time was Raedwald, king of the East Angles it has been suggested the grave was his. Certainly the majestic grave furniture, such as the warrior's helm and exquisitely enamelled armlets shown here bear testimony to the courtly splendour of England's early pagan society.

Below: With King Alfred the Great of Wessex (d. 899) the Anglo-Saxon period of British monarchy reached maturity. This statue to him in Winchester, the ancient capital of the West Saxons, is a modern tribute to the only English king ever to be awarded the title 'the Great'.

Caedwalla (685–8), a war lord adventurer expelled by Centwine, he raided into Sussex killing its king before usurping the crown of Wessex (first so called during his reign). He conquered the Isle of Wight and then resigned the crown (688), dying in Rome (689) 10 days after baptism by Pope Sergius.

Ine (688–726), a major early West Saxon king, noted for his code of laws, the first in a Germanic language, he also extended the frontiers of Wessex and was a notable patron of the Church, e.g. Glastonbury. He abdicated and died a pilgrim in Rome.

Beorhtric (786–802), he married Eadburg, the daughter to Offa of Mercia and died, it is said, of a poisoned drink prepared by the Queen for his favourite.

Egbert (802–39), often considered the first ancestor of the modern English royal house. By his victory over the Mercians at Elendun, Egbert won recognition as king in Kent, Sussex, East Anglia and Essex as well.

Æthelwulf (839–55), son of Egbert, he married Judith, a princess of Francia at Rheims in 856 when she was consecrated as Queen of Wessex by the Archbishop. He was succeeded by his sons **Æthelbald** (855–60), **Æthelbert** (860–6), and **Æthelred** (866–71) who probably reigned jointly. They were succeeded by their delicate younger brother.

Alfred the Great (871–99).

KINGS AND QUEENS OF SCOTLAND

The history of the kingdom of Scotland is conventionally dated from the reign of Kenneth I Macalpin of Dalriada who united the kingdoms of Picts and Scots in the year 843. However, the realm continued to be known by its former name of 'Alba' until the time of Kenneth II (d. 995). Fifty years later, Malcolm II established a kingdom roughly the same in extent as modern Scotland. Succession by primogeniture was established by about 1100 in the line of Malcolm Cranmore. In the late 13th century the line failed and the crown passed successively to the house of Balliol and the house of Bruce. Finally, with the accession of Robert, the hereditary High Steward of Scotland as Robert II in 1371, the family of Stuart was established as Scotland's ruling house. The following list traces these developments and consequently adopts a somewhat different mode of presentation than as for the kings of England.

Kenneth I Macalpin, king of Dalriada 841, king of Picts and Scots, 843–58/9.

Donald I (858/9–62/3), brother of Kenneth I.

Constantine I (862/3–77), son of Kenneth I, killed in battle by the Danes.

Aedh (877–8), son of Kenneth I, murdered by Giric of Strathclyde, Regent for Eochaid.

Eochaid (878–89), son of Aedh's sister, of the house of Strathclyde, possibly with Giric as co-ruler; deposed by Donald II.

(Giric see Eochaid)

Donald II (889–900), son of Constantine I.

Constantine II (900–42; d. 952), son of Aedh, defeated with his allies by Athelstan of England at Brunanburh, 937. Constantine abdicated to become Abbot of St Andrews (d. 952).

Malcolm I (942–54), son of Donald II, assassinated.

Indulf (954–62), son of Constantine II.

Dubh (962–6/7), Malcolm I's son, assassinated.

Culen (966/7–71), son of Indulf, assassinated.

Kenneth II (971–95), son of Malcolm I, one of the kings who rowed Edgar of England on the Dee; received Lothian from Edgar: took title king of Scots in place of king of Alba which seems to have become generally known as Scotland from this time. Assassinated.

Constantine III (995–7), son of Cullen, killed by his successor.

Kenneth III (997–1005), son of Dubh, killed by his successor Malcolm II.

Malcolm II (1005–34), son of Kenneth II, b. 954. Defeating Northumbrians at Carham (c. 1016) he confirmed Scottish possession of Lothian; annexed

King James III and his son kneel in prayer while Scotland's patron saint, Andrew, watches over the King. From a 15th-century altarpiece by Hugo van der Goes.

fita eft fup ripam fluminis tyeue. in loco qui

Left: King David I and his grandson Malcolm IV.

Right: The Royal Company of Archers, Her Majesty's bodyguard in Scotland, give 'Three cheers for the Queen after the royal salute' following Her Majesty's inspection of them in October 1976 to celebrate their tercentenary. Thirty years after their formation, the English and Scottish Crowns were united.

Strathclyde by treaty for his grandson Duncan and thus established realm equivalent to modern Scotland.

Duncan I (1034–40), son of Malcolm II's daughter Bethoc and Crinan Abbot of Dunkeld; killed in battle with Macbeth his successor.

Macbeth (1040–57), Mormaer of Moray, grandson of Kenneth II through his daughter and husband of Gruoch, granddaughter of Kenneth III. Slain in the Battle of Lumphanan near Aberdeen by Malcolm III.

Lulach (1057–8), son of Gruoch (i.e. Lady Macbeth, who is thus known to have had one child), and stepson of Macbeth, killed by Malcolm III.

Malcolm III (1058–93), son of Duncan I, b. *c.* 1031, he married St Margaret of England. Many bloodthirsty raiding wars across the English border ended with his death before Alnwick, though not before he had done homage to William I the Conqueror who led savage counter campaign through the borders to Abernethy. Malcolm's marriage to St Margaret, daughter of Edward Atheling of the English royal house, introduced the beginnings of English customs in Scottish Church and State.

Donald III (Donald Bane) (1093–4; 1094–7), brother of Malcolm III who usurped the crown on the old principle of succession, though his brother had designated as heir his eldest son Duncan II, thus introducing the idea of primogeniture to the Scottish succession.

Duncan II (May–Nov 1094), given as hostage by his father Malcolm III to William the Conqueror. Murdered at the command of his half-brother, Donald III.

Edgar (1097–1107), son of Malcolm III, won the crown with aid of William II of England in exchange for homage. He made Castle Rock, Edinburgh a royal seat.

Alexander I (1107–24), son of Malcolm III, b. *c.* 1077, he married Sybilla, daughter of Henry I of England.

David I (called 'the Saint') (1124–53), English influence further increased under his rule.

Malcolm IV (1153–65), grandson of David I, b. 1142.

William I 'the Lion' (1165–1214), brother of Malcolm IV, b. 1143, he married Ermengard de Beaumont, a cousin of Henry II of England. Joining the English rebels against Henry II in 1174, William was taken prisoner in battle at Alnwick and obliged to do homage to Henry for his kingdom to secure his release. Richard sold him back his homage for 10 000 merks.

Alexander II (1214–49), son of William I, b. 1198, he married (1) Joanna (d. 1238), daughter of John of England; and (2) Mari de Couci.

Alexander III (1249–86), son of Alexander II, b. 1241, he married (1) Margaret of England (1240–75), daughter of Henry III; and (2) Yolande of Dreux. He obtained the Western Isles from Norway; his daughter Margaret married Erik II of Norway and when Alexander died, falling off his horse over a cliff, their daughter the four-year-old Margaret, was acknowledged Queen of Scots.

Margaret 'The Maid of Norway' (1286–90), granddaughter of Alexander III, b. 1283, she drowned when the ship bringing her to Scotland foundered.

First Interregnum (1290–2), the succession was contested by numerous claimants from the Scottish nobility and Edward I of England was called on to arbitrate. In November 1292, presiding over a court of 144 auditors sitting at Berwick, King Edward awarded the crown to John Balliol, a Scotsman.

John Balliol (1292–6), son of Devorguilla, a great-great-granddaughter of David I and John de Balliol; b. 1249, he was declared deposed by Edward when he renounced his submission to the English king.

Second Interregnum (1296–1306), the struggle for Scottish independence was led first by freedom fighter/ terrorist William Wallace, captured and executed by the English, and then by Robert de Bruce who had himself crowned as Robert I.

Robert I (1306–29), son of Robert Bruce, Earl of Carrick, distantly descended from King David I and Robert de Bruis of Normandy; b. 1274, his defeat of the English at Bannockburn (1314) settled the dispute over homage to the English king. He died probably of leprosy.

David II (1329–71), sole surviving son of Robert I; b. 1324, he married (1) Joan of England, daughter of Edward II; and (2) Margaret Drummond. Invasion by Edward Balliol in 1332 with English support drove David to exile in France. Returning to Scotland in 1346 he attempted invasion of England only to be captured and held prisoner for 11 years.

Robert II 'the Steward' (1371–90), son of Marjory Bruce (daughter of Robert I) and Walter FitzAlan, hereditary High Steward of Scotland, b. 1316. He had numerous children by Elizabeth Mure of Rowallan before their marriage, among them his successor.

Robert III (1390–1406), legitimated natural son of Robert II, b. *c.* 1337, named John, he adopted the regnal name of Robert. He left his own epitaph 'the worst of kings and most miserable of men'.

James I (1406–37), son of Robert III, b. 1394, a prisoner in England until being ransomed in 1424, he was assassinated by baronial malcontents.

James II (1437–60), son of James I, b. 1430, he married Mary of Gueldres. A brave and generous king, he was killed by an exploding cannon while attempting to retake Roxburgh from the English.

James III (1460–88), son of James II, b. 1452, he married Margaret of Denmark. An unsuccessful reign ended with his death after battle against rebellious lords near Stirling, possibly a case of assassination.

James IV (1488–1513), son of James III, b. 1473, he married Margaret Tudor, daughter of Henry VII of England. That rare phenomenon in the house of Stuart, a popular and a good king. He died in the defeat of his army by the English at Flodden Field.

James V (1513–42), son of James IV, b. 1512, he married (1) Madeleine of France and (2) Mary of Guise. After the defeat of his army at the battle of Solway Moss he lived long enough to hear the news that his wife had given birth to a daughter, then died with enigmatic remark, 'It came with a lass and it will go with a lass'.

Left: King James V, father of Mary Queen of Scots.

Below: Mary Queen of Scots, by the French court artist François Clouet. Mary spent virtually the first 20 years of her life in France, being briefly queen of the country until the death of her first husband, King Francis II.

Mary (Queen of Scots) (1542–67), daughter of Mary of Guise and James V, b. December 1542, she married (1) Francis [II] Dauphin, later King of France (d. 1560); (2) Henry Stewart, Lord Darnley; and (3) James Hepburn, Earl of Bothwell. When she returned to Scotland from France in 1560, it was to find a turbulent and Protestant nobility which, following the Queen's notably eccentric marital adventures, forced her abdication. She went into exile in England where she lived the self-proclaimed rightful successor to Elizabeth I, before involvement in one plot too many led to her execution at Fotheringhay Castle, Northamptonshire, on 5 February 1587.

James VI (1567–1625), son of Mary and Henry, Lord Darnley, b. 1566, he acceded to the Scottish throne, aged one, at his mother's abdication. From her, through her descent from Margaret Tudor (see above, James IV) he inherited a claim to the throne of England. James's protests at her execution on the orders of Elizabeth were muted since he feared to be cut out of the succession if he offended the English Queen. He married Anne of Denmark, mother of Charles I and Elizabeth of the Palatinate, ancestress of the House of Hanover. In 1603 James acceded to the throne of England as James I.

KINGS AND QUEENS OF ENGLAND FROM ALFRED THE GREAT

Alfred was the only king of England to be accorded the title 'the Great'. As king of Wessex he defeated Danish invaders under Guthrum and forced them to accept baptism.

The list gives the name of the king or queen regnant in the left-hand column, followed in brackets by date of birth; date of accession–date of death. Below each sovereign is given the birthplace, where known, hereditary claim, e.g. 'son of . . .' or other claim to throne, and sobriquet where relevant.

In the right-hand column is the name of the spouse, when known, and the date of marriage.

All dates and periods are to the nearest year except for periods of less than a year, in which cases months are specified.

Alfred (849; 871–99), 'the Great'	**Ealswith**
Edward the Elder (?; 899–925), son of Alfred	
Athelstan (895; 925–39), illegitimate son of Edward the Elder	
Edmund I (?922; 939–46), son of Edward the Elder	**St Ælfgifu**
Eadred (946–55), son of Edward the Elder	
Eadwig (955–9), son of Edmund I	**Ælfgifu**
Edgar (944; 959–75), younger son of Edmund I	**Ælfthryth**, crowned with Edgar
Edward the Martyr (c. 962; 975–8), son of Edgar	
Æthelred II (c. 968; 978–1013 and 1014–16), younger son of Edgar, called 'Unraed' 'lacking counsel', dethroned and exiled by Swegn of Denmark	1002 **Emma** of Normandy
Swegn (Sven) of Denmark (?; 1013–Feb 1014), king by conquest, ousted Æthelred II	
Æthelred II, second reign (1014–Apr 1016)	
Edmund II (?981; Apr–Nov 1016), 'Ironside', son of Æthelred II, defeated at battle of Ashingdon by Cnut, died mysteriously	**Ealdgyth**
Cnut of Denmark (?994; Dec 1016–35), son of Swegn, king also of Denmark and Norway (from 1028)	**Emma**, widow of Æthelred

Above: A coin of Æthelred II *'Unraed'*. The nickname is usually translated as 'Unready', but more properly means 'Lacking in counsel'. The King's real name means 'Noble Counsel'.

Left: The Alfred Jewel. Possibly the head of a reading pointer to help mark the place in a text. The jewel, of gold filigree with the enamel figure of a king mounted behind rock crystal, bears the legend: 'Alfred had me made'. Dating from the late 9th century and found at Athelney, a site associated with King Alfred the Great of Wessex and England, it is confidently assigned to him.

Harold I 'Harefoot' (c. 1016; 1035–40), illegitimate son of Cnut, self-styled regent for Harthacnut, then usurped throne

Harthacnut (1018; 1040–2), son of Cnut

St Edward (1002/5; 1042–Jan 1066), b. Islip, Oxfordshire, 'the Confessor', son of Æthelred II

Edith Earl Godwin's daughter (d. 1075)

Harold II (1022?; Jan–Oct 1066), son of Earl Godwin; king by acclamation, 25 Sept defeated Harald of Norway at Battle of Stamford Bridge, killed at Hastings 14 Oct

Ealdgyth of Mercia

William I (1027/8; 1066–87), 'the Conqueror', b. Falaise, illegitimate son of Duke Robert I of Normandy, and Herleva, a tanner's daughter

1053 **Matilda** of Flanders (despite papal ban; dispensation only in 1059); a remote descendant of Alfred the Great

William II (c. 1057; 1087–1100), 'Rufus' (i.e. 'Redhead'), son of William I, died in hunting accident (possibly assassinated)

Henry I (1068; 1100–35), 'Beauclerc', b. Selby, Yorkshire, son of William I

(1) c. 1100 **Matilda** (also known as Edith) of Scotland (1080–1118)
(2) 1121 **Adela** of Louvain

Stephen (?1097; 1135–54), b. Blois, France, nephew of Henry I

c. 1125 **Matilda** of Boulogne (?1103–52) crowned 1136

Matilda the Empress (1102–(41)–67), 'Lady of England' Apr–Nov 1141, daughter and only surviving legitimate child of Henry I, never crowned or titled 'Queen'

(1) 1114 Emperor **Henry V**
(2) 1130 **Geoffrey** Count of Anjou

Henry II (1133; 1154–89), b. Le Mans, France, grandson of Henry I (his mother was Matilda the Empress)

1152 **Eleanor** of Aquitaine (?1122–1204)

Richard I (1157; 1189–99) 'the Lionheart', b. Oxford, son of Henry II

1191 **Berengaria** of Navarre, m. in Limassol, Cyprus

John (1167; 1199–1216), b. Oxford, son of Henry II, named heir by Richard

(1) 1189 **Avice** (also called Isabella) of Gloucester for her lands; put aside 1200 for
(2) **Isabella** of Angoulême (crowned 1201, d. 1246. (2) Hugh of Lusignan)

Henry III (1207; 1216–72), b. Winchester, son of John

1236 **Eleanor** of Provence (d. 1291)

Edward I (1239; 1272–1307), b. Palace of Westminster, son of Henry III

(1) 1254 **Eleanor** of Castile (d. 1290)
(2) 1299 **Margaret** of France (d. 1318)

Edward II (1284; 1307–27), b. Caernarfon Castle, son of Edward I

1308 **Isabella** of France (1292–1358)

Edward III (1312; 1327–77), b. Windsor, son of Edward II

Richard II (1367; 1377–99), b. Bordeaux, grandson of Edward III (Richard's father, Edward the Black Prince, was the eldest son of Edward III but died in 1376)

Henry IV (1366; 1399–1413), b. Bolingbroke Castle, Lincs, usurper, son of John of Gaunt, Duke of Lancaster, 4th son of Edward III

Henry V (1387; 1413–22), b. Monmouth, son of Henry IV

Henry VI (1421; 1422–61 and 1470–71), b. Windsor, only child of Henry V

Edward IV (1442; 1461–70 and 1471–83), b. Rouen, usurper, son of Richard, Duke of York

1328 **Philippa** of Hainault (1314?–69)
(1) 1382 **Anne** of Bohemia (1366–94)
(2) 1396 **Isabella** of France (1389–1409)
(1) 1368/70 **Mary** de Bohun (d. 1394)
(2) 1403 **Joan** of Navarre (?1370–1437)

1420 **Catherine** of France (1401–37)

1445 **Margaret** of Anjou (1430–82)

1464 **Elizabeth** Woodville (c. 1437–92)

and descended from Edward III's 3rd son Lionel, Duke of Clarence

(Henry VI of the House of Lancaster and Edward IV of the House of York were the principal opponents during the period of English history conventionally called 'The Wars of the Roses'. In March 1461 Henry was declared deposed and his army defeated at the Battle of Towton: in June the same year Edward was crowned king. In September 1470 supporters of Henry forced King Edward to flee England. However, in 1471 he returned and defeated the Lancastrians at the Battle of Tewkesbury in May. Henry died, probably murdered, in the Tower.)

Edward V (1470; Apr–June 1483; d.?), b. in the Sanctuary, Westminster Abbey, son of Edward IV

Richard III (1452; 1483–5), b. Fotheringhay Castle, Northamptonshire, usurper, brother of Edward IV, defeated and killed at the Battle of Bosworth 22 Aug 1485

1470 **Anne** Neville (1456–85)

Left: King Henry V. The victor at Agincourt in 1415, Henry triumphantly maintained England's claim to France. A king was expected to maintain his rights and lead his nobles in victorious (and ransom-rich) war. Devoting his great talents to the job of monarchy with an almost monastic austerity, Henry re-established English rule in Normandy and forced the French king, Charles VI, to name him as his heir. In fact, Charles outlived the English king by a few months. Henry's baby son, Henry VI, grew up weak and incompetent and lost his father's conquest back to the French.

Right: Richard III. Killed at the Battle of Bosworth in 1485 by the adventurer Henry Tudor (Henry VII) and himself ruthless when occasion demanded. Richard was blackened as a monster by Tudor propaganda, accused of the murder of his nephews and of having been horribly deformed.

From the Queen's collection, these priceless miniatures by the renowned Nicholas Hilliard depict, left to right: King Henry VII, Queen Jane Seymour, (Henry VIII's favourite wife and mother of Edward VI), King Henry VIII himself, Edward VI and Queen Elizabeth I.

Below: The young Charles II, in exile at the Hague during the period of the Commonwealth in the 1650s, dances with an unnamed beauty—possibly Lucy Walters, mother of his son, the Duke of Monmouth.

Above: The coronation of King George IV in 1820 was notable for the fact that Queen Caroline, the wife that he hated, was excluded by main force on the King's orders. Londoners, who hated the King, were her vociferous supporters.

Right: Queen Charlotte, wife of George III and with 15 children the most prolific of English queens.

Henry VII (1457; 1485–1509), b. Pembroke Castle, usurper, descended through illegitimate line from John of Gaunt (4th son of Edward III) and his mistress Catherine Swynford

1486 **Elizabeth** of York (1465–1503), daughter of Edward IV

Henry VIII (1491; 1509–47), b. Greenwich, second son of Henry VII, heir apparent on death of his brother Arthur

(1) 1509 **Catherine** of Aragon (1485–1536), [=(i) 1501 Arthur, Prince of Wales (d. 1502), marriage declared null 1509], marriage declared null 1533

(In 1501 Catherine was married to Arthur, Prince of Wales. When he died the following year, she remained in England while her father-in-law, Henry VII of England, and her father, Ferdinand of Aragon, haggled over the terms of outstanding dowry payments and her return. In 1509 the Pope declared her marriage to Arthur had been null and she married Henry VIII. In 1533, after years of legal wrangling had failed to get another annulment from the Pope, Henry had Thomas Cranmer, Archbishop of Canterbury, declare the marriage null and thus, effectively, initiated the breach between the Church of England and Rome. The same year Henry married Anne Boleyn.)

(2) 1533 **Anne** Boleyn (1507–36) marriage declared null 1536, executed
(3) 1536 **Jane** Seymour (?1509–37), died in childbirth
(4) 1540 **Anne** of Cleves (1515–57), marriage declared null 1540
(5) 1540 **Catherine** Howard (d. 1542), executed for unchastity
(6) 1543 **Catherine** Parr (1512–48)

Edward VI (1537; 1547–53), b. Hampton Court, son of Henry VIII by Jane Seymour

Mary I (1516; 1553–8), b. Greenwich Palace, daughter of Henry VIII by Catherine of Aragon

1554 **Philip II** of Spain, titled 'King of England'

Elizabeth I (1533; 1558–1603), sometimes called 'the Great', b. Greenwich Palace, daughter of Henry VIII by Anne Boleyn

James VI and I (reigned 1603–25) (see Scotland), his daughter Elizabeth married a German Prince, the Elector Palatine from whom descended Sophia who married the Elector of Hanover

1589 **Anne** of Denmark (1574–1619)

Charles I (1600; 1625–49), b. Dunfermline Palace, second son of James I, executed

1625 **Henrietta Maria** of France (1609–69)

The Interregnum Kingship declared abolished 17 March 1649
Lords Protector of the Commonwealth: Oliver Cromwell (1599; 1653–8) and Richard Cromwell son of Oliver (1626; 1658–May 1659; died 1712)

The Restoration of the Monarchy declared by Parliament 29 May 1660

Charles II (1630; ruled May 1660–85), b. St James's Palace, son of Charles I

1662 **Catherine** of Braganza (1638–1705)

James II (1633; 1685–88; 1701), b. St James's Palace, son of Charles I

(1) 1660 **Anne** Hyde (1637–71)
(2) 1673 **Mary Beatrice** of Modena (1658–1718)

William III (1650; 1689–1702), b. The Hague, grandson of Charles I, joint ruler with his wife Mary; after her death, sole ruler

1677 **Mary II** (1662; 1689–94), b. St James's Palace, elder daughter of James II

Anne (1665; 1702–14), b. St James's Palace, youngest surviving daughter of James II

1683 **George** Prince of Denmark (1653–1708), refused title of king by Parliament but created Generalissimo and Lord High Admiral

George I (1660; 1714–27), b.

1682 **Sophia**

Queen Victoria in mourning, more or less habitual with her after the death of Albert.

Osnabrück, Germany, son of Sophia, Electress of Hanover, great-grandson of James VI and I

George II (1683; 1727–60), b. Hanover, son of George I

George III (1738; 1760–1820), b. London, Norfolk House, St James's Square, son of Frederick, Prince of Wales and grandson of George II

George IV (1762; 1820–30), b St James's Palace, son of George III

William IV (1765; 1830–7), b. Buckingham Palace, son of George III

Dorothea of Zelle (1666; imprisoned for life 1694, d. 1726)

1705 **Caroline** of Brandenburg-Ansbach (1683–1737)

1761 **Charlotte Sophia** of Mecklenburg-Strelitz (1744–1818)

[(1) Secretly Mrs FitzHerbert]
(2) 1795 **Caroline** of Brunswick-Wolfenbüttel (1768–1821)

1818 **Adelaide** of Saxe-Meiningen (1792–1849)

Victoria (1819; 1837–1901), b. Kensington Palace, daughter of Edward, Duke of Kent, 4th son of George III

Edward VII (1841; 1901–10), b. Buckingham Palace, son of Victoria

George V (1865; 1910–36), b. London, Marlborough House, second son of Edward VII

Edward VIII (1894; Jan–Dec 1936; 1972), b. White Lodge, Richmond Park, son of George V, uncrowned, abdicated and created Duke of Windsor

George VI (1895; 1936–52), b. York Cottage, Sandringham, second son of George V

Elizabeth II (b. 1926; 1952), b. London, 17 Bruton St, W1, daughter of George VI

1840 **Albert** of Saxe-Coburg-Gotha (1819–61)

1861 **Alexandra** of Denmark (1844–1925)

1893 **Mary** of Teck (1867–1953)

1937 Mrs Wallis Simpson, Duchess of Windsor

1923 **Elizabeth** Bowes Lyon, (b. 1900)

1947 **Philip**, Duke of Edinburgh

George Villers
Duke of Buckingham,

The **FRIENDS AND FAVOURITES OF ROYALTY** have ranged from the glamorous George Villiers (left) who attracted James I (notoriously attracted by handsome young men) and was created Duke of Buckingham, to the dour, boorish and generally drunk John Brown, the Scottish ghillie favoured by the widowed Queen Victoria. Charles II's famous Nell Gwynne (above) delighted Londoners with her boast that she was the king's *Protestant* whore as opposed to his French Catholic favourites. George III's sons had numerous affairs. Mrs Mary Anne Clarke (top right) mistress of Frederick, Duke of York, commander in chief, cheerfully sold army commissions in his name while Mrs Jordan the actress bore William [IV], Duke of Clarence (centre right) a large *'bastardise'* as his common law wife. It is said that Edward VII, dubbed 'Edward the Caresser', loved only two women, his wife and Mrs George Keppel (bottom left) who earned the respect of ministers by her discretion and shrewd political sense. Of the numerous mistresses who were favourite with Edward VII, dubbed 'the Caresser', probably the most famous was Lily Langtry, actress and friend of Oscar Wilde (bottom right).

La Promenade en Famille. — a Sketch from Life.

PRETENDERS

According to the dictionary, a royal pretender is 'a person who mounts a claim as to a throne or title'. Which of course leaves unanswered the questions—What kind of persons and what kind of claims? Can anyone be a 'pretender'? Rather surprisingly the answer is technically 'Yes'. It helped if a claim could be presented as a strong one, but more important was a large army and powerful supporters, interested in seeing the pretender succeed and the old regime go down.

Some pretenders made good their claims and so became kings, others did not. History is written by the winners. It is easy to forget that for people at the time, bound like ourselves to regard tomorrow as the future, the stately procession of English royalty presented a number of figures once considered usurpers.

In October 1066, the Battle of Hastings was fought out between two men, neither of whom had more than a shadow of an hereditary claim. One was the Englishman Harold, brother-in-law of the dead King Edward the Confessor and himself king of England since January. The other was William, Duke of Normandy for some 25 years and the illegitimate son of Duke Robert III. Both claimed to have been nominated as his successor by King Edward—in those days the wish of a former king was one important factor in determining the succession. Harold had one great advantage—he had actually been crowned and anointed king by Archbishop Stigand of Canterbury.

But William asserted that Harold had given his oath to recognize William as king when the time came. Furthermore the Pope, for technical reasons, did not recognize Stigand as archbishop and even gave William's plans to invade a Christian kingdom the status of a crusade. So the Norman army could boast it was doing battle for God against a perjured usurper. Those loyal to Harold considered William an alien pretender. It took the Battle of Hastings and some ruthless campaigning afterwards to persuade many Englishmen otherwise. Thus the pretender became king by right of conquest and is remembered to this day as William the Conqueror.

Over the centuries a number of pretenders met with various degrees of success. Stephen of Blois, claiming to have been named successor by King Henry I, got himself crowned by the Archbishop of Canterbury and established his title as king (1135) whereas his rival, Henry's daughter Matilda whom many considered had the better right, never received coronation nor the title of 'queen'. In 1399 Henry of Bolingbroke won the throne as King Henry IV and established the House of Lancaster by forcing his cousin Richard II, the rightful king, to abdicate and by winning support from Parliament. Edward of York, who as Edward IV became the first Yorkist king, defeated the Lancastrian Henry VI. Edward certainly usurped the crown but his claim was somewhat better than a pretence. The Yorkists had persuaded Parliament they had a more direct descent than the Lancastrians from Edward III, common ancestor of both houses, and that they should succeed to the crown on the death of Henry VI.

The most famous medieval pretender to 'make good' was Henry Tudor, Earl of Richmond, who became king as Henry VII. His hereditary claim, such as it was, derived through his English mother's ancestors, the Beaufort family, who could claim a remote connection with the English royal house as the descendants of Edward III's son, John of Gaunt, by his mistress Catherine Swynford. Early in the 15th century, Parliament raised the stigma of bastardy from the Beaufort line. (On his father's side Henry could boast a Welsh grandfather and a French royal grandmother.)

Compared with the legitimate ancestry of the Yorkists, Henry's hereditary 'claim' was laughable. Instead, his supporters, among them the Duke of Brittany and the French King, accepted his assertion he had been adopted as Lancastrian candidate by Henry VI. It was also being rumoured that the Yorkist King Richard III who had succeeded his brother Edward IV in 1483 was ruling harshly and, in some quarters, that he had arranged the killing of his nephews, the boy King Edward V and Richard Duke of York. (When Henry proclaimed his intention to invade England in the summer of 1485 he said nothing about the princes by name. Even if they were dead, and modern partisans of Richard III claim that they were not, there was a good reason for Henry to keep quiet on the subject. Talk about Yorkist princes in the Tower would merely remind people that there were other Yorkists still alive with far better claim to the throne than Henry himself.) With his victory at Bosworth in August 1485 and King Richard's death on the battlefield, Henry Tudor, Earl of Richmond, became King Henry of England.

During the 1480s and 1490s, two pretenders were put up by Yorkists and others in an attempt to rally opposition to Henry. The first, claiming to be the young King Edward V, actually persuaded the Irish to crown him in Dublin. The second, claiming to be the lost Richard of York, took the 'regnal title' of Richard IV. It turned out that the false 'Edward' was in fact a cook boy called Lambert Simnel and after he and his supporters had been defeated at the Battle of Stoke in 1487 Henry, with a rare flash of humour, had him put to work in the royal kitchens. The would-be Richard IV had more success. Known to history as Perkin Warbeck he maintained his pose for four years, from 1493 to 1497. He was actually endorsed not only by the king of Scotland and the Holy Roman Emperor, who had reasons of foreign policy to embarrass Henry, but even by Duchess

Right: The pomp of majesty. Henry VII, or his son Henry VIII, in procession. The Tudors who won the crown by conquest, themselves had to fight off various pretenders.

Below: James, Duke of Monmouth, illegitimate son of King Charles II and his father's favourite.

Margaret of Burgundy, aunt of the real Princes in the Tower. But Warbeck/Richard was eventually captured and executed (1499).

These pretenders were no doubt imposters but they offer something of a conundrum. If it was public knowledge that the wicked King Richard had killed his nephews before Henry VII defeated him at Bosworth, how could anybody claiming to be either of them persuade anyone else to accept the story?

The next and final episode in the annals of English pretenders began almost exactly 200 years after Henry VII's victory at Bosworth. In June 1685 James, Duke of Monmouth, the bastard son of King Charles II and self-styled Protestant champion against his uncle, the Catholic James II, landed at Lyme Regis in Dorset with a small band of followers. Instead of the thousands of eager recruits he expected to flock to his banner, the young Duke raised only a few troops of rustic volunteers. The doomed enterprise was crushed three weeks later at the battle of Sedgemoor and the Duke taken to London for execution. The next Stuart pretenders were to be Catholic rather than Protestant.

The country had been willing to give James II what it considered a fair trial, despite the fact that his religious views were opposed by the majority. However, after a three-year reign he had so antagonized public opinion that William of Orange, husband of the King's own daughter Mary, easily drove James into exile. But James never formally abdicated and the Stuart claim to the throne was maintained by his son, James Francis (1688–1766), known as the Old Pretender and *his* son Charles Edward (1721–88), the Young Pretender.

King James II of England never attempted to return to his realm from his exile in France and Stuart hopes might have ended with his death in 1701 had it not been that Louis XIV, shaping for war with England, recognized James Francis as 'James III' (his British supporters called themselves 'Jacobites' from the Latin 'Jacobus' for James). In 1714 the death of the childless Queen Anne (James's half sister) meant the end of the Stuart occupancy of the British throne. She was succeeded under the terms of Parliament's 1701 Act of Settlement by the Protestant George I, ruler of Hanover in Germany, but also distantly descended from King James I. At the time of Anne's death the 1707 Union of Scotland and England was increasingly unpopular north of the border and this, coupled with hopes of French support, led to the first 'Jacobite' Rebellion of 1715.

The standard of revolt was raised at Braemar on 6 September by 'Bobbing John' Erskine, the Earl of Mar. Initial manoeuvres met with minor successes but when James himself landed in Scotland in December, the impetus had been lost and the rising was all but over. Worse yet, expected French support failed to materialize. On 6 January, James was received in Dundee as 'rightful king', and proclaimed his intention to be crowned at Scone. It never happened. In February he sailed for France. Later he lived in Italy and married the Polish princess Clementina Sobiewska.

In July 1745 their son Charles Edward Stuart 'Prince of Wales', acting against his father's advice and that of most of the Jacobites in Britain and without any hope of French support, set sail for Scotland. His aim was to

This portrait of James Francis Edward Stuart, 'The Old Pretender' (*above left*), recently acquired by London's National Portrait Gallery and never before published, was painted about 1741 by Louis Gabriel Blanchet. Prince Charles Edward Stuart, 'The Young Pretender', by the same artist (*above right*). The Young Pretender called 'Bonnie Prince Charlie', in Highland dress (*below*).

restore his father to the British throne. The dashing young adventurer rallied support in the Highlands, though many clansmen were dragooned by their chiefs. At Prestonpans on the Firth they won a famous victory and occupied Edinburgh.

Crossing unopposed into England in November, the Highlanders now joined by a few hundred Lancashire sympathizers got as far south as Derby by December. There they learnt that three fresh armies were in the field against them, the principal one commanded by George II's son William, Duke of Cumberland. Despite the urgings of the Prince, the council of war decided on retreat. London breathed again, though in truth the outcome for the Highlanders was defeat either way. On a bleak upland moor near Culloden House, by Inverness on the Moray Firth, on 16 April 1746, they were shot to pieces and cut down by Cumberland's forces, among which there were three battalions of Lowland Scots and one raised from the Clan Campbell. Following the victory at Culloden, the government in London unleashed a reign of terror and butchered all resistance. 'Bonnie Prince Charlie' escaped through a haze of Highland myths, ending his days a disappointed dissolute in Rome some 40 years later. What neither he nor his father nor any 'legitimist' could understand was that in England the succession to the throne has depended since the Middle Ages as much on the will and approval of Parliament as on any considerations of blood or family.

SUCCESSION

The strict rules which today determine the exact ranking of any member of the Royal Family in the line to the throne are of comparatively recent origin. In earlier centuries it was often confused and contested and often determined by other than purely hereditary considerations.

By the 10th century, English kings were generally succeeded by their eldest son or nearest male relative, it is true. But inheritance was only one strand in the thread of monarchy and by a combination of factors, occasional shortage of sons, intervention by foreign conquerers and others in England, it took a long time to become established as the main one. However, connection with the blood royal was considered essential so that even the Danish king Cnut the Great thought it advisable to marry into the family by taking the widow of Æthelred II as his queen. William the Conqueror's wife Matilda of Flanders descended from Alfred the Great of Wessex in the seventh generation. William's youngest son, King Henry I, also married a descendant of Æthelred and so brought a more recent infusion of the blood of the Old English house into the royal line.

In this way, Henry brought at least some show of

legitimacy to his accession. At the time, his elder brother Duke Robert of Normandy was still living. In fact their father William I the Conqueror had set the English crown on a collision course with legitimacy when, at his death in 1187 he bequeathed the crown not to Robert but to his second son William II Rufus. The Conqueror had claimed the right to succeed through the will of Edward the Confessor and designation by a predecessor was an important part of the old English succession law. The third element after birth and designation was 'election', better described as the confirmation by the great men of the realm. The king who could secure consecration and coronation established a fact that for some time appeared to be unanswerable.

Henry made his position secure by consecration. At his death he left a daughter whom he wanted to succeed him but she was cut out when a rival, Stephen, moved quickly and got himself consecrated and crowned. Henry II and John both came to the crown by the designation of their predecessor and from John the succession passed regularly for 200 years until in 1399 the forced abdication of Richard II brought Parliament

An idealized portrait of King William III by the German born Sir Godfrey Kneller, court painter to five monarchs. He came to England in 1674 and died in 1723.

to the fore—playing the role of the great men of the kingdom in authorizing the usurpation of the Lancastrian dynasty with King Henry IV. In 1461 force of arms and the acclaim of London and Parliament brought the crown to Edward IV of York. The Tudors won it on the field of Bosworth and James VI of Scotland by the designation (confirming a good hereditary right) of his distant cousin Elizabeth I.

With the 'Glorious Revolution' of 1688, usurpation took a new turn in legitimacy. The Catholic James II had fled his kingdom, but did not renounce his throne. Nevertheless, his nephew William (of Orange) III, married to James's daughter Mary II, received the solemn confirmation of Parliament. Mary died childless in 1697, then in July 1700 the 11-year-old Prince William Henry, Duke of Gloucester, the last child of her sister Anne, tragically also died. Fearful of the prospects for England's Protestant succession in a Europe where reli-

gion still largely dictated policies and Catholic France under Louis XIV was shaping up for aggression, King William looked to Parliament for a bill that would ensure the exclusion of James II and his son, living as pensioners at Louis's court.

The 1701 Act of Settlement laid down that the succession to the English crown would lie with the Protestant Princess Sophia, Electress of Hanover, grand-daughter of James I, her 40-year-old son George (later King George I) and 17-year-old son (later king as George II) and their heirs. The Act was affirmed for Scotland by the Union of Scotland Act of 1707 and confirmed by subsequent acts of Parliament. Not only has the succession to the throne of England never been determined solely on principles of heredity, it has from a very early period depended on the assent of some body (today Parliament) acting for the community of the realm.

GENEALOGICAL TABLES OF ENGLISH KINGS FROM RICHARD I TO JAMES IV

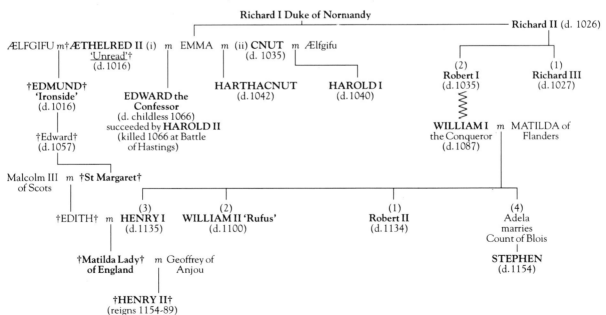

Succession from the Old English to the Angevin line in the century following the Conquest.

Note: the transmission of the English blood royal is marked thus †..†. **KINGS OF ENGLAND** and **Dukes of Normandy** indicated in bold.

For ease of reading children are not always shown in sequence of birth nor are all children shown — sequence indicated by numbers above the name.

≋ Signifies the illegitimate parentage of William I.

Origins of the English claim to the throne of France and descent of the rival houses of York and Lancaster from Edward III

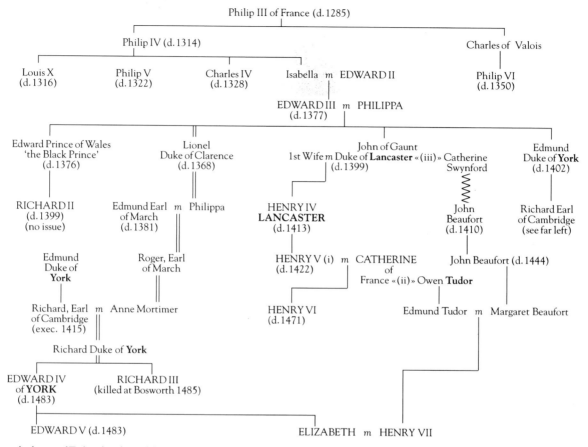

Note: the house of Tudor also claimed descent from Edward through the Beaufort family which originated with John of Gaunt and his mistress Catherine Swynford; the Tudors received their name from the Welsh squire who became the lover (« ») of Henry V's widow, Catherine of Valois of France.

‖ Signifies descent of the House of York from Lionel, Duke of Clarence.

〉〉〉 Signifies descent to the illegitimate child of Catherine Swynford, mistress (later third wife of) John of Gaunt.

Succession of James VI and I to Elizabeth I and his descent from their common ancestor Henry VII.

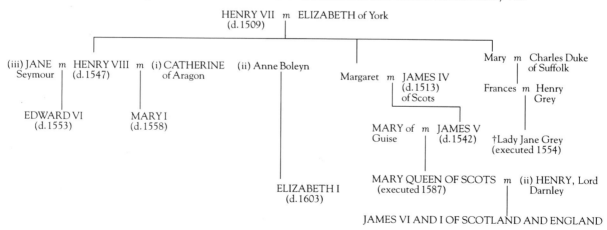

†On the death of King Edward VI on 10 July 1553, Lady Jane Grey was proclaimed Queen by her ambitious father-in-law, the Duke of Northumberland, who hoped to rally Protestant opinion against the Catholic Queen Mary. In fact the popular opinion was entirely opposed to the attempted coup and entirely in favour of Queen Mary. 'Crowned' by her relation in the Tower of London, 'Queen Jane' remained there a prisoner after a nine-day 'reign'. Mary ordered her execution following a rising in her favour in February 1554.
The children of Henry VIII are shown in the order (left to right) that they succeeded to the throne. The order of their mothers' marriages to the King is shown in roman numerals.

FAMILY MATTERS

The death of a monarch is the occasion of great public ceremony and ceremonial, so the treatment of royal funerals will be found in Section III. But births and marriage and the education of royals have also marked them out very definitely from the lives of their subjects. For close on 250 years, from 1688 to the birth of Princess Margaret in 1930, the law required officials representing parliament to be present at a royal birth and it was not until Prince Charles and Princess Anne that it became common practice for the children of the monarch to attend public schools. Over the centuries, royal marriages have traditionally combined the family and the official; monarchs throughout Europe hoped to use the marriages of their sons and daughters to forge alliances and promote foreign policy objectives. All too often the results did not promote the family of nations but instead prepared the grounds for war by providing the sons of such marriage claims to foreign thrones. The most famous case in English history was that of King Edward III, the son of King Edward II and Isabella of France. When the last of his French uncles, King Charles IV, died in 1328 the succession of the throne would have passed, according to English law, to Edward. The French naturally could not allow the succession of the King of England to the throne of France and claimed an ancient law prohibited the succession through the female line. In 1340 King Edward invaded France and the conflict known to history as the Hundred Years War had begun. In modern times royal family connections have been less contentious. In the last century, the marriages of many of Queen Victoria's children established a family network which has spread to include most of the royal families of Europe.

Above: The Duchess of York with Princess Beatrice, March 1989. Photographer: HRH The Duke of York.

Far left: The Prince and Princess of Wales leave St Mary's Hospital, London, December 1984, with their new son, Prince Harry.

Left: The Duke and Duchess of York proudly show off baby Princess Beatrice after her christening in the royal christening robe.

Right: The royal christening robe (detail). Made of Honiton lace for the christening of Queen Victoria's first child, Princess Victoria.

ROYAL BIRTHS

The birth of Princess Beatrice of York in August 1988 was accompanied by the media hype common to such events and followed by great speculation as to the name to be chosen for the new princess. The previous autumn the Yorks had let it be known that they did not expect to start a family for a long time to come. Then, in January, the newspapers got hold of a rumour that 'Fergie' was pregnant. Phonecalls to the Yorks' ski chalet in the Swiss alps produced non-committal responses from a mystery 'baby sitter' whose voice sounded uncannily like that of the Duchess herself. On 25 January 1988 the Palace announced that a baby was due in August. From then on public expectations built up just as they had back in 1982 when the Wales's first son, Prince William of Wales, was born.

Then, Princess Diana continued with her official engagements, opening a community centre in south-east London just a month before she went into hospital, early on 21 June. At 9.03 p.m. on the same day she gave birth to a baby boy who weighed in at a healthy seven pounds. Since it could be assumed that he would one day be king, the birth was greeted with even more than usual of the 'royal rigmarole', to use his grandfather's term. The bells of Westminster Abbey rang out for one and a half hours, while salutes were fired by the Royal Horse Artillery in Hyde Park and the Honourable Artillery Company at the Tower of London. Prince William of Wales, restless and energetic, can be endear-ing or assertive at will, above all completely self-assured. Within the royal family circle, apparently, he earned the nickname William the Wombat.

At all events, the childhood of this probable 'William V' is bound to be better documented than that of his great ancestor William the Conqueror. Love child of Duke Robert II of Normandy and a tanner's daughter from Falaise, almost nothing is known about his childhood. However, the obscure circumstances of his birth do not seem to have prejudiced his prospects. The same can hardly be said of the most notorious birth in the history of Britain's royalty.

In November 1687 Mary Beatrice of Modena, the lovely Italian queen of James II, all of whose children had died young, announced with delight that she was again pregnant. It seems that Mary conceived sometime in September but delayed the announcement. Thus the child was expected sometime in late July or early August 1688.

In the spring of 1688 spiteful gossip led by Princess (later Queen) Anne rumoured that the Queen was not pregnant at all. On 20 June 1687 Mary lay in labour in St James's Palace. Although it was a hot day, a warming pan was called for to ease the Queen's pain. In due course she was delivered of a healthy son but, because of the heat and stuffiness of the chamber, the midwives took the child into an adjoining room where, suitably cleaned up and swaddled, he was shown to the thirty-

odd people who had assembled to witness the royal birth—unfortunately there were no prominent members of the government present.

Until this moment the succession to the crown seemed certain to pass to the staunchly Protestant Mary, James's eldest daughter by his first wife. Now, with a boy born to Catholic James and his still more committed Catholic wife the Protestant cause seemed in jeopardy. It began to be rumoured that the young prince James Francis Edward Stuart was in fact a changeling, introduced in the warming pan by Jesuit plotters. The King only gave credence to the rumour when, with a misplaced gesture of openness, he ordered an inquiry.

From that time on by the insistence of Parliament, every royal birth had to be witnessed by at least one representative of Parliament or the Crown, by convention the Home Secretary, actually in the labour room. The practice continued until Prince Albert, who thought it demeaning and ruled that the 'witness' be content to wait in an adjoining room.

The last royal birth at which even this part of the official protocol was observed was that of Princess Margaret in 1930. The Duchess of York insisted on returning to her family home of Glamis Castle for the birth; the witnesses were to be Jim Clynes, the Labour Home Secretary, and a Mr Boyd, Ceremonial Secretary at the Home Office. The two went up to Scotland well in advance of the event, being put up at Cortachy Castle by the Duchess's friend Lady Airlie. A special

Above: One of the official christening photographs of Princess Elizabeth (the Queen Elizabeth II to be) with her parents, the then Duke and Duchess of York, May 1926.

Left: The christening of Queen Victoria's first child, Victoria Adelaide Mary Louise, at Buckingham Palace on 10 February 1841. Immediately after her birth she had been presented for inspection by assembled dignitaries charged with authenticating the birth, being laid upon a table for all to see and yelling all the time before being taken off to be dressed. Being born to a reigning sovereign, the child was named 'Princess Royal' (the title reserved for the eldest daughter of the sovereign) in the year of her birth. At the age of 14 she was betrothed to Crown Prince Frederick William of Prussia (1831–1888), their son succeeding his father as emperor, being the famous Emperor William II.

Right: Princess Elizabeth poses with her daughter Anne for the official christening photograph of the baby Princess, 21 October 1950.

The Tower of London, 22 June 1982. The guns fire a loyal salute to celebrate the birth of Prince William of Wales, the day before.

telephone line was installed and a dispatch rider stood to day and night.

After days of waiting, which visibly frayed the nerves of the Ceremonial Secretary, a call came through on the evening of 21 August. Driven at speed, the two men arrived at Glamis with half an hour to spare for Mr Boyd to do his witnessing, such as it was. He records that the father, his in-laws and his wife's sister were crowded round the cot. They at once made way for the man from the ministry who 'peeping in, saw a fine chubby faced girl lying wide awake'.

When Prince Charles was born in Buckingham Palace at 9.14 p.m., 14 November 1948, no minister of the Crown nor Member of Parliament even viewed the cradle, let alone attended the birth. Mr Chuter Ede, Labour's Home Secretary, agreed (warming pans being long out of fashion) that the birth of a royal child, like that of any other, could safely be left to its mother and her gynaecological advisers.

In any case, high officers of state had not always proved reliable. As King George III paced his room in St James's Palace in the evening of 12 August 1762 awaiting the birth of his first child, he let it be known that whoever should bring him notification of the birth of a girl should receive £500, but if the child should be a boy the messenger would receive £1000.

Queen Charlotte was in labour in her own room in the same palace but it was thought improper for a man to witness his own wife giving birth. Instead the witnesses included, beside the Ladies of the Bedchamber, the Archbishop of Canterbury, the First Lord of the Treasury, the two Secretaries of State, the Officers of the Privy Council and the Officers of the Royal Household. Among these latter, it was customary for the Lord Chamberlain to announce a birth to the sovereign. However, on this occasion an eager Master of the Horse, the Earl of Huntingdon who had evi-

dently heard only the King's first offer, rushed into his chambers breathlessly to announce the birth of a daughter. On going to see for himself, however, the King discovered that he in fact had a 'strong, large, pretty boy'; the future George IV had entered the world an object of controversy . . . as he would remain.

With 15 children (all but three of whom survived to adulthood) Queen Charlotte is the most prolific mother in the history of English royals. Her husband's ancestress Elizabeth, Queen of Bohemia and daughter of James I, through whom the House of Hanover inherited the throne, came a good second with 13; Edward III's Queen Philippa of Hainault (1312–69) had 11 children while Victoria had nine. (Queen Anne (b. 1665; 1702–14) is in a tragic category all her own. Of her six children one was still-born and of the other five only William Duke of Gloucester achieved the age of 11 before succumbing, like his siblings, to hydrocephalus; in addition Anne had 12 miscarriages.)

It was not because she doted on children that Victoria had so many. She 'positively' thought that 'those ladies who are always enceinte are quite disgusting: it is more like a rabbit . . . and is really not very nice'. Worse, regular pregnancies made one's life wretched, wore a woman out and endangered her looks. She was dismayed at the age of 20 to find herself already pregnant; barely three months after Princess Victoria's birth the Queen was pregnant again—and was furious, Prince Albert later told a friend.

As to the act of giving birth, Victoria hated it. Talking to her granddaughter Queen Marie of Romania, whose mother-in-law who wrote poetry under the name Carmen Sylva, to Victoria's amusement, considered the act a moment of poetical rapture, the Queen confided that she 'deeply deplored' the fact that she had to bring eight children into the world 'without the precious aid of chloroform'.

THE EDUCATION OF ROYALTY

One of King James VI of Scotland and I of England's contemporaries dubbed him 'the wisest fool in Christendom'. He was well read, a diligent author on the dangers of smoking, the power of witches and the nature of kingship, but his judgement of men and affairs was, by and large, disastrously inadequate. Queen Elizabeth, his predecessor on the English throne was, by contrast, not only the most successful monarch of her century but also one of the most brilliant members of a brilliant family. It was an age when people valued education and few monarchs in the history of Europe have been better educated than the Tudors. But King James's example shows that book-learning is not everything and the debate over the proper education for princes has swayed back and forth over the centuries.

Above: Off to school. The Prince and Princess of Wales, with Prince William and his brother Prince Harry on Harry's first day at school. They are welcomed by headmistress Jane Mynors.

Left: Prince Charles escorts his young sister, 1954.

THE QUEEN AND HER FAMILY

The Queen and Princess Margaret were educated at home. They were taught to read by Queen Elizabeth the Queen Mother and then, when Elizabeth was seven, Marion Crawford was appointed as nursery governess. She appears to have received a fairly explicit briefing from the Duchess of York (as the Queen Mother then was). The princesses were to be outdoors as much as possible and to be encouraged in country pursuits. They were 'to acquire good manners and perfect deportment and to cultivate the feminine graces'. The Duchess wanted her children to have a civilized appreciation of the arts and music and to acquire as much book learning as might be within their capabilities.

Following this brief Miss Crawford supervised their lessons—helped by the Belgian lady Mme Antoinette Bellaigue, who taught them French and remained an intimate of the family for several years. When she finally left the royal service 'Crawfie', as she had been affectionately known to everyone, published a gossipy book of reminiscences much to the anger of the family. Princess Elizabeth, as heir to the crown, received tutorials in the constitutional history of Britain from Sir Henry Marten, vice-provost of Eton.

Prince Charles began his formal education at the age of five with his governess Helen Lightbody in the palace schoolroom. But the Queen and the Duke wanted their children to have a real if privileged education and after time at Hill House, a London pre-preparatory school, Charles went to Cheam, his father's old prep school. Homesick like any small boy, he was plagued by the press and then at the age of 10 found himself proclaimed Prince of Wales and Knight of the Garter—the notion that one was just like other boys must have been difficult to maintain.

After Cheam came Gordonstoun, again his father's old school. Gordonstoun is successor to the school founded in 1920 at Salem, Germany, by the progressive educationalist Kurt Hahn. The school buildings were on the estate of the Margrave of Baden, the husband of Philip's older sister Theodora. Hahn's educational principles were based on the development of the whole personality, combining tough physical and intellectual discipline and cultivating self reliance, service to the community and independence of judgement.

The choice of school was left to Prince Charles. The pressure, and challenge, to follow in the footsteps of his extrovert father must have been strong but it may be doubted whether his days there were the happiest time of his life. However, two terms at Timbertop, the country branch of Geelong Church of England Grammar School, Victoria, Australia, sandwiched into his Gordonstoun stint, may well have been. Within days of

his arrival, the Pommie Prince had been perfectly at ease with his Australian classmates. Returning to England after an extensive holiday tour of Australia he finished off at Gordonstoun as head boy ('Guardian') and with two 'A' levels to add to the seven 'O' levels notched up before he went down under. His sister, meanwhile, went to boarding school at Benenden in Kent, where she got six 'O' and two 'A' levels.

From Gordonstoun, Charles went up to Trinity College, Cambridge, to read archaeology and anthropology. To the public at large his period as a student was chiefly noticeable for his participation in undergraduate theatricals. His academic programme was not assisted by the decision to send him for a term to the University College of Wales at Aberystwyth. Many, and not only Welsh nationalists, regarded this as a gimmick, but at least Charles learnt Welsh to such effect that he was able to deliver a five-minute speech in the language at his investiture as Prince of Wales in July 1969. After the ceremony he returned to Cambridge, completing his studies with a second class honours degree.

Andrew followed the family footsteps to Gordonstoun and a spell overseas, in his case at Lakefield, a smart Canadian school east of Toronto. After graduating at the Royal Naval College Dartmouth, the Prince joined the navy on a 12-year commission. A qualified helicopter pilot, he saw active service with HMS *Invincible* during the Falklands Campaign of 1982.

Prince Andrew is the third Duke of York to serve in the navy, a traditional career for second sons, though

Left: The Queen and Princess Margaret as debutantes.

Right: Prince Charles, 14 November 1951, pushed by nurse Helen Lightbody and accompanied by Prince Richard of Gloucester, is taken for a third birthday outing in the Park.

Below: Princess Elizabeth in 1933, outside the miniature cottage given to her by the people of Wales in 1931.

Below right: Elizabeth, now HM Queen Elizabeth II, welcomed to the cottage by her grandson Master Peter Phillips, Princess Anne's three-year-old son, 1980.

Queen Victoria had none too high an opinion of it: 'The very rough life to which boys are exposed on shipboard is the very thing not calculated to make a refined and amiable prince.' Prince Edward after Gordonstoun and a spell as a student teacher at Wanganui in New Zealand, went up to Jesus College, Cambridge, graduating with a 2.1 in archaeology and anthropology, and, like his brother Charles, distinguishing himself in college theatricals. At six foot two—the tallest member of the family, he joined the Royal Marines as a commando. Since some form of military career is deemed proper for members of the royal family, Prince Edward showed courage of a rare kind when, having decided such a career was not for him, he wasted no further time on it and resigned.

Traditionally, kings and princes have been required to train for warfare as part of their role in society but for the most sophisticated and greatest king of the house of Wessex from which the present royal family descends, a good ruler kept the arts of war in perspective.

CHRONICLES OF ROYAL SCHOOLROOMS

Alfred the Great had been so concerned with the education of his son, and indeed of the young nobles of his kingdom, that he himself turned author and translator of text books in geography and philosophy.

In the 1320s an elaborate and beautifully illuminated copy of the *Secretis Secretorum* was presented to the teenage Edward III by Walter de Milemete of Oxford. It was the most admired treatise on the education and duties of princes at the time, and the illustrations must have delighted Edward—lavish heraldic ornamentation in the borders and, fittingly for a soldier prince, Europe's first known illustration of a gunpowder artillery weapon.

Edward's grandson Richard II, who as a patron of Chaucer was one of the most cultivated of England's medieval kings, seems to have been deeply impressed by the teachings of his tutor, Sir Simon Burley, a strong believer in the aura which surrounded the office of king. When Richard himself became king he behaved with such high-handed authority that the barons rose in opposition. Some of the King's closest friends and advisers were arraigned and executed for encouraging the young King to tyranny, among the first being his old tutor.

No dynasty made higher intellectual demands of its children than the Tudors. Henry VII appointed Thomas Linacre, the renowned Greek scholar, as tutor for his son Arthur and the old man was recalled by Henry VIII to teach the Princess Mary [I]. Her brother Edward [VI] is said to have loved only two people in the whole of his short life and one of them was his tutor Sir John Cheke. Edward, who died aged just 16, was very much a child of his age—a bigot in religion with an intellect of breadth and penetrating power.

Elizabeth [I] matched her brother in learning and was far beyond him in tolerance. Her principal tutor, the enlightened educationalist Roger Ascham, opposed the use of corporal punishment and published a treatise on archery. He did not want his pupils always poring over books but urged them 'to delight in all courtly exercises' for the Muses were 'ladies of dancing, mirth and minstrelsy' as well as learning.

Elizabeth was a brilliant pupil. She spoke four modern languages; 'scoured up her old Latin' for an impromptu and withering harangue to a Polish ambassador; danced the leaping dance *la volta* when young; did three or four galliards at a Twelfth Night party in her mid-sixties, was an outstanding keyboard player and a noted markswoman with the crossbow.

Her successor, James I, did not like shooting and had absolutely no idea of statecraft, though he ponderously wrote *Basilikon Doron* on the topic for the instruction of his eldest son. It contained precepts of the 'Divine right of Kings' calculated to antagonize anyone who followed them to the Parliament in London. 'My son,' wrote the king, 'learn to know . . . that God made you a little God to sit on his Throne and rule over other men.' Tragically Henry Prince of Wales died before his father. His younger brother Charles [I] learnt the lessons all too well.

The young Charles [II] profited variously from private tuition. His governess Mrs Wyndham may have provided the teenage prince with his first lessons in love while he certainly took to heart the words of his tutor, that outstanding horseman, William Cavendish, Earl (later Marquis) of Newcastle: 'I would not have

The boy king Edward VI.

Below left: Prince Charles at work in his Cambridge 'set' (i.e. rooms), June 1969.

Below: Like many a male royal before him, Prince Andrew made his career in the Navy. Here he is seen with his helicopter aboard HMS *Invincible*, after his return from the Falklands campaign, 1982.

Queen Elizabeth I, one of the most intellectually brilliant, as well as politically successful, of England's monarchs. The painted tableau behind her records the defeat of the Spanish Armada.

you too studious for too much contemplation spoils action.' He went on, '. . . to women you cannot be too civil especially to great ones.'

George III had Lord Harcourt as governor but Andrew Stone, his sub-governor, was said to be a Jacobite. He introduced his biddable pupil to books which defended James II's unconstitutional measures, and asserted the right of kings to choose their own ministers and claimed they had in times past been the people's protectors against the aristocracy and could be so again.

His granddaughter Victoria was no blue stocking, but she received a respectable education. Besides German she could speak (and write) in French and was taught Italian, arithmetic, drawing and music. Like other young ladies of her time, Victoria kept up her art and improved her modest talent with lessons from Edward Lear. (His first visit to Windsor took his breath away. 'Where did you get all these wonderful pictures?' he asked. 'They belonged to my family, Mr Lear', came the amused reply.)

Later in life, Queen Victoria wrote of her governess Baroness Lehzen that she '. . . devoted her life to me from my fifth to my eighteenth year . . . never taking a day's leave. I adored her'. The daughter of a Lutheran pastor, Louise Lehzen had also been a staunch ally against the attempts by Victoria's mother to establish herself as the power behind the throne before her daughter's accession.

In the years that followed, Albert presided over his family with increasing authority under the adoring eyes of his wife. Their chief disappointment was their eldest son, whom the consort aimed to educate into England's ideal king. There are few more obvious cases in history of a father endeavouring to fulfil his ambitions through his son and few more frustrating or unhappy tales. From boyhood Edward was subjected to the strictest of regimens. The one tutor for whom he had real affection was removed for not being sufficiently strict.

At Oxford he lived with his entourage in a private mansion; when he entered lectures the undergraduates stood and remained standing until he sat. His brief attendance at Oxford was followed by a still briefer one at Cambridge and from there he was sent to the Army camp at the Curragh in Ireland with 10 weeks in which to pass his promotions from ensign to battalion commander. It was an absurd programme and the boy acquired his first mistress instead. Albert Edward was not meant for desk work but he had other talents which, coupled with diplomatic tact, were to impress Prime Minister Gladstone.

While it is true that today's generation of young royals is the first to have had a conventional schooling, they were not the first to encounter 'real life' during the course of their education. Their grandfather, George VI, great-uncle Edward VIII, and great-grandfather King George V spent time in naval training establishments which provided harsh encounters with real life. 'It never did me any good to be a Prince', wrote King George V, recalling his days on the Royal Navy training ship. '*Britannia* was a pretty tough place and the other boys made a point of taking it out of us on the grounds that they'd never be able to do it later on.'

At the age of six he had joined his elder brother Prince Albert Victor with the Reverend John Dalton as tutor. Mr Dalton's view was not over-flattering: 'Prince George lacks application . . . and his sense of self-approbation is almost the only motive power in him.' He also noted that the older boy needed the stimulus of his brother's company to work at all. George's self confidence stood him in good stead during his naval training. In fact, while in no way brilliant, he proved a capable student in things nautical. At Greenwich he achieved first class marks in gunnery and torpedo work as well as well as seamanship and he won promotion on genuine capacity up to the rank of commander.

But if the navy gave George V some sense of his equality with other people (by whom, his son Edward [VIII], always known in the family as David, would observe, 'he meant the children of the well-born'), it hardly gave him an education. And not having had one himself, George V saw no need for his two elder sons to have one, although his third son Prince Henry [later Duke of Gloucester] was sent to Eton.

Their childhood tutor, a yachting and golfing crony of the King's who reckoned the boys would have been better sent to a good preparatory school, at least tried to provide the setting of a schoolroom on the first floor of York Cottage, Sandringham, with blackboard, desks, bookshelves and a strict timetable. Unfortunately, as he admitted, he was a poor and uninspiring teacher. He was assisted by visiting tutors in German and French. Neither boy was bright and 'Bertie' was not only inattentive at German but when scolded merely pulled his tutor's beard!

At the naval college of Osborne on the Isle of Wight the physical conditions were more primitive even than an Edwardian boarding school. Whereas Prince Henry was to have a room of his own at Eton, the two future kings shared dormitories with some 30 other boys—it was a rude break with their life thus far. Woken by bugle call at 6.30 in the morning they followed a tight daily curriculum at the double. Neither was entirely immune from bullying and because school rules forbade seniors to mingle with new boys, even brothers, they had to make secret rendezvous when Bertie wanted brotherly comfort and advice.

Shy and inhibited Bertie, given the incognito of 'Mr Johnson', was treated with almost exaggerated disregard for his status, being brusquely disciplined and, though left-handed, being constantly harried at Osborne to use his right. His marks were appalling—it was a matter for congratulation when he was out of the bottom 10. However, at Dartmouth he revealed himself as a useful tennis player, and while there, he began to lose something of his awkwardness as the staff encouraged him to use his left hand. There were those who thought that his education in self confidence and preparation for kingship were completed by his wife. Whatever the elements that went to form his character and judgement, King George VI proved equal to the challenge of war, the classic test of kingship.

The business of educating the royal heir has been tackled, it would seem, with mixed success. In the days when monarchs exercised real power, the usual problems of growing up and the conflict between children and parents were made worse by the young princes' knowledge that they were sure to succeed to a crown. Even as a schoolboy, the heir could be sure that the day would come when none of his 'elders and betters' would be likely to criticize his actions; his class mates might find him a bit bumptious too. Things do not change all that much if we are to believe the gossip in the French press about Prince William of Wales (presumably to be one day King William V). *Paris Match* reported that he earned the nickname William the Bruiser ('le cogneur') at his prep school and was liable to silence opposition with a peremptory 'My Dad'll thump yours, my Dad's Prince of Wales!'

King George III wrote to his son Prince William (later King William IV), about to begin his training as a naval cadet, to remember that though he was a prince at home, on board he was just a boy learning the trade of the sea. But just because he was a prince, he must always remember that there were things other boys might do that he must not do and because he was a prince, higher standards of behaviour, if not necessarily of achievement, would be expected of him.

Queen Victoria, photographed in July 1897 with her great-grandson, Prince Edward of York, aged three. He was later king as Edward VIII.

The young Prince Albert, later king as George VI, in sailor suit. Like his father, King George V, he was principally educated in naval colleges.

MARRIAGES

In earlier days marriage of royals was an important part of foreign policy; often with the worst results. Edward II's marriage to Isabella of France, for example, provided their son Edward III with a claim to the French throne which provided a pretext for the Hundred Years War. But then love matches were rarely more successful. Edward IV's secret marriage to Elizabeth Woodville, the beautiful widow of an impoverished Lancastrian knight, could perhaps have been a gesture of reconciliation in the rivalries of the Roses. In fact, it not only alienated the King's great minister Warwick but, more important, admitted the new Queen's rapacious relatives to the opportunities of royal patronage and antagonized many.

Marriage of royals was in those days primarily to beget sons and the failure of St Edward the Confessor (d. 1066) and his Queen Edith to have children had far-reaching consequences. The Normans claimed Edward had designated their duke William as his heir. The Battle of Hastings was needed to convince the English on the point.

William the Conqueror's own marriage to Matilda of Flanders was in defiance of the Church and for the first five years of the marriage, until a dispensation was finally forthcoming from the pope, they lived in sin. The marriage of William's youngest son Henry I to Matilda of Scotland was intended to secure the legitimacy of the Norman kings beyond question since she was descended through her mother from the old English kings whose blood thus returned to the royal line.

From that time, by devious but traceable routes, it has continued to flow in the veins of England's kings and queens. The remarkable marriage saga of King Henry VIII, ending as it did in the glorious but childless Queen Elizabeth I, proved a cul-de-sac in dynastic terms. Since George III's Royal Marriage Act of 1772 the royals of Britain have been governed by unique rules of permission. Its provisions are described below. First we look at the marriages of the present Queen and her immediate family, some of the happiest events in the history of modern Britain.

Above: The coats of arms of the Prince and Princess of Wales. (Copyright is reserved.)

Right: The wedding of the Prince and Lady Diana Spencer, St Paul's, 29 July 1981.

Left: The Duke and Duchess of York, after their wedding in Westminster Abbey, July 1986.

ANDREW = SARAH
HRH Prince Andrew, Duke of York
To Sarah Ferguson
On Wednesday 23 July 1986
At Westminster Abbey

As with most modern royal 'eligibles', speculation was rife in the press as to whom Prince Andrew would eventually marry, long before the event. Then, in February 1986, Miss Sarah Ferguson, daughter of Major 'Ronnie' Ferguson, manager of Prince Charles's polo team, was among the visitors to HMS *Brazen*, the ship on which Andrew was serving. The public quickly decided that 'Fergie' would be the next royal bride; on 19 March the Palace confirmed they were right.

Late in June, Andrew and Sarah made a visit to Northern Ireland. The young royals signalled new departures when Sarah and Princess Diana, lightly disguised as policewomen, raided Andrew's stag party. On the morning of the ceremony the Queen had followed old traditions by creating her second son Duke of York. The service followed the old Prayer Book with its bridal promise to obey. The *decolletée* dress was of old fashioned white satin with encrustations of jewelled embroidery in a pattern of thistles and anchors on the bodice and train and bows on the shoulders of the same material. The bride wore a single row of pearls with a diamond drop, her veil held in place with a diamond and pearl tiara. Prince William of Wales made a bumptiously cherubic page boy.

There were an estimated 500 million telespectators world-wide.

CHARLES = DIANA
HRH Charles, Prince of Wales
To Lady Diana Spencer
On Wednesday 29 July 1981
At St Paul's Cathedral

The day dawned bright and glorious as security men, policemen and dog handlers moved to their positions. Bellringers prepared for the four-hour 5000-change stint to be rung on the Cathedral bells. The groom with his two supporters Prince Andrew and Prince Edward, the Queen and members of the royal family left Buckingham Palace in a cavalcade of carriages shortly after 10 o'clock. They and the bride's family were in their places in the Cathedral when the cheers outside announced the arrival of the bride and her father Earl Spencer in the magnificent glass coach. Like every wedding, it had its hitch when Lady Diana got her husband's numerous Christian names muddled.

The dress by David and Elizabeth Emanuel was of ivory silk taffeta with a 25-foot-long (7.6 m) train; the bouquet falling near to the floor, was of white flowers, roses, trailing ivy and the traditional myrtle and veron-

ica. Returning with cavalry guard escort to the Palace they delighted the crowd with a new precedent for royal weddings—a kiss on the balcony.

The honeymoon began at Broadlands; then on the Saturday by an Andover of the Queen's Flight to Gibraltar; thence by HMY *Britannia* to Egypt; then by air to Scotland and the privacy of Balmoral.

The cake of five tiers was made by the catering corps of the Royal Navy.

Television audience world-wide estimated at 750 million.

ANNE = MARK
HRH The Princess Anne
To Captain Mark Phillips
On 14 November 1973
At Westminster Abbey

The wedding, classed by the Palace as a private event, was attended by no fewer than 4000 police and celebrated by a 1500-guest reception by the Queen with some 25 members of royal families among the guests, though no foreign monarchs attended the Abbey service. Mark was made one of her aides-de-camp by the Queen but was not ennobled. The Princess had only one bridesmaid, Lady Sarah Armstrong Jones, for as she said, she knew what it was like 'having yards of uncontrollable children'. The dress, designed by Maureen Baker, Princess Anne's dressmaker at Susan Small Ltd, was of an exquisitely fine ivory silk. The bodice and skirt were cut in one and embroidered in silver thread, seed pearls and mirror jewels; the long sleeves were pleated.

Anne and Mark honeymooned in the Caribbean on HMY *Britannia*, Princess Margaret's island retreat of Mustique being among their ports of call.

The cake of four tiers, weighing 145 lb (65.7 kg), was made by the Army catering corps.

Television audience world-wide estimated at 530 million.

MARGARET = TONY
HRH The Princess Margaret
To Antony Armstrong-Jones, created Earl of Snowdon
On 6 May 1960
At Westminster Abbey

The first major royal event since the Queen's coronation, her sister's wedding was a brilliant affair with closed circuit TV screens in remoter parts of the Abbey. At Princess Margaret's wish, the bridesmaids were dressed in replicas of her first childhood ball gown, a favourite with her late father. Her own dress of white silk organza was by Norman Hartnell. It had a 'V' neck bodice and a skirt of broadly flaring panels; the veil was secured in a superb tiara. On their way to Rotherhithe dock for the royal barge to take them aboard HMY *Britannia*, their limousine was so mobbed by the crowd that it slowed to a walking pace and someone found time to scratch a heart into the maroon paintwork.

They honeymooned in the Caribbean on board *Britannia*.

Television audience world-wide estimated at 320 million.

ELIZABETH = PHILIP
HRH The Princess Elizabeth
To Philip, Duke of Edinburgh
On 20 November 1947
At Westminster Abbey

The first great royal event after World War II, at a time when rationing was still in force, Princess Elizabeth's wedding was less glamorous than some but, in the conditions of post-war Britain's austerity made a glittering display. Like any other bride, the Princess received a bonus of 200 clothing coupons and many female admirers sent her their treasured coupons as a present. But it was illegal to give away coupons and the ladies in waiting at the Palace returned each generous gift with a personal note.

The Norman Hartnell dress could truly bear a 'Made in Britain' label, its ivory satin spun from English silkworms, the crystal, pearl and thread embroidery of roses, stars, ears of corn and orange blossom twinkled like stars, brightening up the lives of the thousands who braved the rain to watch the procession go by. The pattern was repeated on the silk tulle train, borne by six attendants down the aisle of the Abbey, packed with visiting royalty, peers and peeresses, politicians and other commoners. The groom had the day before been created Duke of Edinburgh, Earl of Merioneth and Baron Greenwich, but too late to be included in the order of service.

The royal couple began their honeymoon at Broadlands, the home of Philip's uncle 'Dickie' Mountbatten, but harassed by the press and sightseers they fled north to Birkhall on the Balmoral estate.

Left: The famous first royal kiss on the balcony at Buckingham Palace when Prince Charles, to the delight of the crowd, kissed Princess Diana following their wedding on 29 July 1981.

Right: Dartmouth Naval College, 22 July 1939. This was probably the first photograph showing the then Princess Elizabeth (furthest from camera) and the Duke of Edinburgh together. King George VI and Queen Elizabeth (front row) at the King's old College with their daughters. At the back, the uniformed Philip can be seen sharing a joke. On his right stands his uncle, Lord Louis Mountbatten —who, characteristically, is fully aware of the camera's presence.

Above left: The then Princess Elizabeth and the Duke of Edinburgh take time off together in Malta where the Duke was posted soon after their marriage.

Above right: The ill-starred marriage of George, Prince of Wales (later King George IV) to Caroline of Brunswick (1794). He loathed her from the start and his attempt to divorce her by a bill in the House of Lords (after his accession in 1820) outraged society, delighted the London mob and for a time seemed to threaten the monarchy as an institution. George had in fact been secretly married to the Catholic widow Mrs FitzHerbert since 1785.

Left: Queen Victoria's marriage to Prince Albert of Saxe-Coburg-Gotha, often known as 'Albert the Good' and once called 'the finest king Britain never had'. The young Queen's devotion to him was complete.

THE ROYAL MARRIAGE ACT

Since 1772 all British royal marriages have required the permission of the sovereign, under the terms of the Royal Marriage Act of 1772, framed on the instructions of George III. His sense of royal propriety was, it appears, outraged by the secret marriage to a commoner, contracted by his brother, Henry, Duke of Cumberland. The terms of the Act made it illegal for descendants of George II, other than the issue of princesses who married into foreign families, to marry without permission of the reigning sovereign. Severe penalties were attached, including the loss of civil rights, the loss of land and goods and the possibility of imprisonment. Such a marriage becomes null and void and any children illegitimate. However, anyone subject to the terms of the act and over the age of 25 could, if refused the consent, give 12 months' notice to the Privy Council and marry at the end of that time provided Parliament raised no objections.

Despite the Act, King George's eldest son George [IV] contracted a secret union with the Catholic widow Mrs FitzHerbert, while the King's sixth son Augustus, Duke of Sussex, secretly married Lady Augusta Murray—the King had the Church courts rule the marriage void.

George III's own wedding to Charlotte of Mecklenburg-Strelitz was preceded by a proxy betrothal ceremony conducted in her German home on the King's behalf by an English diplomat. After dinner the witnesses adjourned to a drawing room where the princess was symbolically 'put to bed' upon a couch. This done, the diplomat, representing her royal suitor, placed his leg bare to the knee upon the couch.

The wedding itself was held in the Chapel Royal at St James's in the evening of 8 September 1761. It must have been an occasion of acute embarrassment for the new Queen. Despite her dress of white and silver, her train of violet coloured velvet, its ermine lining and the brooch of enormous pearls at her shoulder, she could not outshine the ravishing Lady Sarah Lennox, one of the bridesmaids and the not so secret heart's desire of King George. The ceremony was held, as was usual then, in the evening and no doubt the young lady looked the more dazzling in the candlelight. Among the courtiers, the ageing Earl of Westmorland had to be prevented physically from paying his respects and doing homage to her as Queen of England, while the Queen herself stood mutely by.

The time of the wedding is significant. For centuries it had been customary for weddings to be celebrated late in the day so that the marital couple could be literally put to bed in the presence of the guests who became witnesses, as near as possible, to the coupling which, it was hoped, would produce an heir in due course. It was not until the wedding of Albert and Victoria in 1840 that the evening hour was abandoned in favour of the afternoon.

The extramarital and amorous life of George's heir George [IV] kept the nation entertained for years. His marriage to Caroline of Brunswick, in St James's Palace in the evening of 8 April 1795 was a disaster. At their first meeting on her arrival in England shortly before, George had recoiled in shock. Not only was the lady not beautiful, she seldom washed and rarely changed her underclothes. But Parliament was prepared to clear the Prince's debts amounting to more than £600 000 only if he married. It was said he had drunk the best part of a bottle of brandy before the ceremony. After the egregious goings on of the Hanoverians, the Victorian age must have come as a refreshing change.

VICTORIA = ALBERT
HM Queen Victoria
To HH Prince Albert of Saxe-Coburg-Gotha
On Monday 10 February 1840—in the afternoon
At The Chapel Royal, St James's Palace

Queen Victoria looked radiant as a bride, the low cut of her gown of white satin and Honiton lace revealed her shoulders and the short puff sleeves ornamented with large bows left her arms bare. She wore her splendid Turkish diamond necklace with matching earrings and, a present from Albert, a sapphire brooch. Both bride and groom were only twenty. He was dressed in the uniform of a British Field Marshal and entered to the strains of Handel's anthem *See the Conquering Hero*, a bible rather than a baton in his hand. The chapel was too small to accommodate the spectators, most of whom were seated on stands and boxes specially erected outside the chapel. After the service, he led Victoria back to the crimson and gold throne room, where brooches were presented to the bridesmaids. The cake is reported to have weighed 300 lb (136 kg), to have cost 100 guineas and to have been 9 ft 4 in (2.84 m) in circumference. The honeymoon was spent at Windsor but Victoria primly cut the proposed two weeks to three days with the words: 'Parliament is sitting and something occurs almost every day for which I am required.'

VICTORIA = FREDERICK
HRH Victoria, Princess Royal of England
To Frederick William of Prussia
(later Emperor Frederick III of Germany)
On 25 January 1858
At Chapel Royal, St James's

The 18-year-old Princess Royal, known in the family as 'Vicki', wore a dress similar to her mother's of 18 years

Right: A coach of the royal train in the 1930s. The occasion was the honeymoon of the Duke and Duchess of Gloucester in November 1936 and the photograph shows workmen putting finishing touches to the preparation of the train at Willesden Junction.

Over page: The marriage of her son Edward, Prince of Wales (later King Edward VII) to Alexandra of Denmark was a trial for Queen Victoria, still mourning her own beloved Albert (died 1861). She watched the ceremony, a gloomy presence, from the wooden gallery in St George's Chapel, Windsor (right of picture).

before. Like hers it was off the shoulder with short, puff sleeves but fashion had moved on and now demanded more decoration. The skirt, semi-crinoline, in white silk was scooped and caught up in garlands of ribbons and flowers, with the motif repeated on the shoulder and on the decolletage neckline. To counter this, her jewellery was simple, a single strand necklace and matching bracelets on each wrist. Her veil of fine silk tulle was held in place by a toque of flowers. This is the first wedding at which Mendelssohn's Wedding March is known to have been used. Their children included William II, Emperor of Germany, and Sophie, wife and queen of Constantine I of Greece.

ALICE = LOUIS
HRH Princess Alice, third child and second daughter of Victoria
To Louis of Hesse (later Grand Duke)
On 1 July 1862
At Osborne House, Isle of Wight, in the Dining Room

The death of her father six months before was a double misfortune for Princess Alice, since Victoria refused all but the very quietest of ceremonies. It might have been postponed had the date not been fixed by the Prince. The gentlemen were dressed in black and the ladies in half mourning of grey or violet. The service was con-

ducted under a family portrait dominated by the figure of the dead *pater familias*, from whom his widow hardly shifted her gaze throughout the ceremony.

The offspring of the marriage were to include Alix, the future wife of Tsar Nicholas II, and Victoria, grandmother of the present Duke of Edinburgh.

EDWARD = ALEXANDRA
HRH Albert Edward, Prince of Wales
To Alexandra, daughter of Prince Christian of Denmark
(from November King as Christian IX)
On 10 March 1863
At St George's Chapel, Windsor

Although Edward's father had been dead some 15 months, his marriage, like that of his sister Alice, was overshadowed by the Queen's mourning. When Edward had gone to greet his bride on her landing at Tilbury only weeks before, she had been cheered to the echo by the London crowds. By contrast, the ceremony at Windsor was dirge-like. Victoria could not bear to join in the nuptial celebrations and instead watched the ceremony from Catherine of Aragon's closet in the gallery, overlooking the chancel. At 18, Alexandra was tall and beautiful and already enormously popular with the British public. Her crinoline dress of white silk had four lace flounces on the skirt decorated with garlands

of flowers and caught up with ribbon bows. The *decolleté* neckline showed off the magnificent diamond and drop pearl necklace. Her lace veil was held in place with a coronet of flower. Her groom wore dress uniform and the regalia of the Order of the Garter.

ALFRED = MARIE
HRH Prince Alfred, Duke of Edinburgh
To HIH Grand Duchess Marie Alexandrova of Russia
On 23 January 1874
At Winter Palace, St Petersburg

Their children included Marie, wife and queen of Ferdinand of Romania.

BEATRICE = HENRY
HRH Beatrice, youngest daughter of Victoria
To HSH Henry, Prince of Battenberg
On 10 July 1885
At Whippingham parish church, Osborne, Isle of Wight

The Queen gave her consent to the marriage of her 'baby' to 'Liko' on condition the couple lived with her. Their children included Victoria Eugenia, wife and queen of Alfonso XIII of Spain.

GEORGE = 'MAY'
HRH George, Prince of Wales
To HSH Princess Mary of Teck
On 6 July 1893
At Chapel Royal, St James's

The bride wore a dress of white satin brocade embroidered with roses, thistles and shamrocks festooned with orange blossom, and made her entry to the bridal march from Wagner's *Lohengrin*. After the ceremony, the wedding party drove through crowded streets to Buckingham Palace, where the wedding breakfast was held in the throne room. It was a hot and sultry day and although the wedding followed tradition by being held in St James's and by being a family affair, there was a carriage procession which drew huge crowds. From the Palace, bride and groom took the train from Liverpool Street station for Norfolk to honeymoon at York Cottage on the Sandringham estate.

This was the last major royal wedding to be celebrated at St James's. On 27 February 1919, Princess Patricia of Connaught, the daughter of Victoria's third son Arthur, Duke of Connaught and Strathearne, and Commander the Honourable Alexander Ramsay got married in Westminster Abbey. It was exactly 650 years since the marriage of Henry III's son Edmund to Aveline of Aumale, the last time the old church had been used by a royal couple. Princess Patricia, the Abbey's first modern royal bride, was immensely popular both in Britain and in Canada, where the Duke had

served as Governor General. During his period of office, the beautiful 'Princess Pat', as she was known to the Canadians, had presided with great panache as hostess at Government House following the death of her mother. Her wedding day saw the crowds and royal family out in force. (The King and Queen even waived court mourning for their epileptic young son Prince John who had died the previous month.)

The Princess was driven to the Abbey from Clarence House in one of the standard road landaus from the royal mews. It suited her mood and her new station in life for, uniquely among royals, she had decided that following her marriage, she would renounce the title of Princess and all style of HRH, rather than outrank her husband in the social pecking order. She made a fairy tale bride in her white ermine cloak, Venetian style wedding gown, embellished with silver lace and with its cloth of silver train embroidered with lilies and her royal corsage of heather and myrtle. But she left her dream day for a golfing honeymoon to live happily ever after in modest obscurity.

The next Abbey royal wedding was in February 1922 when George V's charming daughter Princess Mary (later Princess Royal) married the unprepossessing Viscount 'Lucky' Lascelles, 15 years her senior. The bride was driven with her father from Buckingham Palace in the Irish State coach. Her dress was of silver lamé, embroidered in English roses worked with thousands of tiny diamonds and seed pearls in a faint lattice work design, girdled with a silver cord studded with triple rows of pearls and from the left-hand side of the waist hung a trail of orange blossom with beautiful, delicate silver stems.

ALBERT = ELIZABETH
HRH Prince Albert George, Duke of York
(later King George VI)
To Elizabeth Bowes Lyon (the present Queen Mother)
On 26 April 1923
At Westminster Abbey

The Abbey wedding of the decade was on 26 April 1923. On that day Prince Albert George, Duke of York, married the Lady Elizabeth Bowes Lyon. It is said, one million people lined the streets of London; the bells pealed for four hours; the guests included the then Prime Minister, Bonar Law, his great predecessor Lloyd George and still greater successor Winston Churchill. As the bride's landau arrived at Westminster Abbey the sky as if on cue miraculously cleared, after 24 hours' rain and murk. The bride wore a simple dress of ivory crepe silk with low square neck and short sleeves, made by the court dressmaker Madame Handley Seymour; the long veils of old lace were loaned by Queen Mary. She laid her wedding bouquet of white roses and

Lady Elizabeth Bowes-Lyon (later Queen Elizabeth the Queen Mother) leaving for her marriage to the Duke of York (later King George VI).

heather on the tomb of the Unknown Warrior before beginning her walk down the aisle.

The last pre-war royal wedding in the Abbey was also perhaps the most unusual. In the summer of 1934, the Duke of York's younger brother Prince George [Duke of Kent] had, quite unannounced, flown out to Yugoslavia to visit Prince Paul (later the Regent) and his wife Olga of Greece at their villa in the Julian Alps. Among their house guests was Olga's sister, the exiled Princess Marina of Greece. It soon became apparent that she had been the object of the Prince's unexpected journey.

On 29 November 1934, Marina and George were married in the Abbey by the Archbishop of Canterbury, with a Greek Orthodox prelate in attendance. The groom arrived in full naval uniform escorted by his supporter, Edward, Prince of Wales, while members of the British and Greek royal families faced one another across the chancel. The bride's sheath-like gown was designed by Captain Edward Molyneux. The most beautiful bride of that and many another year, Marina was a vision in delicate white and silver brocade ornamented with an English rose design, crowned in a magnificent fringe tiara, a present from the City of London.

The couple returned to Buckingham Palace for the Greek wedding ceremony in the private chapel. They honeymooned in the West Indies and while in the Americas met President Roosevelt.

Another royal wedding was scheduled for the Abbey in the 1930s but never took place because of the sudden and unexpected death of the bride's father. On 6 November 1935 Prince Henry, Duke of Gloucester married Lady Alice Montagu-Douglas-Scott, daughter of the Duke of Buccleuch, in the private chapel at Buckingham Palace. The Prince was resplendent in the gold braided uniform of the 10th Royal Hussars, the bride in a Norman Hartnell creation, a long gown of palest pink satin with a full tulle veil to match. In the eyes of Queen Mary, two of the bridesmaids 'looked too sweet'; they were the Princesses Elizabeth and Margaret Rose.

The next royal event in the Abbey would be the funeral of old King George who had but two months to live. Even the drama of the abdication and marriage of an ex-king was to be horribly eclipsed by the turmoil of world war before Westminster would see another royal wedding. Then it was the elder of those two young bridesmaids. Only five years later she would become Queen.

Left: Earl Mountbatten of Burma, the loved and respected uncle of Prince Philip, attending the inaugural service for the Guards Chapel at London's Wellington Barracks in November 1963.

Below left: The beautiful and popular Princess Alexandra of Kent.

Below right: The Queen, the Duke of Edinburgh and the Queen's cousin, the Duke of Gloucester, Grand Prior of the Order of St John, at the centenary celebrations of the Order in Hyde Park, in the summer of 1987.

Above: The Duke and Duchess of Kent at the final of the Men's Singles, Wimbledon in 1985. The Duke is President of the All England Lawn Tennis and Croquet Club.

Above right: The young Kents, Princess Alexandra, Prince Edward and Prince Michael (his first birthday) at the then family home of Coppins, Iver, Buckinghamshire.

Right: Prince Charles and the Queen with her grandchildren Zara Phillips, Prince William and Peter Phillips. Sandringham, January 1988.

Below: The official wedding photograph of Prince Charles and Lady Diana Spencer.

Above left: A fascinating collection of royal relations, this photograph taken in 1907 shows King Edward VII with his niece, Queen Victoria Eugenie (seated on his right), his nephew, the German Emperor William II and the German Empress Augusta (seated between the two monarchs). In the centre of the picture stands Edward's Queen Alexandra with Queen Amelie of Portugal (seated on her left), King Alfonso XIII of Spain and Queen Maud of Norway (daughter of Edward VII) complete the group.

Above right: King Edward VII (centre) and his family with their cousins, the Russian royal family. Edward was uncle to the Tsarina (here seated on his right) while Queen Alexandra (third from the left) was aunt to the Tsar (seated to her left). On the extreme left of the picture stands Prince Edward of York (Edward VIII); seated next to him is his mother, the Duchess (later Queen) Mary. Directly behind the Tsar can be seen Princess Mary of York (later Princess Royal) while seated on the ground between the two monarchs is the haemophiliac Tsarevitch, with his sister Anastasia on his left. On the right of the picture sits George, Duke of York (later George V) with his arm round Grand Duchess Tatyana.

Left: King Edward VII, with Queen Alexandra (standing to his right) and Empress Augusta of Germany (seated to her right), poses with family members and guests during a shooting party, possibly at Holly Grove, Windsor, 1904. Behind the King stands his nephew, the German Emperor William II while Edward's son and heir, George, Prince of Wales (later George V) can be seen standing third from the left.

Right: Taken about 1912, this delightful family photo shows King Haakon VII of Norway and Queen Maud, daughter of King Edward VII, with their son Crown Prince Olav. Haakon, who lived in exile in England during the German occupation of Norway in World War II, died in 1957 when the Prince succeeded as Olav V.

Above: The monarchs of Belgium (who shares a distant common ancestor with the Queen), Norway, Sweden and Denmark (who all number King Edward VII among their ancestors) leave St Paul's after the wedding of the Prince and Princess of Wales, 1981.

Left: Queen Victoria with her children and their children at Windsor Castle in her Golden Jubilee year of 1887.

THE DESCENT AND DESCENDANTS OF QUEEN VICTORIA

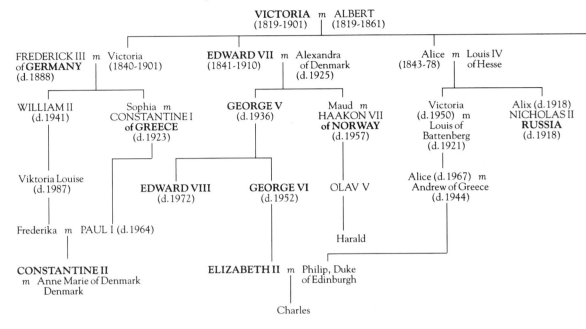

European monarchs and their descent from Queen Victoria

VICTORIA *m* ALBERT
(1819-1901)   (1819-1861)

FREDERICK III *m* Victoria
of **GERMANY** (1840-1901)
(d.1888)

EDWARD VII *m* Alexandra
(1841-1910)   of Denmark
(d.1925)

Alice *m* Louis IV
(1843-78)   of Hesse

WILLIAM II
(d.1941)

Sophia *m*
CONSTANTINE I
of **GREECE**
(d.1923)

GEORGE V
(d.1936)

Maud *m*
HAAKON VII
of **NORWAY**
(d.1957)

Victoria
(d.1950) *m*
Louis of
Battenberg
(d.1921)

Alix (d.1918)
NICHOLAS II
RUSSIA
(d.1918)

Viktoria Louise
(d.1987)

EDWARD VIII
(d.1972)

GEORGE VI
(d.1952)

OLAV V

Alice (d.1967) *m*
Andrew of Greece
(d.1944)

Frederika *m* PAUL I (d.1964)

Harald

CONSTANTINE II
m Anne Marie of Denmark
Denmark

ELIZABETH II *m* Philip, Duke
of Edinburgh

Charles

Over the centuries Europe's royal families formed numerous marriage alliances to produce numerous foreign connections. The charts on these pages show the links resulting from the marriages of Victoria's children and how the English determination secured a Protestant succession in 1688 and brought the German Hanoverian House, of which she was the last member, to the English throne.

The picture (left) shows Victoria's descendant, Queen Elizabeth II, arriving in Britain for the first time as Queen in February 1952.

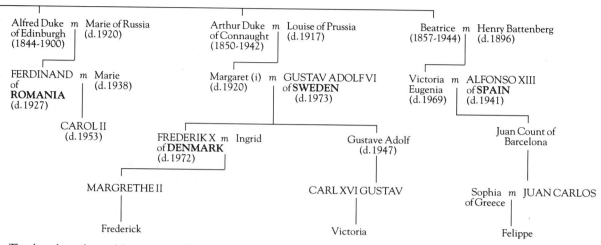

Alfred Duke *m* Marie of Russia
of Edinburgh   (d.1920)
(1844-1900)

FERDINAND *m* Marie
of   (d.1938)
ROMANIA
(d.1927)

CAROL II
(d.1953)

Arthur Duke *m* Louise of Prussia
of Connaught   (d.1917)
(1850-1942)

Margaret (i) *m* GUSTAV ADOLF VI
(d.1920)   of **SWEDEN**
               (d.1973)

FREDERIK X *m* Ingrid   Gustave Adolf
of **DENMARK**   (d.1947)
(d.1972)

Beatrice *m* Henry Battenberg
(1857-1944)   (d.1896)

Victoria *m* ALFONSO XIII
Eugenia   of **SPAIN**
(d.1969)   (d.1941)

Juan Count of
Barcelona

MARGRETHE II   CARL XVI GUSTAV   Sophia *m* JUAN CARLOS
                                               of Greece

Frederick   Victoria   Felippe

The chart shows the royal descendants of Queen Victoria; spouses from out of the family shown only when themselves royal or to clarify names or relationships. Only death dates are shown. MONARCHS SHOWN IN CAPITALS, BRITISH MONARCHS IN **BOLD CAPITALS.**

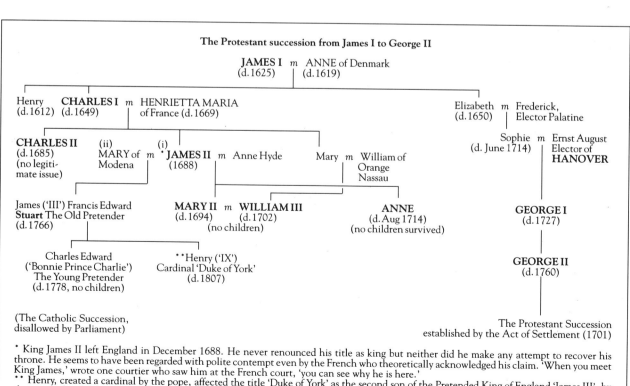

The Protestant succession from James I to George II

JAMES I *m* ANNE of Denmark
(d.1625)   (d.1619)

Henry   **CHARLES I** *m* HENRIETTA MARIA   Elizabeth *m* Frederick,
(d.1612)   (d.1649)   of France (d.1669)   (d.1650)   Elector Palatine

CHARLES II   (ii)   (i)   Sophie *m* Ernst August
(d.1685)   MARY of *m* * **JAMES II** *m* Anne Hyde   Mary *m* William of   (d. June 1714) Elector of
(no legiti-   Modena   (1688)   Orange   **HANOVER**
mate issue)   Nassau

James ('III') Francis Edward   **MARY II** *m* **WILLIAM III**   **ANNE**   **GEORGE I**
Stuart The Old Pretender   (d.1694)   (d.1702)   (d. Aug 1714)   (d.1727)
(d.1766)   (no children)   (no children survived)

Charles Edward   **Henry ('IX')   **GEORGE II**
('Bonnie Prince Charlie')   Cardinal 'Duke of York'   (d.1760)
The Young Pretender   (d.1807)
(d.1778, no children)

(The Catholic Succession,   The Protestant Succession
disallowed by Parliament)   established by the Act of Settlement (1701)

* King James II left England in December 1688. He never renounced his title as king but neither did he make any attempt to recover his throne. He seems to have been regarded with polite contempt even by the French who theoretically acknowledged his claim. 'When you meet King James,' wrote one courtier who saw him at the French court, 'you can see why he is here.'
** Henry, created a cardinal by the pope, affected the title 'Duke of York' as the second son of the Pretended King of England 'James III', by the same token his brother was held by Jacobites to be Prince of Wales. When he died, Henry liked to be known as Henry IX of England.

CEREMONY AND CELEBRATION

It is almost as though the celebration of royal events has increased as the power of the crown has diminished. Coronations have usually been great occasions but the first time a monarch celebrated a golden jubilee year with any great ceremony was in 1887. A number of English sovereigns had reigned for 50 years and more before that time but none marked the anniversary with any great show. The list on page 105 gives the names of kings and queens who lived to see jubilee years, both silver and golden but, just as Victoria was the first to celebrate a golden jubilee, so King George V and Queen Mary were the first to celebrate a silver jubilee. The section also traces the development of the ceremonial and significance of the coronation service and, with a specially drawn series of heraldic illustrations, shows how the history of the crown can be traced through the most obvious emblems of royal ceremony—the shields, coats of arms, crests and badges that go to make up the full heraldic achievement (page 26).

Above: The return of HM Queen Elizabeth II with her consort Philip, Duke of Edinburgh, from the Abbey to Buckingham Palace, June 1953.

Left: The coronation of Queen Elizabeth II, Westminster Abbey, 2 June 1953.

Right: The coronation banquet of George IV, 1820. The last such gargantuan event on the grand scale, it was also noted for the exclusion of the Queen, whom King George hated. It was also the last occasion on which the royal champion rode in to challenge anyone who might contest the King's right to the crown.

CORONATIONS

ELIZABETH II

The summons of the peers to the coronation of Queen Elizabeth II on 2 June 1953 followed archaic formulae: 'Right Trusty and Well Beloved Cousin, We greet You well . . . and command You all Excuses set apart, that you make your personal attendance upon Us [for the Solemnity of Our Coronation] . . . furnished and appointed as to Your Rank and Quality appertaineth, . . . to perform such services as shall be required.'

The organization of the event fell to the 16th Duke of Norfolk as hereditary Earl Marshal of England. The coronation committee was under the chairmanship of the Duke of Edinburgh. The Queen was deeply involved in the planning. When any point of optional procedure arose, her reaction was always 'Did my father do it?' and if the answer was yes, 'Then I will do it' decided the matter.

But in one startling respect she was determined on innovation. In 1937 the BBC, having broadcast the world's first television programmes the year before, made an outside broadcast of George VI's coronation procession—another first. Only a few thousand sets within a 65-mile (105 km) radius of Hyde Park Corner had been able to receive the pictures and the cameras had not been allowed in the Abbey. Sixteen years later, the audience was country-wide and at the young Queen's insistence, overruling Prime Minister Sir Winston Churchill, the entire ceremony, all but the Queen's private communion, was televised. To adapt the words of an Italian observer of Edward IV's coronation in 1461, 'the entire kingdom kept holiday'.

PROCESSIONS

On 6 July 1483 Richard III, pilloried by Tudor historians as monster, tyrant and usurper, enjoyed the most magnificent coronation of his century, escorted by more members of the nobility than ever before, rich in ermines, velvets and cloth-of-gold. As a sign of humility, King Richard walked to the Abbey barefoot from the Tower of London. It had become an established tradition (Charles II, 1661, was the last to observe it) that a new sovereign lived for a few weeks in the Tower before the coronation and then never resided there again. As the King paced the carnival streets some must have given a thought to the 12-year-old boy who had been ceremonially lodged in the Tower only weeks before as King Edward V, but now stayed there apprehensive and disgraced, having been proclaimed bastard by his uncle's order.

Northumberland bore 'curtana', the 'sword of mercy'; Lord Stanley—the treachery of whose family would cost Richard his life and crown at the Battle of Bosworth two years later—bore the constable's mace; the Duke of Suffolk the sceptre; John, Earl of Lincoln, the orb; then came Lord Howard, newly created Duke of Norfolk, carrying the crown; Thomas Howard, Earl of Surrey (his son), the Sword of State; now came the King flanked by two noblemen carrying swords of Justice and with the Duke of Buckingham holding his train. A group of earls and barons preceded Queen Anne, barefoot like her husband, her regalia borne by two earls and a viscount, her train by Margaret Beaufort, Countess of Richmond and mother of Henry

Left: King George VI and Queen Elizabeth acknowledge the cheers of the crowd from the balcony of Buckingham Palace after their coronation, 1937. With them are Princess Margaret and Princess Elizabeth, already an adept at the royal wave!

Above right: Queen Elizabeth II poses for a formal coronation picture in the Throne Room, Buckingham Palace, with her maids of honour, June 1953.

Tudor, the victor at Bosworth. At the high altar Richard and Anne, stripped to the waist, were anointed with the chrism; they then changed into cloth of gold and Cardinal Bourchier set the crowns upon their heads. A Te Deum being sung, the royal couple received communion and returned to Westminster Hall for their coronation banquet. It appears that most of the nobility of England turned out to celebrate the event—a remarkable tribute indeed to a man who, two years later, lay dead on the field of Bosworth, a tyrant and usurper.

THE CEREMONY

A reign is dated from the day of the monarch's accession, but some form of solemn inauguration has been customary from very early times. Among the Germanic and Celtic tribes from which modern European monarchies derive, the king in his capacity as warleader was commonly hoisted shoulder high on a shield by his companions in arms. With the coming of Christianity elements of church involvement crept in.

The service used for Queen Elizabeth II displayed elements going back to the coronation of Edgar the Peaceful of Wessex at Bath in 973, notably the coronation oath and the coronation anthem 'Zadok the Priest'. Handel's setting of the words has been used ever since the coronation of George II in 1727. The music is a vibrant reminder that the coronation of Solomon as described in the Bible provided ideas for the clerics who helped devise the very earliest European coronation rituals.

Edgar's rite provided the model for centuries. The principal features were: the *presentation* to the people; the *oath*; the *anointing* with oil and chrism (a mixture of oil and balsam) or consecration; the *crowning* and presentation of the regalia; the homage of the peers; the invocation; and finally the *banquet*.

The *presentation* of William I at his coronation on Christmas Day 1066 in Westminster Abbey (since that time the traditional site for an English coronation) was greeted with such a shout of acclaim that the Norman soldiers guarding the Abbey thought he was being attacked. The *oath* of the medieval period was a threefold promise to maintain the church, restrain crime and ensure justice to all comers. Centuries later, King George III refused assent to Catholic emancipation because by his time the coronation oath bound a king to uphold the Protestant succession and George genuinely believed he would perjure his soul if he opened careers in public life to Catholics.

In the Middle Ages the *anointing* was a thorough business: one manuscript illumination shows a bishop tilting a sizeable vase of oil over a king's head. In 574 Aidan the Scottish king of Dalriada was anointed by his distant Irish relation St Columba, the first example known in Britain. The earliest English example was Egfrith son of King Offa of Mercia, consecrated in 787 during his father's lifetime to secure the succession, though unhappily he died shortly afterwards. The

As we know it today, Westminster Abbey was built by King Henry III in the 13th century. Like its predecessor, London's west minster, built by St Edward the Confessor (d. 1066), it is England's traditional coronation church.

Above: George V's coronation 22 June 1911.

Right: The coronation of Queen Victoria 20 June 1837.

magical-religious aspect of the consecration with the holy oil—still the most important part of a coronation—was felt to imbue the monarch with spiritual power and set him or her as the Lord's anointed, apart from others. Matilda's failure to get herself crowned in her struggle with Stephen was an important factor in her defeat.

In 1399 Richard II, who had the most exalted view of the king's functions and nature, proclaimed the discovery of a vial of holy oil, supposedly given to the martyred Thomas à Becket by the Virgin Mary. Ironically, the magic potion was used to consecrate his cousin, the usurping Henry IV who almost certainly ordered Richard's murder.

When Edgar went to his famous coronation he was 30, and had already ruled for some 14 years. The ceremony seems to have been a semi-mystical rededication of the King to his kingdom. Edgar's *crowning* was more a recrowning, since he had entered the church wearing the diadem which he put aside after prostrating himself before the altar. After a Te Deum, prayers, the anointing and the singing of the antiphon 'Zadok the Priest', he was presented with ring and sword—symbols of power—solemnly crowned and then given sceptre and staff. There followed the acts of allegiance from his leading subjects and then the invocation 'Vivat rex, vivat rex, vivat rex in aeternam'—'may the king live for ever'. At the coronation (1625) of Charles I this was sung by the boys of Westminster school.

At his crowning, Richard I handed his crown from the altar to the archbishop, for him to place on his head. Edward I (1274) had removed the crown the moment Archbishop Kilwardby had completed the act of crowning him, swearing that he would not wear it again until he had recovered lands of the royal domain granted away by his father. George III gained points for piety by removing his crown when receiving the sacrament; Queen Victoria chatting with Lord Melbourne after her coronation, told him how heavy it had been; while King George VI recorded that he 'had taken every precaution as I thought to see that the crown was put on the right way round, but the dean and the Archbishop had been juggling with it so much that I never did know whether it was right or wrong'.

BANQUETS

When Edward I went to his coronation on 19 August 1274, the preparations for the banquet had been under way for at least six months. Orders for food went out to a dozen counties in February, the returns from Gloucestershire alone included 60 head of cattle, 60 swine, two fat boars, 40 bacon pigs and 3000 capons. Religious houses throughout the country were instructed to bring on as many swan, peacock and crane as they could, along with rabbits and kid. Westminster Palace was refurbished throughout, two new stone thrones were carved and installed in Westminster Hall, and scores of temporary buildings were run up in the Palace grounds for kitchens, stabling and the like. On the day itself, the water conduit in Cheapside ran with wine.

Just 22 when he came to the throne in 1760, George III was a vigorous and good looking young man, not averse to effects. His banquet had a dramatic opening. Westminster Hall was kept in darkness until the arrival of Queen Charlotte when, of a sudden, a thousand little lights blazed on the scene. The effect was achieved by putting tapers to waxed strings which hung from one lantern to the next; for a minute or so the company was showered with burning wax but the light revealed mounted stewards and glinting gold plate, the jewels of the ladies and embroidered vestments of bishops, peers in velvet and ermine, judges in scarlet, the pageantry of pursuivants and heralds.

As at all great occasions there were some awkward moments: the sword of state having been forgotten, the lord mayor's had to be used instead; and when the Lord High Steward rode up to the high table to make his obeisance, his horse, trained for weeks in the art of walking backwards so it might make a properly deferential exit, insisted on making its solemn entrance in the new fashion and advanced up the hall rump first.

An important part of the banquet was the challenge by the king's champion to any who contested the right of the monarch to his throne to do battle. The office of champion, for generations hereditary in the Dymock family, enjoyed its most glamorous moment at the restoration crowning of King Charles II on St George's Day 1661. Pepys, who attended the banquet, describes how Dymock rode into Westminster Hall 'all in armor on horseback, with his Speare and targett [i.e. shield] carried before him. And a herald to proclaim that if any dare deny Ch Steward to be lawful King of England, here was a Champion that would fight him and with those words the Champion flings down his gauntlet'.

The flourish was given three times as Dymock curvetted up the banqueting hall between the tables to approach the high table. When he arrived, the King drank his health from a gold cup which he gave him as his perquisite for his service. It is said that at the coronation of George III Prince Charles Edward, the Young Stuart pretender (having slipped incognito across the Channel), was among the congregation in Westminster Abbey. He did not challenge the champion.

Both champion and banquet were abandoned by William IV, disgusted by the gross expense and excesses of his brother George IV. William's admirable contempt for excessive flummery earned his modest coronation the derisive nickname of the 'half crownation' (from the 'half crown' coin).

THE CROWN JEWELS

This popular term for the royal regalia is commonly used to refer only to the crowns and other items held in the Tower of London, i.e. the Crown Jewels of England. In addition there are the regalia of Scotland (known as the Honours of Scotland), kept in the Crown Room of Edinburgh Castle, and the regalia of the Principality of Wales, held in the National Museum of Wales, Cardiff.

THE REGALIA OF ENGLAND

The principal items are: the **Imperial State Crown**, made for Queen Victoria. Among its thousands of precious stones are three historic gems: the sapphire, said

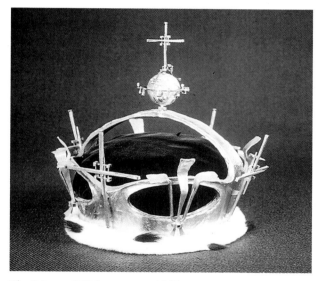

The Prince of Wales coronet, 1969.

The crown and regalia of the Kings of Scotland.

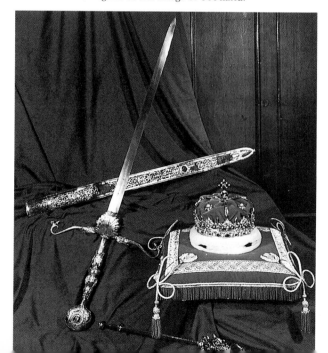

to have belonged to Edward the Confessor, the Stuart sapphire and the Black Prince's balas ruby; **St Edward's Crown**, called after St Edward the Confessor, this is the crown with which the actual coronation ceremony is performed; the **jewelled Sword of State**; **curtana**, the blunted Sword of Mercy; the **golden spurs** of Knightly virtue; the **sceptre with the dove**, to symbolize equity and mercy; the **royal sceptre with the cross**, *the* symbol of royal authority and power; the gold **ampulla**—a container for oil in the shape of an eagle; the silver-gilt anointing **spoon**; the coronation **ring**, to symbolize the wedding of the monarch to the realm; the **golden orb** surmounted by a jewelled cross, symbolizing commitment to Christianity; and the golden bracelets or armills.

None of these is as old as the monarchy itself and only the ampulla and the spoon date back before the 1660s. The former is probably from the early 14th century. The bowl of the spoon, possibly used at the coronation of King John, is thought to have been made in the 12th century, though it was clearly embellished at the time of the Restoration remake of the other jewels. (The ancient regalia of the English crown were broken up and sold during the Cromwellian period. New pieces were commissioned over the centuries.)

Beside the Imperial State Crown, subsequent additions include the Great Diamond mounted on the royal sceptre between the golden shaft and the miniature crown, supporting the Maltese cross. This diamond, cleaved from the Cullinan Diamond, is known as the Star of Africa. It was presented to King Edward VII by Sir Thomas Cullinan, in 1907. At 530.2 carats, it is (in 1989) the largest cut diamond in the world. The Cullinan also provided stones for the Imperial State Crown. The armills used at the coronation of Queen Elizabeth II represented the revival of a part of the ceremony last used for the coronation of Elizabeth I and were specially made with gold donated by the countries of the Commonwealth.

THE REGALIA OF SCOTLAND

These comprise: the Lord High Treasurer's mace and jewels bequeathed by Henry Stuart, Cardinal of York (brother of Prince Charles Edward and second son of James Francis Edward Stuart, the 'Old Pretender'), who died in 1807.

The Honours of Scotland
The Crown dating in its present form from remodelling commissioned by King James V in 1540; the Sword of State, presented to King James IV by Pope Julius II in 1507; and the Sceptre also presented to James IV, by

Above: Some of the British Crown Jewels. Top: St Edward's Crown. Left to right, top to bottom: The eagle ampulla and the anointing spoon. The Imperial State Crown. The orb. Royal sceptre with the dove. The armills; communion chalice and paten (or communion plate); the bracelets of St George: the jewelled sword of state; coronation ring; the spurs of St George; and in the front of the case the sceptre with the cross.

Below left: A crown jewel that got away. Made probably for Richard II's beloved wife, Anne of Bohemia (d. 1394), it was sent to Germany by Henry IV with his daughter Blanche when she married the Count Palatine of the Rhine.

Pope Alexander VI 'Borgia' in 1494. During the Coronation of Queen Elizabeth II in June 1953, the Honours of Scotland were carried in state from Edinburgh Castle to St Giles's Cathedral, where a solemn service of dedication was being held to coincide with the coronation service in Westminster Abbey.

REGALIA OF THE PRINCIPALITY OF WALES

These comprise two coronets, the sword, the ring and rod made of Welsh gold for Edward's [VIII] investiture in 1911. When preparations were beginning to be made for the investiture of Prince Charles in 1969, it was discovered that the coronet could not be adjusted to fit. The Queen accepted the offer by the Goldsmiths' Company of the City of London to commission and present a new one for the investiture. Made from 22-carat gold and weighing 1361 g (3 lb), the coronet takes the form of a circlet, bearing alternate crosses and fleurs-de-lys, with a single arch surmounted by an orb and cross.

HERALDS AND CHIVALRY

ORDERS OF CHIVALRY

British honours are technically conferred by the sovereign as the fount of honour but most are in the gift of the prime minister: to such a degree that Edward VII once complained that the 'fount' was in danger of becoming a pump! The Royal Victorian Order, founded by Queen Victoria in 1896 for members of the royal household, and the Order of Merit, established in 1902 by Edward VII, restricted to just 24 members—among them were Edward Elgar the composer and Bertrand Russell the philosopher—are in a class of their own. So are the three ancient orders of chivalry, the Garter (instituted in 1348), the Thistle (the Scottish order founded in the 15th century and refounded by Queen Anne in 1703; it comprises 16 Scottish knights and the sovereign) and the Bath (established in its present form in 1725).

The Most Honourable Order of the Garter

What attracted Lord Melbourne about the Order of the Garter was that 'there's no damn merit about it'—he also declined to recommend Queen Victoria to make him a member since 'I can hardly bribe myself'. The Garter was certainly not founded as a reward, rather as an encouragement to good behaviour—membership made one a close companion of the sovereign

Above: The Queen at the ceremony of the Garter, Windsor.

Below: Officers of the College of Arms (1560s) in the reign of Queen Elizabeth I. To the left are two Kings of Arms, Clarencieux and Norroy and then six heralds; from left to right: Lancaster, Windsor, Richmond, York, Somerset, Chester. Headed by Garter King of Arms and assisted by various pursuivants, the College of Arms is the final court in all matters concerning heraldry and the right to bear arms.

and advertised the fact to the world at large. The world's oldest order of chivalry, it is still the most distinguished.

INSTITUTION OF THE ORDER

In the year 1344, King Edward III announced as his intention, 'to begin a Round Table in the same manner and conditions as the Lord Arthur, formerly King of England, appointed it'. For a century or more the Arthurian legends had provided a colourful backdrop to the business of war. The tournament, from being a form of battle training, had become a kind of *concours d'élégance* of the medieval martial art and the code of knighthood an ethical gloss on the laws of war. Some 300 knights were to be invited to Edward's event. By the symbolism of the Round Table, they would be accounted equals.

The King was preparing to invade France to make good his claim to the French crown and was no doubt on a morale-raising exercise. In 1346 the royal army returned from France with the battle honours and booty of Crécy but a few knights had been impoverished by the campaign. On St George's Day (23 April) 1348 Edward announced the foundation of a chantry and almshouse for those Poor Knights (since 1833 called the Military Knights).

It seems that the Order of the Garter—a select body of 25 Companion Knights and the sovereign—was inaugurated at jousts held in Windsor that spring in conjunction with the founding of the new charity in 1348. The Garter itself was worn as a badge by two teams of 12 knights, led by the King and the Black Prince. The King certainly celebrated a feast on this day and he and his knights were 'clad in gowns of russet sprinkled with blue garters, wearing the like garters on their right legs, and mantles of blue with escutcheons of St George'. A famous legend may explain how the badge was chosen.

At a ball held in Windsor, went the story, the King was dancing with Joanne, Countess of Salisbury, when her garter slipped off. Edward gallantly retrieved it. Teased by his courtiers, he responded sharply with the words 'Honi soit qui mal y pense', literally 'shame to him who thinks evil of it'. (For the modern English version see page 97.) As the ribaldry continued, the King added that in a short time they would 'see the garter advanced to so high honour as to account themselves happy to wear it'. The early statutes of the order are lost, but the story is entirely plausible and fully in keeping with the mood of 14th-century courtly pageantry.

The oldest surviving heraldic plate in the stalls of the Order's chapel of St George, Windsor, is that of Lord Basset of Drayton, who fought alongside the Black Prince at Poitiers in 1356 (when the prisoners included King John II of France). The earliest depiction of the leg band, or garter, is the one on the effigy of Sir William Fitzwaryn (d. 1361; Wantage parish church, Berks); the earliest surviving garter dates from about 1489 and belonged to Maximilian I [Holy Roman Emperor] elected to the Order in that year. And the earliest surviving Garter mantle is the one that James I sent to his brother-in-law King Christian IV of Denmark, installed in 1605.

The warlike St George was made patron of the Order which was given as its home the chapel which Henry III built in honour of St Edward the Confessor.

By the later 14th century, the chapel was in a ruinous condition. The repairs were put in the charge of Geoffrey Chaucer, whose poetry had delighted the court for a generation but whose income derived from his post as Clerk of the Works in the Palace of Westminster.

Early in the next century, St Edward was displaced in his role as patron of the English by the martial St George. He it was who inspired the army of King Henry V to their great victory at Agincourt (1415) and Henry made the first notable change to the institution of the Order by appointing William Bruges first Garter King of Arms. He compiled his Garter Book some time about the year 1430, depicting the founding 25 knights and King Edward III. The first register of the Order, now lost, was compiled in Henry V's reign.

In 1478 King Edward IV ordered the chapel of St George to be demolished and a new one built on the site. Edward also completed the establishment of the Order's officers with the appointment of the first Chancellor. Under Henry VII work continued on the chapel of St George (thanks in part to handsome legacies by Sir Reginald Bray, d. 1503)—he stipulated the addition of a cap of honour and an elaborate collar to the regalia of the knights. His son Henry VIII completed work on the chapel, building the wooden oriel viewing gallery near the high altar so that Queen Catherine might watch the ceremonial. Henry also specified the precise form and materials of the collar and provided that it should be adorned by the Great George. The first surviving Register of the Order, known as 'The Black Book' from the colour of its binding, was begun. It contains the statutes, in Latin, an account of the founding of the Order and accounts of ceremonies and installations—among them the Kings of Spain, France and Scotland and the Emperor.

After Henry, the order suffered certain vicissitudes of fortune. The puritanical Edward VI condemned it for 'despicable ceremonies of papish origin'. But his sister Elizabeth exploited its mystique and ceremonies to the full in furthering the cult of courtly magnificence and her courtiers' loyalty. When in 1572 Thomas Howard, fourth Duke of Norfolk, was convicted of plotting with Mary Queen of Scots, his heraldic plate was removed from his stall in the chapel and his degradation from the Order pronounced with awful solemnities. In the 1950s, the plate was recovered and secured to the last bay of the choir wall.

In the Civil War, the town of Windsor having opened its gates to the Parliamentary army, a garrison was installed in the castle—the commander being given strict instructions to guard the chapel against any excesses by his troops and 'preserve the records of the Order of the Garter from defacing'. He followed orders.

At the Restoration, the Order enjoyed another golden age. At its banquets held in St George's Hall, King Charles II sat in state alone at a high table on the dais. The Companion Knights, with high hats adorned with rich plumes and dressed in elaborate new robes designed by the King himself, had their places down a long table backed by a beautiful arras. Between the high windows on the opposite wall stood pier tables, one for each two knights, from which their food was brought by their servants who had to make their way across the breadth of the hall between the 12 officers of the College of Arms who stood in double file with Garter King of Arms at their head, facing the dais with the high table where the King ate in solitary state.

In the 19th century, to honour his Reform prime minister Lord Grey, William IV created him an extra member at a time when there were no vacancies. Foreign rulers and potentates had been enrolled in the order since the Middle Ages and from about 1800 have been admitted to the Order as extra or supernumerary members. Victoria installed both the Shah of Persia and the Sultan of Turkey, while in the 20th century Emperor Hirohito of Japan received the honour, withdrawn during World War II but reinstated in the 1970s.

SOVEREIGN OF THE ORDER   Her Majesty the Queen

MOTTO OF THE ORDER
Honi soit qui mal y pense—translated as 'evil be to him who evil thinks'

CHAPEL
Chapel of St George, Windsor Castle

OFFICERS OF THE GARTER and the reign in which they were first appointed
Prelate, traditionally the Bishop of Winchester (Edward III)
Gentleman Usher of the Black Rod (Edward III)
Register, Dean of Windsor (Edward III)
Garter King of Arms (Henry V)
Chancellor (Edward IV)

CEREMONIAL DRESS AND INSIGNIA
Garter leg band worn on the left leg just below the knee; on the left arm by lady members and associates
Mantle of blue with the Cross of St George enclosed in a Garter, embroidered on the left shoulder
Collar, consisting of 26 enamelled roses, separated by gold knots with, suspended from it, the Great George
Great George, a jewelled pendant of St George
Lesser George, non-ceremonial pendant

Insignia of the Order of the Garter.

Above: The Ball Room inside Buckingham Palace with the thrones, the room where the Queen holds the Investitures.

Left: The Queen in the robes of the Order of St Michael and St George, founded in 1818 and reserved mainly for diplomats.

Above right: Some of the Queen's Beasts, heraldic and mostly fabulous animals which feature on various badges of the monarch and her family.
The devising of such heraldic charges and all matters concerning heraldry is the responsibility of the College of Arms, founded by King Richard III in 1483.

Right: Henry VII's Chapel, Westminster Abbey.

The Military Knights of Windsor

Founded in 1348, to help knights impoverished by ransom payments during the Crécy and other recent campaigns in France, it is thought; it consisted of 26 knights to match the number of Garter knights. Each was provided with lodgings at Windsor and with a pension. Henry VIII made a special provision in his will to reduce the number to 13; Elizabeth I provided the statutes which presently govern the Order while in 1833 William IV ordained the change of name from Alms Knights or Poor Knights to Military Knights. The badges of the Order are the shield of St George and the Star of the Order of the Garter. The knights have apartments in Windsor Castle, take part in the ceremonies of the Garter and are required to attend Sunday morning services at St George's Chapel, Windsor, as representatives of the Garter Knights.

The Order of the Bath

Although the knightly ritual of purification by bathing can be traced as far back as the 12th century, the present chivalric Order of the Bath dates from the reign of King George I, its statutes being devised by the Garter King of Arms and modelled on those of the Garter, and its ceremonies consisting of a procession, an investiture, and a banquet. The order was instituted on 17 June 1725 in Henry VII's Chapel, Westminster Abbey—the first knight to be installed being King George II's four-year-old son, Prince William Augustus, Duke of Cumberland.

The Collar and Star of the Order of the Thistle.

SOVEREIGN   Her Majesty the Queen

GREAT MASTER   Prince Charles, Prince of Wales

MOTTO OF THE ORDER
Tria juncta in uno—'Three in one'

CHAPEL
Henry VII's Chapel, Westminster Abbey

OFFICERS OF THE BATH
Secretary
Register
Gentleman Usher
Genealogist
Bath King of Arms
Blanc Coursier Herald
Dean to the Order: the Dean of Westminster

DRESS AND INSIGNIA OF THE BATH
Mantle of red bearing a star
Surcoat for ceremonial occasions
Collar of gold, suspended from it the Order's badge
Badge, a star
Pendant for non-ceremonial occasions

Since 1847 the order has comprised three classes: Knights Grand Cross, Knights Commanders, Companions, each organized into military and civil divisions.

As indicated above, in one sense the Order of the Bath looks back to more genuinely chivalric antecedents even than the Order of the Garter. In very early times, admission to the order of knighthood was an initiation rite of the young noble warrior into the fraternity of war. It followed years of physical training in the management of weapons and of horses and the conventions of courtly living. The final rite itself often took place on the field of battle and might take the form of a simple blow from a senior knight—the last blow the apprentice knight could receive without retaliation and without loss of face. This 'dubbing' became formalized as the tap of the accolade as we know it today. Other rites might be the girding of a belt, the hanging of a shield round the neck or by an elaborate ceremony involving a night's vigil in a chapel, preceded by the ritual purification of a bath. The ritual, known at least since the 12th century, came to be used for the ceremonial creation of knights at coronations or royal weddings at least as early as the reign of Henry IV.

A number of knights were created in ceremonies preceding the marriage of Henry VII and Elizabeth of York in 1487. Such knights had acquired a distinctive style of robes to which were added, at the time of James I, a badge of three crowns and the motto *'Tria juncta in uno'* (i.e. 'three joined in one') celebrating the union of the crowns of England, Scotland and Ireland under one monarch. Knights of the Bath were created at the coronation of Charles II, but thereafter the practice lapsed.

CELEBRATIONS

In the Middle Ages the accession, and/or the coronation of the sovereign, his marriage and that of his heir or his eldest daughter were the principal occasions on which the community of the realm might be expected to celebrate the sovereign if only by paying special feudal dues. There were also certain special events: examples were London's reception for King Henry V's victory at Agincourt in 1415, and the celebration of the house of Hanover's English centenary in 1814.

In our own day, the June celebration of the official birthday of the sovereign is the most notable pageant of the year with the Trooping the Colour on Horse Guards Parade. The first sovereign to be honoured with an annual commemoration of his birthday (by parliamentary decree 1660) was Charles II. Charles's return and the restoration of the monarchy in 1660 was a notable event indeed and duly celebrated but on the whole formal celebrations were much less frequent when kings and queens wielded real power. The progresses of Queen Elizabeth I must have been dramatic events for the localities she visited, and George III enjoyed similar popularity, being serenaded with band music on his birthday and on the celebration of the 50th year of his accession. What today would be a dramatic Golden Jubilee was, in 1810, the occasion for a modest concert of band music on the North Terrace at Windsor. Queen Victoria's Golden and Diamond Jubilees were events of a quite different order.

The first monarch to celebrate a silver jubilee was George V. That of his granddaughter in 1977 marked the half way point of a decade noted for its royal celebrations. November 1972 saw the Queen and Prince Philip's silver wedding, marked by a Service of Thanksgiving followed by a Guildhall luncheon; July 1981 the wedding of Prince Charles and Lady Diana Spencer and August 1982 the happy 80th birthday of Queen Elizabeth, the Queen Mother.

Charles II: The Restoration of the Monarchy, 8 May 1660

Charles II's courtiers considered him king from the moment of his father's execution on 30 January 1649. However, it was not until Parliament had voted for the restoration of the monarchy on 1 May 1660—'the happiest May Day that hath been many a year' wrote Samuel Pepys—that the scene was set for the reign to begin: Parliament declared Charles king on 8 May 1660. The new King and his brothers James [II], Duke of York and Henry, Duke of Gloucester crossed over from Scheveningen, Holland, in ships sent over by Parliament and landed at Dover on 25 May. They entered London on 29 May, Charles's 30th birthday, 'with a triumph of above 20 000 horse and foot, brandishing their swords and shouting with inexpressible joy' wrote the diarist John Evelyn. The streets were strewn with flowers, carpets and tapestries hung down

Jubilee Day 1977. The official celebrations in Britain opened on 7 June. The Queen was guest of the City of London in Guildhall. Here, she and the Duke of Edinburgh are preparing to enter their coach.

Top left: The view of the Mall from the Centre Room giving on to the famous balcony at Buckingham Palace.

Top centre: Crowd scenes outside the Palace, at the wedding of the Duke and Duchess of York.

Far left: The Queen, the Queen Mother and Princess Margaret at Clarence House to celebrate the Queen Mother's birthday, August 1986.

Left: Ten years on from her Jubilee year, the Queen in happy mood at Covent Garden, August 1987, as she opens the Jubilee Market there. It is a listed building, begun in 1897, the Diamond Jubilee year of Queen Victoria.

Above: George V and Queen Mary celebrated their Silver Jubilee with a simple but moving service in St Paul's.

VE Day 8 May 1945, great crowds assembled outside Buckingham Palace to celebrate Victory in Europe after World War II. King George VI and Queen Elizabeth, accompanied by the Princesses, came out with Winston Churchill to acknowledge the cheering.

from the windows which, like the balconies, were 'all set with ladies', the bells of the city churches pealed and the fountains spouted wine. There were myriads of people flocking the streets, as far as Rochester. As the King entered London, a deputation of clergy presented him with a Bible which, the Merry Monarch solemnly assured them, 'he would make the rule of his life and government'. To fanfares of trumpets and other festival music he advanced into the city to be received by 'the Lord Mayor, the aldermen and all the companies in their liveries, and chains of gold'. The procession took seven hours to pass.

JUBILEES

Elizabeth II: Silver Jubilee, 6 February 1977
While the actual accession was commemorated in church services in February, the Queen spent the weekend at Windsor with her family and the full British celebrations were held in the summer in the hope of better weather and better tourist revenue. As a result the first official visit of Jubilee year was to Western Samoa, where the Queen's plane made a stop on the way to Australia and New Zealand. The royal yacht *Britannia* took the royal party to Tonga and Fiji and there were visits to Tasmania and Papua New Guinea.

Meanwhile, in Britain souvenir production was getting under way and, for the first time, large retail chains were taking out insurances on the Queen's life and those of other members of the royal family for anything up to £1 million, lest death or disaster should put an end to the bonanza before it could begin.

Prince Charles now left the navy to head the Queen's Silver Jubilee Trust 'to help the young to help others'.

The English tennis star Virginia Wade won the Wimbledon Ladies' Singles.

On 4 May, both Houses of Parliament presented loyal addresses to their Queen in Westminster Hall, to the accompaniment of pageantry and trumpets.

A bonfire beacon lit by the Queen at Windsor started a chain of beacons across the country.

Outdoing the famous progresses of Elizabeth I (thanks in part, it must be admitted, to the new royal train!) the Queen travelled more than 7000 miles (11 265 km) through her United Kingdom of Scotland,

Wales, England and, in August (despite an IRA bomb threat) Northern Ireland, though she lived aboard the royal yacht, being flown to her official engagements by helicopter—the first time this form of transport had been permitted for the Queen. Both Prince Philip and Prince Andrew accompanied her on parts of this tour. Later she visited Canada and the West Indies, flying back by Concorde—her first flight on the plane.

On 7 June, the Royal Family attended a Service of Thanksgiving in St Paul's after which the Queen and Prince Philip walked to Guildhall for a luncheon in their honour. Then they went walkabout all over London where plaques let into the paving stones still recall the occasion.

The Queen finished her Jubilee travels on 2 November. During the year, it was estimated, the Queen travelled 56 000 miles (90 120 km) world-wide.

More than 100 000 congratulatory cards were received. Some 30 000 Jubilee medals were distributed.

Monarchs with jubilee years since Alfred the Great (d. 899)

> **England and UK:** *Æthelred II (978–1016); Henry I (1100–35); Henry II (1154–89); Henry III (1216–72) SG; Edward I (1272–1307); Edward III (1327–77) SG; Henry VI (1422–60); Henry VIII (1509–47); Elizabeth I (1558–1603); George II (1727–60); George III (1760–1820) SG; Victoria (1837–1901) SGD; George V (1910–36); Elizabeth II (1952–   ).
>
> **Scotland alone:** Constantine II (900–42); Malcolm III (1058–93); David I (1124–53); William I (1165–1214); Alexander II (1214–49); Alexander III (1249–86); David II (1329–71); James I (1406–37); James III (1460–88); James IV (1488–1513); James V (1513–42); James VI (1567–1625) and I of England.
>
> All the monarchs with silver jubilee years (i.e. at least 25 years) are listed: 'SG' = silver and gold; 'SGD' = silver, gold and diamond jubilee years. It was only with Victoria that the celebration of jubilees as such began.
>
> * Æthelred II called 'the Unready' was forced into exile in 1013 by the Danish King Swegn 'Forkbeard', who had himself proclaimed king; but he died in February 1014 and Æthelred succeeded in reestablishing himself.

Victoria: Golden Jubilee, 20 June 1887; Diamond Jubilee 1897

For Mark Twain, Queen Victoria's Diamond Jubilee celebration of 1897 (see p. 6–7) 'set one reflecting on what a large feature of this world England is today'. He thought the very scaffolding built to accommodate the spectators along the no less than 10 miles (16 km) of terraced benches seemed designed to endure until Doomsday. As far as the eye could see the windows, 'a multitudinous array of bright colours suggested the boxes in a theatre'. The procession itself 'stretched to the limit of sight in both directions—bodies of soldiery in blue, followed by a block of soldiers in buff, then a block in red, a block of buff, a block of yellow, and so on, an interminable drift of swaying and swinging splotches of strong colour sparkling and flashing with shifty light reflected from bayonets, lance heads, brazen helmets and burnished breastplates'.

The procession, thought Mark Twain, was 'the human race on exhibition'. Apparently it was the Indian princes, 'men of stately build and princely carriage', in their splendid, ceremonial dress who made the greatest impact on the crowd. Twain also noted Prince Rupert of Bavaria in the procession, whose mother as lineal descendant of the House of Stuart was considered by some eccentrics as rightful Queen of England, what Mark Twain, the American, called in surprisingly monarchist style, 'The microbe of Jacobite loyalty'. Thirty more foreign kings and princes paid their homage along with the prime ministers of Britain's colonies and dominions overseas. All were escorted by troops of soldiers so that the first carriages did not appear for an hour and a half.

'The excitement was growing now; interest was rising to the boiling point. Finally a landau driven by eight cream-coloured horses, most lavishly upholstered in gold stuffs, with postilions and no drivers . . . came bowling along, followed by the Prince of Wales, and all the world rose to its feet and uncovered. The Queen Empress was come.'

George V: Silver Jubilee, 6 May 1935

The day was marked by a Service of Thanksgiving held in St Paul's Cathedral. According to the King's own diary, the temperature was 75°F (23°C) in the shade and 'there were the greatest number of people in the streets that I have ever seen'. The celebrations, modest when compared with those for his granddaughter in 1977, continued throughout the country for about a month with official receptions, loyal addresses in and around London and street parties. The King was astonished by the obvious popularity of himself and the Queen: 'I really think they like me for myself', he commented. He was always aware of his limitations as a man but did not realize how his own good will and paternal concern for his subjects had communicated itself. Queen Mary was even surprised to find how many people in the East End recognized them on one of their unannounced car visits to various parts of London. Media coverage of royalty was not so extensive as today and it was possible for people not to be absolutely sure about the appearance of even famous personalities.

FUNERAL CEREMONIES AND ACCESSION

'The King is Dead! Long Live the King!'

As the life of old King Edward VII drew to its close early in May 1910, George, Duke of York and his family were at their London home of Marlborough House. On the morning of the 7th, the 16-year-old Prince Edward (later King Edward VIII) woke up his brother Albert (later King as George VI) and pointed across the way to Buckingham Palace where the Royal Standard was flying at half mast.

The old King had in fact died a little before midnight and the two princes' father, now King George V, had passed a sleepless night desolate with grief. Nevertheless, he saw it as his duty to give the boys the portentous news and had them summoned to his room as soon as they were dressed. Barely attempting to hold back his tears he told them their grandfather had died. Prince Edward tried to help the new King through an obviously painful duty and to ease his distress, explained that they had already seen the Royal Standard over the Palace and understood the significance. Exhausted and perhaps a little confused, King George asked his son to repeat what he had said. And then, to maintain constitutional propriety, he gave orders that a flagstaff be immediately raised on Marlborough House. 'The King is Dead! Long Live the King!'

In the long history of British monarchy the last time the old familiar saying was given the lie was at the turn of the year 1688/9. Between 11 December 1688, when King James II fled his kingdom, and 12 February 1689, when William of Orange and his wife Mary Stuart accepted the rule of England as joint sovereigns (Wil-liam III and Mary II), England was without a monarch. Indeed it would appear that between 11 and 24 December, when the peers assumed executive functions, she was without even a government. Today it is assumed that from the moment of the monarch's death, the successor is in place but the idea of automatic succession took some time to establish.

A HISTORY OF DEATH AND CONTINUITY

The details of a medieval royal funeral could be grisly. When William the Conqueror died unexpectedly in

Right: The Vigil of the four Princes at the lying in state of the body of King George V.

Left: The glorious tomb of King Edward III, Westminster Abbey.

Below left: The pomp of death. The official 'icon' of the dead King Edward III on his tomb in Westminster Abbey.

Below centre: The Eleanor Cross at Gedney, Lincolnshire. One of the memorials set up by King Edward I, to commemorate the journey of the body of his dead wife, Eleanor of Castile, to London in 1296.

Below right: The Mausoleum at Frogmore, Windsor.

Normandy, his corpse was abandoned as the nobles of his entourage rode back to their castles in anticipation of civil war—but only after they had stripped the body of all its valuables and most of its clothes. On its way to burial in the Abbé aux Hommes at Caen, the coffin exploded under pressure from gases released in the decaying hulk of the dead duke-king.

Some three centuries later another conqueror, this time the English conqueror of Normandy Henry V, was brought back in doleful splendour to his last resting place in Westminster Abbey. This time, though the cortège took weeks to travel from Vincennes where the King had died on 31 August 1422, there were no explosions. In the absence of embalmers, the body was dismembered, the flesh boiled off the bones and the resulting royal salmagundi packed with herbs and spices in a lead coffin. The remains were borne in state first to St Denis, the traditional burial place of the French kings, from there to Rouen, Henry's Norman capital where it was joined by Queen Katherine and from there to the English town of Calais, via Abbeville and Boulogne. Atop the coffin on its ponderous wooden chariot drawn by four black horses, brooded a more than life size effigy of the dead King. Across the Channel, the towns along the Dover road, like their French counterparts, accompanied the cortège with tolling bells and the priestly chanting of the office of the dead.

The death and funeral obsequies of Queen Victoria tolled the knell of an era and, as we can now see, the passing of the British Empire's brief epoch of greatness. The Queen Empress herself ended her life in the routine of commemoration and business that had governed it for decades. On 14 December 1900 she paid her annual homage at Albert's Mausoleum in Frogmore and then took train with members of her family for Christmas at Osborne. There, on 22 January, she died in the arms of her grandson, the German Emperor William II. Soon, as was her wish, she would rest next to her beloved husband, robed in white and her wedding veil.

The encoffined body was conveyed from Cowes to Portsmouth aboard its yacht between a double line of battleships of the Fleet to the flat thud of the minute gun. From there the route lay to London where the crowds lined the streets for the last time in her honour to watch the cortège make its way to Paddington and the special train of the Great Western Railway to bring the coffin to Windsor. From there, following the Queen's express wish, it was to be taken on a gun carriage to the mausoleum in Frogmore. But the long wait at the station had made the horses restive and the honour guard of naval ratings tailed on to drag ropes to haul the body of the great lady to her last resting place.

The funeral of her son King Edward VII who died on 6 May 1910 was organized with the same impressive pomp and accompanied by an almost equal warmth of emotion, affectionate rather than awed, as it had been for his mother. As his subjects mourned the passing of

The funeral cortège of King Edward VII was followed by the Crown Prince of the Austro-Hungarian empire and the kings of Greece, Spain, Portugal, Denmark, Norway and Bulgaria, among numerous dignitaries. They were headed by the dead monarch's son, King George V, and nephew, Emperor William II of Germany, the two figures in plumed helmets at the extreme right of the picture. Behind and to the left of King George can be seen his second son, Prince Albert (later George VI) while behind the Kaiser walks Prince Edward (later King Edward VIII).

'our dear Dad' his funeral cortège was followed by the last great display of Europe's monarchy: King George V, The Kaiser, Crown Prince Franz Ferdinand, representing the Austro-Hungarian Empire, the Grand Duke Michael Alexandrovitch representing the Tsar of Russia, the Kings of Spain, Portugal, Denmark, Greece, Belgium, Bulgaria and Norway, and Prince Henry representing the Netherlands.

King George V died at his home of Sandringham on 20 January 1936. Working up to the last, he died after struggling in vain to put his signature to the proclamation setting up a council of state. Apologizing to the grieving courtiers for being so slow, he at length made two crosses. The newspapers appeared with black borders of mourning, radio programmes were cancelled and theatres and cinemas closed. On 23 January, after lying in Wolferton Church for the estate workers to pay their respects, the coffin was taken to London where it lay in state for four days in Westminster Hall. A vigil was mounted throughout the period by members of the Household Troops, the Yeomen of the Guard and the Gentlemen-at-Arms. Close on a million people, it was estimated, filed past the catafalque. As midnight approached on the evening of Monday 27 January people were still shuffling past. Shortly after the guard changed, King Edward VIII and his brothers the Dukes of York, Gloucester and Kent took up position between the guards and for some 20 minutes mounted 'the Vigil of the Princes'.

THE KING IS DEAD! LONG LIVE THE QUEEN!

The death of every monarch is followed by the accession council of his or her successor. News of her father's death reached the Queen when she and Prince Philip were outside Nairobi, Kenya, on the first leg of a Commonwealth Tour. On Wednesday 5 February they checked in at the Treetops in Kenya, less a hotel than a suite of rooms amongst the branches of a huge wild fig tree. The next day everything changed 'for the lady we must now call Queen', in the words of her private secretary. Letters and telegrams had to be dispatched, cancelling arrangements for the rest of the tour; the sealed Accession documents had to be opened and the Queen had to decide her official regal name. Her father, known as Albert to the family, had chosen his fourth name as 'George VI' to assert the continuity of the dynasty; his daughter, whose third name Mary was never used, chose to be known as Elizabeth II: 'My own name, of course,' she answered the formal question, 'What else?' Twenty-four hours later she was disembarking from her BOAC Argonaut at London airport (arrival 4.19 p.m., Thursday 7 February). The following day she read her declaration of sovereignty at her Accession Council, in St James's Palace. It was followed by the heralds' proclamation of the new reign at the palace, at Temple Bar and elsewhere in London and by officials through the length and breadth of the land, according to the time honoured pattern.

Right: 'The three Queens', a remarkable study in grief at the funeral of King George VI in February 1952. The dead King's mother, Queen Mary, stands between her daughter-in-law, Queen Elizabeth the Queen Mother, and her granddaughter, HM Queen Elizabeth II.

Far right: The funeral of the Duke of Windsor at St George's Chapel, Windsor, on 5 June 1972 was an occasion for reconciliation of ill feelings, dating back to the Duke's abdication when King as Edward VIII in 1936. The picture shows the Queen, the Duchess of Windsor and the Queen Mother as mourners at the service.

ROYAL LIFE STYLE

The constitutional role of the sovereign is dealt with elsewhere in another section; here the focus is on the glamour of the public and official life style of the monarch. Paid for, by one means or another, out of the public purse, it is reckoned to recover its costs several times over in the foreign earnings brought into the country by the tourist industry. Over the centuries, most parts of Britain have had what might be called a 'local' royal residence and the section opens with a survey of these palaces and houses past and present that have provided homes for royalty. In earlier ages, monarchs like the 12th-century Henry II travelled widely over the country in the day-to-day business of government or, like Queen Elizabeth I, showed themselves to their people in royal progresses. Today's Royal Family travels as never before; equally it has the most elaborate and luxurious transport section of any of its predecessors. The royal mews provides classic coaches and carriages for state receptions and well appointed limousines for royal journeys; the Royal Yacht is an essential unit in the Queen's overseas tours, little as she enjoys sea travel, while the Royal Train and Royal Flight are both fully exploited. Tools of the trade, they are also the luxurious accoutrements of a high profile and glamorous public life style. This reaches its apogee in the magnificent state banquets hosted by Her Majesty for visiting heads of state and the organization of and preparations for such a banquet form the centrepiece of this section.

Below: Buckingham Palace, the Throne Room.　　　　*Right:* Royal yacht *Britannia* from the bows.

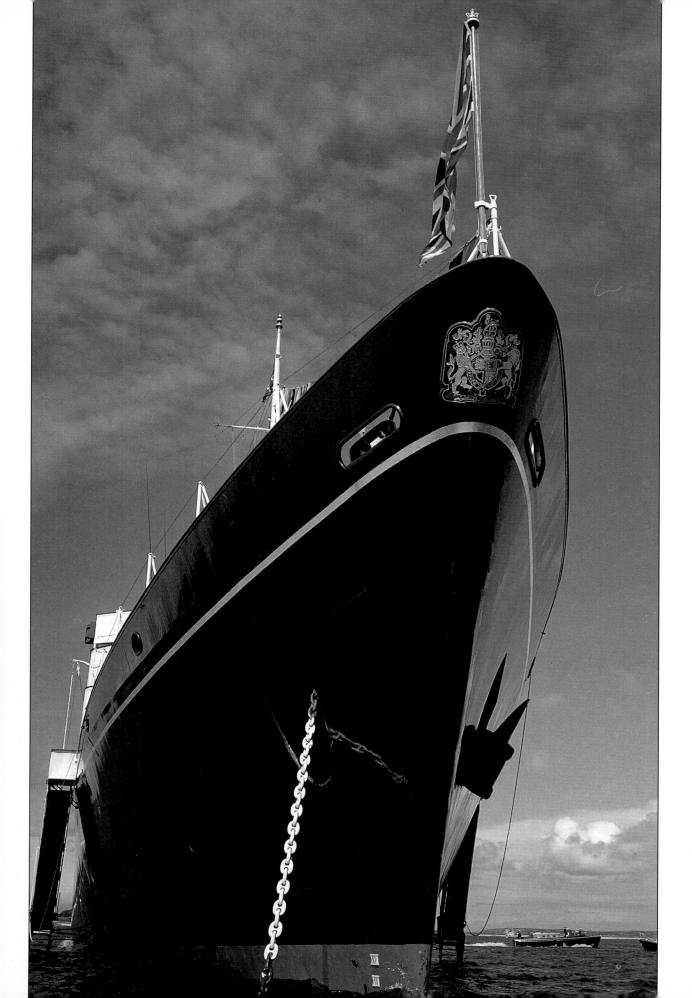

RESIDENCES PAST AND PRESENT

Balmoral Castle and estate near Ballater in Aberdeenshire, Scotland, one of the two private residences of Queen Elizabeth II (the other is Sandringham). Prince Albert and Queen Victoria leased the house and its estate in 1848 and the following year converted and enlarged a cottage some 5 or 6 miles (8–9 km) from the castle where they could live in absolute seclusion. In 1852, they bought the estate (with part of the money left to Victoria in the will of the eccentric John Camden Nield) and by 1856 the castle was rebuilt to designs by Prince Albert, and carpeted in the red and grey Balmoral tartan which he designed. A marble statue of the Prince in full highland regalia stands in the entrance hall, and the Gillies' Ball, which he instituted, remains an annual event, the Queen and Duke joining the dancers. On their visits, the Queen and Prince wear the tartan and dine to the skirl of bagpipes. There are a number of other houses on the estate, among them the Queen Mother's residence of Birkhall, and Craigowan which is used by the Prince and Princess of Wales.

Baynard's Castle, Thames Street, London. A medieval fortress house of the Yorkist kings, made into a comfortable family town house by Henry VII, both 'beautiful and commodious'. In the 1980s archaeologists revealed extensive medieval timber quaysides.

Beaumont Palace, Oxford. Birthplace of Richard I. Built by Henry I, it was frequently visited by his grandson Henry II, medieval England's great lawgiver, on the road to the royal hunting lodge at Woodstock. In fact the Palace may have contributed to the birth of the University. During the 12th century, the Palace and hence the town of Oxford was frequently host to the court and so a magnet for the ambitious. Law, newly fashionable, was an essential qualification for a career in the royal service and among the earliest teachers at Oxford were masters of law. By 1200 masters in all faculties were there, attracted by the swelling numbers of students.

Brighton Pavilion, Sussex. Thanks to the supposedly medicinal qualities of sea bathing, various coastal resorts can date the beginnings of their prosperity from the later 18th century. In 1783 George [IV], Prince of Wales made his first visit to Brighton and commissioned Henry Holland to build a house for him. Early in the 1800s, he engaged John Nash to realize the extravagant oriental style fantasy known as the Brighton Pavilion. From the outside an eccentric Mogul palace, within it was an Aladdin's Cave of *objets d'art*, and chinoiserie decorations and bamboo. The fabulous chandeliers of the music room cost more than £4000 and the astounding great kitchen offered even 'modest' dinner parties more than 100 dishes. Coupled with his 'secret' marriage to Mrs FitzHerbert, whose wedding ring is on display here and whose Brighton house was a favourite retreat for the Prince, it seemed to flaunt his contempt for the British public. They responded with hatred and a simmering republicanism, outraged by such royal extravagance at a time of economic depression and near-starvation. With the coming of the railway in 1841, Brighton began to be oppressively popular. Boarding houses jostled the Pavilion, making it 'quite a prison' as Victoria confided, while trippers jostled the little Queen when she walked the front, for a look at her face under her poke bonnet. In 1850, having removed parts of the decorations, she and Albert sold it to the Brighton Town Commissioners.

Buckingham Palace, London. Formerly called 'Buckingham House', it was built for John Sheffield, Duke of Buckingham, 1703. George III bought it in 1762; all but three of Queen Charlotte's children were born there and it came to be known as The Queen's House. At this time, 'Buck House' was a much smaller, brick built residence. George IV commissioned a rebuild by John Nash which was not completed at his death. William IV, like most of its 20th century occupants, considered it an 'ill-contrived house'. In fact he detested the place, suggesting it be converted into a barracks. In 1834, when fire destroyed the old Palace of Westminster he wistfully offered it to Parliament, as its new home. The principal state rooms are on the first floor and they comprise the Throne Room, with its seven magnificent chandeliers; the great 100-foot-long (30 m) Ballroom; and the state Dining Room with its great mahogany table to seat some 60 guests.

When in London, William and Queen Adelaide had lived either at St James's Palace or at Clarence House. To Victoria, Buckingham Palace was the answer to a prayer. As she advanced to womanhood, her happy childhood home at Kensington Palace had become oppressive with the jealous tutelage of her mother. She moved to the big house at the end of the Mall within three weeks of her accession. She continued with her own programme of additions. They included the new E. front, replaced in 1913 by the present façade of Portland stone. King George IV's grand entrance archway, which obscured much of the front, was moved as 'Marble Arch' to its present site. During World War II, a lone German bomber deposited a stick of bombs on the Palace which destroyed the chapel. The Queen's Gallery, open to the public, displays pictures from the royal collection.

The Chinese luncheon room is decorated with furnishings and fabrics in Chinese style from the ban-queting and music rooms of George IV's Brighton Pavilion. The Queen's apartments including her work room with its bow window are on the north side. Princess Anne has a small suite of rooms on the second floor, immediately above the central balcony, with rooms for her private secretary and her personal secretary. Besides its own swimming pool and cinema, Buckingham Palace is probably one of the few residences in the land with a nuclear fallout shelter and liveried footmen to serve afternoon tea.

Carlton House, a former royal residence (now demolished) to the east of St James's Palace. It was the home of George III's widowed mother, which her son considered needed only 'a touch of paint and handsome furniture where necessary'. Her grandson George [IV] transformed it into a palace (1780s), with Henry Holland as his consulting architect. Its features comprised a classical portico, now adorning the National Gallery, Gothic conservatory of cast iron; and a Chinese salon hung with yellow silks.

Castle of Mey, a private residence of Queen Elizabeth the Queen Mother, between Thurso and John o'Groats in the north of Scotland. 'Barrogill Castle' as it was then called, had been unoccupied for years when she bought it from the Earl of Caithness and was in a literally ruinous state. Its new proprietor instituted what amounted to a military campaign of restoration and rebuilding and devoted much time to creating the beautiful garden.

Clarence House, adjoining St James's Palace, London. Residence of the Queen Mother. Built (1825–9) for William IV when Duke of Clarence, by John Nash. 'Billy Clarence is rigging up in a small way in the stable yard', wrote the diarist Creevey in 1826. Later it was the home of Queen Victoria's son the Duke of Connaught,

Left: This photograph, printed from a glass negative found in the studio of James Reid, the village photographer of Ballater near Balmoral, shows the aged Queen Victoria with her Indian orderly, Abdul Khayrim, a lady in waiting and a Highlander, George Gordon. There is no record of the date or occasion of the photograph but, from the apparent age of the Queen, it would seem to have been taken after the death of the gillie John Brown, notoriously the Queen's confidant.
Right: Clarence House, London.

Top left: Balmoral Castle.

Top centre: The Chinese Dining Room, Buckingham Palace.

Top right: Castle of Mey, Caithness, Scotland.

Left: Royal Falkland Palace, Fife, Scotland.

Above: Hampton Court Palace, Surrey.

Right: The Palace of Holyroodhouse, Edinburgh.

until he went to take up his appointment as Governor General of Canada in 1911. From then, it stood virtually derelict until brief occupation by the Red Cross during World War II. In 1949 Princess Elizabeth and Prince Philip of Greece, together with their baby son Prince Charles, moved in. They installed bathrooms and replaced the gas-lighting which did not work with electricity and refurbished it throughout. Here Princess Anne was born on 15 August 1950. In 1953, following her accession the year before, the Queen and Prince Philip moved to Buckingham Palace, and Queen Elizabeth the Queen Mother and Princess Margaret went to Clarence House.

Edinburgh Castle, Scotland. Malcolm III Canmore, King of Scotland 1058–93, built a castle on the site, though nothing now remains. The present Great Hall dates from the 1500s. James VI was born here but he abandoned his own capital for London on becoming King of England in 1603. Charles II, fugitive from republican England, visited the place in 1650 and George IV wore the tartan here early in the 1820s. The regalia of the Scottish kings, the 'honours of Scotland', are kept here and every year the great parade ground is the site for the world famous Edinburgh Military Tattoo, closing ceremony of the Edinburgh Festival.

Eltham Palace, Kent. A prosperous yeoman's house here was bought for Edward II's Queen Isabella, but it was their son Edward III who, in the mid-14th century, enlarged the house and opened up the gardens to make it one of the Plantagenets' favourite palaces. It was modernized with bathrooms by Richard II. The principal surviving building is the Great Hall, built for Edward IV.

Falkland Palace, Fife. Originally a royal hunting lodge and castle, it was improved and enlarged by James II and his queen Mary of Gueldres. The Gatehouse dates from about 1500, but the south façade and much of the French Renaissance style building (including the tennis court) were done in the 1530s by craftsmen brought over from France by James V. The place was a favourite residence of himself and his two French queens Madeleine and her successor Mary of Guise. As he lay dying here in December 1542, James received news that Queen Mary had given birth to a daughter, the future Mary Queen of Scots.

Gatcombe Park, near Minchinhampton in Gloucestershire, the 18th-century mansion built in Bath stone bought by the Queen for the newly married Princess Anne and Captain Mark Phillips in 1976. The house has some 30 rooms, including four main reception rooms. There is also a large conservatory, a library and billiard room. There is an adjoining farm of some 500 acres.

Greenwich Palace, London. Now the home of the National Maritime Museum, Greenwich, this was the birthplace of King Henry VIII and a favourite palace with the Tudors—Elizabeth I spent much of her time here. However, the first palace on the site was built (1430s–40s) by Henry V's brother Duke Humphrey of Gloucester, who called it Bella Court. On his death, it was taken over by Henry VI's queen, Margaret of Anjou. Henry VII, refaced it with red brick, and also gave the place the name it still bears. The beautiful 'Queen's House' was commissioned from Inigo Jones by James I's queen, Anne of Denmark. Charles II established the Royal Observatory here—hence unwittingly preparing the world's base meridian of longitude—but William and Mary had Sir Christopher Wren build extensions before making the place a seamen's hospital. In the 19th century it became a naval college.

Hampton Court, Surrey. A royal residence from the time of Henry VIII to George II, Hampton Court dates from 1514 when Thomas Wolsey, Archbishop of York, began to build a magnificent palace on this Thameside site. The following year he was created cardinal by the Pope and appointed chief minister by King Henry VIII. In 1525, aware of the King's jealousy of his prince-like wealth and power, the cardinal accepted a royal house at Richmond in exchange for his palace—in 1530 he fell from favour nevertheless. Henry ordered substantial enlargements and alterations. He was always impatient and work on his Great Hall was pressed on, even at night in the glow of a thousand candles. He also laid out gardens and a deer park, a tilt yard and the tennis court. It was the site of happy days for Henry and Anne Boleyn; but a gallery behind the chapel is said to be haunted by the ghost of Henry VIII's wife Catherine Howard who tried to escape her guards pending her execution for adultery in an attempt to plead with the King. It was the honeymoon palace of Queen Mary and her Spanish husband Philip II and of Charles II and his Portuguese wife Catharine of Braganza. Lord Protector Cromwell used it but William III commissioned Wren to rebuild Hampton Court to surpass Versailles. The plans proved over-ambitious. Later improvements and embellishments included work by the architect Sir John Vanbrugh and the wood carver Grinling Gibbons. George III never lived here and Victoria opened it to the public. There are a number of grace-and-favour apartments in the Palace; a fire broke out in 1986 in which one of the residents died and much beautiful and historic work was destroyed.

Highgrove House, Gloucestershire. Residence of the Prince and Princess of Wales. An unassuming classical style, embellished with pilasters and so forth, to Prince Charles's design. In the late 1980s, the Prince began to introduce organic methods on the estate farm.

Holyroodhouse, Edinburgh. The sovereign's official residence while in Scotland where the Queen holds her court each July. The name derives from an abbey founded in 1128 by King David I to honour a piece of the True Cross (the 'rood'), given him by his mother St Margaret. The palace was begun in the late 1490s by James IV. Here Mary Queen of Scots held court and here her Italian confidant David Riccio was murdered by her courtiers. The present building dates largely from the reign of Charles II, though the apartments of the 'James IV Tower' are original. The palace provided accommodation for 'Bonny Prince Charlie', the Young Pretender, during his attempt to seize the crown in the 1745 Highland Rising. In 1822 George IV, wearing a placatory kilt, held court here. Queen Victoria instituted the tradition of the annual visit. The annual Scottish royal garden party is held in the grounds each July.

Kensington Palace, London. So many members of the Royal Family have their London residences here, it might be called a royal apartment house. Much of the building, then known as Nottingham House, was redesigned by Sir Christopher Wren for William III when he bought it in 1689. He was brought here to die, at his own request, after his fatal riding accident at Hampton Court. Queen Anne, who also died here, added the Orangery. George I had the state apartments designed by William Kent, and commissioned the King's Staircase, adorned with *trompe l'oeil* paintings of courtiers looking over balconies, among them the King himself with his Turkish servants. King George II died here (he had once been robbed of his silver watch by a venturesome footpad while walking in the gardens). Victoria was born here and lived here until her accession. She looked back on Kensington, at that time a pleasant village surrounded by rich villas well beyond the urban sprawl of London, as 'My dear native town'.

Mary of Teck, later Queen Mary, was born at the Palace. Its royal occupants number Princess Margaret, the Wales's, the Gloucesters, and Prince and Princess Michael of Kent. Some senior members of the royal household also live here.

Kew House, Surrey. The home of Frederick, Prince of Wales, father of King George III, is now known as Kew Palace and is open to the public as part of the Botanical Gardens. The 'White House' at Kew, long destroyed, provided an occasional retreat for George III and Queen Charlotte. The famous pagoda by Sir William Chambers was done for the old house in 1760 while the gardens owe their initiation to George III's mother Princess Augusta. On 13 July 1818 The Old Palace at Kew was the scene of a double royal wedding when the Duke of Clarence and the Duke of Kent married respectively Princess Adelaide of Saxe-Meiningen and Princess Victoria of Leiningen and Saxe-Coburg-Saalfeld, the former the future queen Adelaide and the latter the mother of Victoria.

Linlithgow Palace, West Lothian, Scotland. The birthplace of Mary Queen of Scots—and also of King James V—Linlithgow had been a Scottish royal residence since David I (1124–53) built a house by the loch here. The present palace dates largely from the 15th century. Together with the neighbouring St Michael's church the fortress palace towers impressively over its loch.

Marlborough House between the Mall and Pall Mall, London. Now the Commonwealth Secretariat and Conference Centre. Built by Wren in the reign of Queen Anne for the Duke and Duchess of Marlborough. The widowed Queen Adelaide, Edward VII and Alexandra while Prince and Princess of Wales, George V as Prince of Wales and the widowed Queen Alexan-

The Princess of Wales with Prince William in one of the rooms of their home in Kensington Palace, 1982.

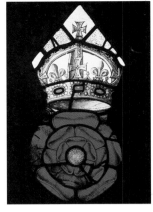

Above: Window roundel with a red 'Tudor-style' rose, rescued from Henry VIII's destroyed palace of Nonsuch.

Left: The old Kew Palace and a re-creation of the 18th-century 'Queen's Garden'.

Right: Sandringham House, Norfolk.

Far right: The King's State Bed Chamber, Windsor.

Left: Inside the Armoury, St James's Palace, London.

Right: Ceiling of the Queen's Audience Chamber, Windsor, painted by the 18th-century Italian artist Antonio Verrio.

dra all lived here. During the occupancy of Edward and Alexandra as the Wales's, it was the setting for entertaining on the grand scale, becoming the focus of a second court during the prolonged mourning of Queen Victoria for her beloved Albert. Queen Alexandra's dogs' cemetery is in the garden while much of the antique furniture was chosen by Queen Mary.

Nonsuch, Surrey. Built by Henry VIII 1538 onwards, a fantasy palace comparable to the château of Chambord on the Loire, built by Henry's contemporary Francis I. Many of the artists and craftsmen had worked at Fontainebleau. Charles II presented the palace to his mistress Barbara Villiers who demolished it and sold the contents.

Osborne House, Isle of Wight. Purchased by Prince Albert as a holiday retreat for his and Victoria's growing family (1845). To the delight of the Queen, who had become very disillusioned with Brighton, the estate included 'a charming beach quite to ourselves'. By 1851 a new Italianate style house had been built to designs by the Prince Consort in collaboration with the architect Thomas Cubitt. Additions to the grounds included the Swiss cottage and the model dairy, where the royal children spent happy hours. With Windsor, it was the Queen's principal home and retreat during her

long period of mourning after Albert's death. She herself died here. Edward VII hated the place and gave it to the nation.

Richmond Lodge, Surrey. Rebuilt by Lord Ormonde in 1704, on the site of the lodge to the old Richmond Palace, it was granted by George I to George [II] Prince of Wales in 1722. George III and Queen Charlotte began their married life here. The Lodge was awarded by Parliament to the Queen.

Richmond Palace, built by Henry VII to replace the old palace of Sheen which burnt out on 21 December 1498. He named the new building after the Yorkshire honour whose title he had borne before his usurpation. Queen Mary restored the Priory at Sheen and Elizabeth I gave her last public audience here in February 1603. Henry, Prince of Wales (d. 1612) was the last royal to live at the Palace. In the 1720s the lodge was briefly occupied by George [II], Prince and Caroline, Princess of Wales.

Sandringham House, Norfolk. A private royal residence, the large red-brick mansion set in 17 000 acres (6885 ha) of pines and heathland, is largely the work of Edward [VII], Prince of Wales. It was bought from the accumulated revenues of the Duchy of Cornwall, at a price of £220 000. During the summer seasons it saw a

York Cottage, the house in the grounds of Sandringham where the future George V and Queen Mary raised their sizeable family. Their eldest son Edward VIII, always known to the family as David, told a friend in later life 'You will never understand my father until you have seen York Cottage'. By royal standards, and considering that besides the family it had to accommodate numerous live-in servants, it provided cramped quarters indeed. Yet George always preferred it

above his other residences. This popular souvenir picture, dating from 1905, depicts him and Mary when Prince and Princess of Wales with their children (left to right) David (i.e. Edward VIII, later Duke of Windsor), 'Bertie' (later King as George VI), Mary (later the Princess Royal), Henry (later Duke of Gloucester), George (later Duke of Kent) and John (who died in 1919).

round of house parties, delivered by train from London nicknamed the 'Prince of Wales Special'. Up to 30 people regularly sat down to 12-course dinners. In 1977, Queen Elizabeth opened the house and estate to the public and exploited the estate commercially. The cramped York Cottage in the grounds provided the family home for George [V], Prince of Wales. People were astonished that royalty would tolerate such accommodation. Edward VIII told a friend 'You will never understand my father until you have seen York Cottage'. For George V, Sandringham provided a retreat from the care of monarchy. (He used to say 'I have a house in London and a home in Norfolk'.) It was from here that he made the first ever royal Christmas radio broadcast in 1932. Here, too, he died as did his son George VI. The Queen made her first Christmas TV broadcast from Sandringham in 1952. The Princess of Wales, Lady Diana Spencer, was born in York Cottage, too!

St James's Palace, London. The official residence of the English royal court since 1698, when fire gutted the palace of Whitehall. On the death of a monarch the accession council convenes here and the proclamation of the new reign is made in Friary Court. The original red and blue brick Palace was built by Henry VIII for himself and Anne Boleyn on the site of a former leper hospital. The gateway with its entwined monograms of 'A' 'H' for Anne and Henry is all that remains. It provided Charles II with a bijou residence in which to house various successive mistresses. The clocktower gatehouse remains from the Tudor period. The Palace houses the central chancery of the orders of knighthood, the headquarters of the Gentlemen at Arms and the Yeomen of the Guard, among other offices, and is the London home of the Duke and Duchess of Kent.

Sheen, Surrey. The original manor house at Sheen was a favourite resort of the medieval English monarchs. Edward III ended his days here in the care of his beloved mistress Alice Perrers. Richard II, Shakespeare's unhappy king, found here an idyll of love with his young Bohemian Queen Anne. When she tragically died at the palace, he ordered the destruction of the entire wing that housed her apartments.

Stirling Castle, Scotland. On its great outcrop of volcanic rock in the Scottish lowlands, Stirling is one of the most dramatic places in the United Kingdom. In 1174 it was ceded to Henry II in return for the liberty of King William the Lion, forced to acknowledge Henry as Scotland's overlord at the Treaty of Falaise. In 1651 the Parliamentary armies discharged the historic obligation of more or less any new English regime of defeating the Scots at least once by storming the place—a feat which Prince Charles Edward, or Bonnie Prince Char-

lie, crucially failed to achieve in 1746. The present structure dates mostly from the 16th century, when it saw the birth (1594) of the tragically short-lived Prince Henry, eldest son of King James VI and I.

Tower of London. Begun by William the Conqueror to secure the capital city of his newly conquered kingdom, the White Tower was completed about 1100. From the start it was intended as a residence as well as fortification. In the late 12th century, King Richard added further outer defences. In the following century, Henry III was housed in the Lion Tower whose private menagerie included lions. Edward III extended the royal apartments so that it was more or less palatial in its amenities, although the place was used for high ranking state prisoners and occasionally their executions on Tower Green. The fact that the boy king Edward V was lodged here in 1483 in anticipation of his coronation, lacked the sinister implications read into it later. Traditionally, all kings stayed here at least on the night before their coronation—Charles II was the last to observe the tradition. The armouries and the Jewel House where the Crown Jewels are kept are reminders of a dramatic history. Each night, the ancient Ceremony of the Keys takes place, with the Chief Yeoman Warder ceremonially locking the Gates of the Tower.

Westminster, London. The palace of Westminster, today comprising the Houses of Parliament, Westminster Hall (built by William II Rufus and roofed by Richard II) and the 14th-century Jewel Tower, remains, in theory at least, what it was in the days of Edward the Confessor—a royal residence. In fact it was the principal royal residence until the time of Henry VIII. The crypt church of St Mary's Undercroft is all that survives of St Stephen's church. This was once the Commons' meeting house, from 1547 to 1834, when it and most of the rest of the palace was destroyed by fire. St Thomas More, Guy Fawkes and Charles I were among those tried in the great hall. A statue of Lord Protector Cromwell, who led Parliament's armies to victory over King Charles in the Civil War, overlooks Parliament Square from the precincts of the royal palace. Not since 1642 has a sovereign been permitted to enter the Commons chamber. However, following heavy damage by German bombers in World War II, the 1834 House of Commons was rebuilt (to its original design, following Winston Churchill's urging). The then King George VI expressed the wish to see the restored chamber and, since it was technically not yet in use, permission was granted and the monarch and his heir, the Princess Elizabeth, were allowed in. The Houses of Parliament were the work of Sir James Barrie and Arthur Pugin while Prince Albert, as chairman of the Royal Commission for Redecoration, was largely responsible for the design of the frescos.

Windsor Castle, a dramatic view of the Castle under floodlighting.

Whitehall, London. The first palace on this site, as at Hampton Court, was the property of Cardinal Wolsey in his capacity as Archbishop of York. Inevitably, Henry VIII expropriated it from the owner, adding his tilt yards and tennis courts. The palace banqueting hall, designed by Inigo Jones in the 17th century, is the magnificent but only survival of a once immense complex of royal buildings, following a fearful fire in the late 1690s. The present structure houses government offices.

Windsor, Berkshire. The world's largest inhabited castle and the oldest royal residence still in use as such, Windsor stands on a low hill on the south bank of the Thames, with the shops and houses of the little town of Windsor coming up to the gates. Away to the south, the 3-mile (5 km) long walk leads to Windsor Great Park. Eastward, Home Park runs down to the Thames, more than a mile away, with the royal mausoleum and Frogmore House. North-west, across the river, lies Henry VI's foundation of Eton College, originally intended for poor scholars. Eastward, on the same bank, is Datchet where Charles II watched and joined in the races and to the south-west runs the road to Ascot, established in royal favour by Queen Anne.

More or less in the middle of Great Park stands George III on his copper horse. Nearby is Royal Lodge. Today the Home Counties retreat of the Queen Mother, it was originally 'Lower Lodge' and renamed and taken over by George IV during his renovation of the castle. The castle proper is a rough figure of eight, comprising the Upper Ward, with the state and private apartments dating from the 17th to 19th centuries; the Lower Ward, dominated by St George's Chapel, home of the Order of the Garter; and Middle Ward, from which rises the ancient defensive mound and the Round Tower, the lower courses built by King Henry II and the upper stages part of George IV's rebuilding.

Windsor is a treasure house of paintings, drawings, books, archives and works of art. Other immensely popular features are the Savile Gardens near Cumberland Lodge in Great Park, the Valley Gardens by Virginia Water and in the castle itself, Queen Mary's Dolls' House. Designed by Sir Edwin Lutyens and first exhibited at the Great Empire Exhibition of 1926, it is a miniature country mansion in which 'everything that should work does'.

York House a suite of apartments on the north and west side of St James's Palace which provide the London residence of the Duke and Duchess of Kent and offices for the Lord Chamberlain's department.

A STATE BANQUET

Historically, receptions for visiting royalty, of which the state banquet was the high point, were occasions as much if not more on which to impress one's friends, neighbours and possible enemies as to entertain them. The gold and silver accoutrements of the dining table were a form of investment and measure of wealth, their display a public relations exercise. The sideboard on which to display one's treasures was an essential piece of equipment. Pleasing to relate, it still is. Ostentation remains an honoured tradition at the Palace.

At the state visit of the President of Turkey, on Tuesday 12 July 1988, some of the gold-plate on display were: two large gold wine flagons dating from 1690 and two made in 1828 and engraved with emblems of the kingdoms of England, Scotland, Ireland and Hanover; and a great dish (diameter 31 in, 78.7 cm) made by Paul Storr in 1814, depicting 'The Triumph of Bacchus and Ariadne'. In addition to this, of course, the tables were laid with pieces from the 'royal gold', including massive candelabras of the Grand Service founded by George IV. Some of the table centres take four men to lift and position. It is said that the entire gold and silver gilt banquet dinner service weighs some five tons. Naturally, the porcelain and glass matches the plate in quality. On this Tuesday, the table glass was a service of English cut crystal, hand engraved with the cipher 'E II R' while the sweet course (as the pudding is called at a Palace banquet) was served in a Minton service of turquoise (literally, 'Turkish') and gold with floral motifs made for Queen Victoria in 1876.

The tables were decorated with summer flowers in shades of cream, yellow, pink and blue and hidden among the roses, sweet peas, lilies and other flower arrangements were, no doubt, the 'traffic lights' (it is the only word) that ensure the smooth running of such occasions. Using a code based on amber for 'get ready' and green for 'go', a steward standing behind the Queen, sensing when Her Majesty is coming to the end of a course or when she is ready to begin her next course can usually ensure that each course is served to the scores of guests at the moment it is placed before the Queen.

As always on these occasions, the regular Palace staff was supplemented by scores of 'temp' footmen, chefs and kitchen staff, hired through agencies. For the evening, all are members of the same staff, the regulars have their pay raised to the high hourly rates of the part timers whilst they, of course, are dressed in state livery. For senior staff (all regulars) this comprises black and gold braided coats with fine white knee breeches,

The Ballroom, Buckingham Palace.

stockings and black buckled pumps. The footmen wear scarlet gold braided livery, scarlet plush knee breeches, pink stockings and black buckled pumps.

After the banquet, which on this occasion was held in the ball room rather than the state dining room, after the last speech and the departure of the guests the treasures, the gold plate and centrepieces are carefully taken down and, like the table settings which are carefully washed, returned to store only when they have been checked off in their books by the Yeomen of the Gold, the Silver and the Glass and China Pantries.

The seating plan and menu for the State Banquet in honour of the President of Senegal in November 1988.

STATE BANQUET

IN HONOUR OF

**THE PRESIDENT
OF THE
REPUBLIC OF SENEGAL
AND
MADAME ABDOU DIOUF**

BUCKINGHAM PALACE

TUESDAY, 8th NOVEMBER, 19[...]

Menu

Bisque de Homard

Crêpes de Volaille
à l'indienne

Caneton Bigarrade
Fèves au beurre
Fleurettes de Chou-fleur Glacées
Pommes Croquettes

Salade

Bombe Glacée Coppelia

Les Vins

Fine Old Amontillado
Hochheimer Königin Victoria Berg 1980
Château Talbot 1975
Veuve Clicquot 1979
Dow's 1966

THE PRESIDENT OF THE REPUBLIC OF SENEGAL
QUEEN ELIZABETH THE QUEEN MOTHER

THE QUEEN

THE PRINCE PHILIP, DUKE OF EDINBURGH
MADAME ABDOU DIOUF

Archbishop of Canterbury
Madame Ibrahima Fall
The Prince Edward

The Duke of Kent
Mrs. Runcie
Monsieur Pape Diouf

The Princess Margaret,
Countess of Snowdon
Monsieur Ibrahima Fall
Prime Minister
The Duke of Gloucester
Lady Mackay of Clashfern
Prince Michael of Kent
Mrs. Weatherill
Lord Great Chamberlain
Madame Idrissa Fall
Earl of Dalhousie
Lady Farnham
High Commissioner for
the Gambia
Lady Somerleyton
Chief Secretary to
the Treasury
Mrs. Monday
High Commissioner
for Australia
Lady Mayoress
Cledwyn of Penrhos
Mrs. Zenined
Right Hon.
William Heseltine
Lady Fieldhouse
Henri Mendy
Lady Heseltine
of the Fleet
Fieldhouse
Kershaw
Colonel
[...]e Diop
[...]lewitt
[...]unt
[...]rr
[...]ll

The Duchess of York
Lord Chancellor
The Duchess of Gloucester
Right Hon. the Speaker
The Duchess of Kent
Lord Privy Seal
Princess Michael of Kent
Monsieur Djibo Ka
Marchioness of Cholmondeley
Earl of Airlie
Lady Howe
Monsieur Bruno Diatta
Madame Stathatos
Dr. Geoffrey Young
Lady Bramall
Monsieur Babacar Mbaye
Mrs. McClelland
Right Hon.
James Molyneaux, M.P.
Mrs. Leigh-Pemberton
Ambassador of the
Kingdom of Thailand
Lady Grimthorpe
Right Hon. Robin Leigh-Pemberton
Mrs. Prasasvinitchai
Admiral Sir John Woodward
Lady Kennedy
Lieutenant-General
Sir John-Richards
Mrs. Macrae
Colonel Lamine Cisse
Mr. Roger Hervey
Lady Gibb
Major-General Christopher Airy
Mrs. Baker
Lieutenant-Colonel George West
Sir Frank Gibb
Mrs. McLeod
Lieutenant-Commander
Sir Richard Buckley, R.N.
Professor Anthony Kirk-Greene
Mrs. Shelley
Mr. Alfred Shepperd
Mr. Michael Miller
Mrs. Rimmer ·

Earl of Westmorland
Mrs. Panayides
Secretary of State
for Foreign and
Commonwealth Affairs
Countess Alexander
of Tunis
Monsieur Famara
Ibrahima Sagna
Mrs. Parkinson
Lord Farnham
Mrs. Major
Ambassador of Greece
Baroness Young
High Commissioner
for Sierra Leone
Lady Lane
Lord Somerleyton
Mrs. De Mel
Field Marshal
Lord Bramall
Lady Burgh
Ambassador of the
Kingdom of Morocco
Lady Chapple
Sir Patrick Wright
Madame Sourang
Sir John Burgh
Lady Buckley
Sir Francis Kennedy
Lady Wright
Colonel Boubacar Wane
Mr. Kenneth Scott
Mrs. Airy
Monsieur Cheikh Sylla
Mrs. Angus
Mr. Brian McGrath
Mr. John Baker
Mrs. Gilbart-Denham
Mr. Robert Bauman
Mr. Douglas Rimmer
Hon. Mrs. Leatham
Mr. Michael Coates
Mr. Alan Shelley
Miss Sarah Cruise O'Brien

Viscount Davidson
Duchess of Grafton
High Commissioner
for the Republic
of Cyprus
Viscountess Davidson
Mr. John Macrae
Madame Fatoumata Ka
Secretary of State
for Energy
Lady Susan Hussey
Ambassador of the
Republic of Senegal
Lady Cledwyn of Penrhos
Lord Chief Justice
of England
Mrs. Aubee
Right Hon.
the Lord Mayor
Mrs. Kinnock
Ambassador of the
Republic of Côte d'Ivoire
Countess of Airlie
Right Hon.
Neil Kinnock, M.P.
Lady Woodward
Monsieur Abdou Sourang
Lady Hunt
General Sir John Chapple
Lady Richards
Monsieur Jean-Noël
de Bouillane de Lacoste
Lady Neill
Sir David Orr
Hon. Mary Morrison
Sir Anthony Kershaw
Madame de Bouillane
de Lacoste
Monsieur Simon Dioh
Lady Camoys
Mr. Hugh Balfour
Professor Roland Smith
Mrs. Miller
Mr. Michael Angus
Mrs. Birch
Dr. Malcolm McLeod
Mrs. Vallance
Mr. Geoffrey Coates
Rear-Admiral Sir Paul Greening

[...]en
Lieutenant-Colonel
Seymour Gilbart-Denham
Mrs. Smith
Mr. Iain Vallance
Mrs. Shepperd
Mr. Kenneth Birch
Lieutenant-Colonel Blair Stewart-Wilson

HER MAJESTY'S GUESTS ARE REQUESTED TO REMAIN SEATED DURING THE SPEECHES OF THE QUEEN AND THE PRESIDENT OF THE REPUBLIC OF SENEGAL

THE ROYAL YACHT HMY BRITANNIA

The present royal yacht, latest in a long line of ceremonial royal boats, was completed at John Brown's Clydebank shipyard in 1953, named and launched by Her Majesty the Queen in the same year and commissioned on 11 January 1954. It had taken two years to complete at an estimated cost of £2.1 million.

Unlike her predecessors with their swan bow and counter stern, *Britannia* has a clipper bow and modified cruiser stern. The modification of design reflects the decision to build a boat that could be used as a hospital ship in time of war—though in fact she was not used in this capacity during the Falklands war of the early 1980s. However, she did see action in the Queen's 60th birthday year, while on passage to Australia in connection with Her Majesty's visit there. On 13 January fighting broke out in the southern Arabian state of South Yemen and the international community in Aden, representing more than 50 nationalities, was in dire danger. Four days later the royal yacht steamed into sight. Over the next 48 hours she coordinated the evacuation of more than 1300 civilians and herself took off 1082 men, women and children, many of them Soviets.

In her royal blue and white livery, royal arms at the bow, royal cipher at the stern, *Britannia* seems a floating palace—an attractive honeymoon transport for the younger royals as well as a mobile base for royal tours overseas. More than once Her Majesty has held investitures on its decks and on major tours a 26-piece Royal Marines Band is embarked for entertainment and official music—for example it regularly performs the Beating the Retreat.

With annual running costs of well over £1 million and a 1987 refit, aimed at extending its life well into the next century and running into several millions, the yacht is a periodic target for critics of royal expenditure. She has a complement of more than 250 officers and men, all of them Royal Navy volunteers.

The royal apartments are abaft the mainmast. Access is down a wide mahogany staircase to the anteroom which gives into the drawing room through tall mahogany doors. The doors can be folded back so as to throw the two rooms into a single reception room which can hold up to 200 people. The dining room, which seats up to some 60 people, can double up as a cinema. The furniture of the yacht includes some of the pieces from its predecessors, among these being a gimbal table designed by Albert, the Prince Consort and the binnacle from the *Royal George* of King George IV. The Queen and the Duke of Edinburgh have private sitting rooms which connect with their bedrooms on the uppermost deck by lift.

DIMENSIONS OF HMY *BRITANNIA*
Length: 412 ft 3 in (125.65 m)
Beam: 55 ft (maximum) (16.76 m)
Draught: 17 ft (at load displacement) (5.18 m)

Britannia's immediate predecessor as the official royal yacht, the *Victoria and Albert* (third of the name) 1935.

Left: *Victoria and Albert II.*

Right: *Britannia's* state launch.

Below left: The drawing room aboard the royal yacht.

Below centre: The dining room.

Below right: One of *Britannia's* 17th-century predecessors.

Mast head height: 123 ft (37.49 m)

Gross tonnage: 5769 tons (5862 tonnes)

Deep load displacement: 5280 tons, with 430 tons of diesel fuel and 199 tons of fresh water

Main machinery: Geared Steam Turbines, 12 000 shaft horsepower. 2 shafts

She can maintain a continuous seagoing speed of 21 knots and has a range of 2500 miles at 14 knots. *Britannia* can carry a 40-ft (12 m) barge, and a Rolls Royce.

YACHTS OF YORE

Among her predecessors was Charles I's *Sovereign of the Seas*. In 1782 King George III, apprehensive over the state of affairs in Britain on the resignation of Lord North following the loss of the American colonies, ordered the royal yacht to be at readiness to evacuate the royal family to Hanover should need arise. In 1814 Louis XVIII of France, restored to his Bourbon throne by the defeat of Napoleon at the Battle of Leipzig was shipped, rather prematurely as it transpired, across the Channel to Calais in Britain's royal yacht. When he became king, George IV used the *Royal George*, built for him while still Prince of Wales, for his visit to Scotland in 1822. (*Britannia* is often used to take the Queen and members of the family round the coast to Balmoral, stopping at various of the lesser British Isles en route.)

William IV, who loved sailing his yacht down the Thames to Greenwich, appointed Adolphus, one of his illegitimate sons, commander of the royal yacht. As befitted a half blood royal, he became a rear admiral and, surprisingly perhaps, an aide-de-camp to the young Queen Victoria. However, the *Royal George*, last of the sail royal yachts, fell out of favour with the Queen on her 1842 visit to Scotland when it had to be towed virtually all the way to Leith because of light winds. Victoria ordered a steam yacht, the first *Victoria and Albert*, so powerful that it easily outpaced its naval escort on its trials. Over her reign there were three successive boats of the name, one of them a paddle steamer. When he came to the throne, Edward VII commissioned the *Alexandra*, though 'V & A' (III) remained the official boat.

This had no appeal for Edward's son and successor, George V, who commissioned a racing yacht *Britannia* which, after his beloved queen, was probably the nearest thing to his heart. By the 1930s the old *Victoria and Albert* was virtually unseaworthy and George VI planned to commission a new yacht; however, the outbreak of World War II and the years of austerity that followed meant that work had to be delayed.

The royal yacht, like every other aspect of modern royalty, is changing with the times. An innovation on royal tours introduced during the 1980s has been the holding of 'Sea Days' on board to promote British and Commonwealth trade and financial services overseas. Given the mystique that still surrounds Britain's royalty overseas they must be unique opportunities for selling and, it is claimed, do indeed generate millions of pounds worth of business.

THE ROYAL COACHES

The royal mews houses the world's finest collection of state coaches, landaus and barouches still in active service. In addition it usually stables some 30 horses, 10 greys (i.e. white horses) and 20 bays.

The Gold State Coach   Used by George IV at his coronation in 1820 and at every coronation since that time, the coach was built for King George III in celebration of England's victories in Germany, Canada and India in the Seven Years War over France and her allies. Inelegant and impractical, it burgeons with baroque ornaments of triumph. Gilded tritons symbolize Britannia's rule of the waves; three gilded cherubs support the crown on the roof; a gilded bundle of lances forms the pole. One of the panels, which were painted by G. B. Cipriani, a founder member of London's Royal Academy, depicts classical figures of victory bearing St Edward's Crown up into the sky. Originally, the coach had a driving box but this was removed on the orders of King Edward VII so that the occupants could be seen more easily. Since his time, there being no coachman, the horses have been led by grooms and footmen. King George V noted the ride in the coach in this entry in his diary on his coronation day: 'May [i.e. Queen Mary] and I left B.P. in the coronation coach at 10.30 with 8 cream coloured horses. There were 50 000 troops lining the streets . . . There were hundreds of thousands of people who gave us a magnificent reception.'

The Irish State Coach   Bought by Victoria after she had seen it on display at a Dublin exhibition in 1852, it was rebuilt in 1911 after a fire destroyed the original woodwork. It was used to carry Princess Elizabeth to her wedding, and conveyed the sovereign to every State Opening of Parliament this century up to 1988, when it was displaced by the Australian State Coach.

The Australian State Coach   Presented to the Queen by the Commonwealth of Australia in May 1988, during her Bicentennial tour, it is a modern masterpiece of the coach builder's art. Armorial decorations were done by the Queen's heraldic painter brought over from England. They include the emu and kangaroo supporters of Australia, while the coach-lamps, surmounted by miniature St Edward's crowns, have lenses of fine hand-blown and cut Waterford crystal. All the other craftsmanship and materials, such as the timber and aluminium and craftsmanship of the coach, built at Dubbo, New South Wales, under the supervision of Jim Frecklington, a former royal household groom, are of Australian provenance. Once steam-bent to shape, the hardwood elements of the timber and aluminium undercarriage were left to season to the correct moisture consistency and at every stage the workmanship was monitored to the highest standards to give the vehicle a working life of over 200 years.

Left: An 18th-century state Thames River barge.

Right: The Queen with Prince Charles and Princess Diana on the way to the State Opening of Parliament.

Above: Queen Elizabeth II on her coronation day in the gold state coach.

Left: The Royal Mews with the gold state coach, furthest from the camera, the glass coach, the Irish state coach and a state landau.

Right: The royal coachmen in scarlet (out rider), full state, black and scarlet (walking groom) liveries.

Queen Alexandra's State Coach This was first used by King Edward VII's queen, and was used at Queen Elizabeth's coronation to carry the crown from the Tower of London to Westminster.

The Glass Coach This was bought for use in George V's coronation procession. This was the coach that brought Princess Elizabeth and Philip, Duke of Edinburgh, and years later Prince Charles and Princess Diana, back to Buckingham Palace after their weddings.

King Edward VII's Town Coach A regular standby at royal weddings, it is also made available to foreign ambassadors when they make their ceremonial visit to St James's Palace to present their official papers of accreditation to the Court of St James on beginning their tour of duty.

The 1902 State Postilion Landau This was built for Edward VII, and is commonly used by the Queen for welcoming visiting heads of state.

THE ROYAL TRAIN

The fleet of 12 vehicles which constitute the modern royal train, was officially handed over to the Queen at London's Euston Station on 16 May 1977, the Queen's Silver Jubilee year. The Queen and the Duke of Edinburgh first boarded it for the overnight journey to Scotland which inaugurated their numerous tours in that year.

There is no royal locomotive as such, the appropriate power unit being drawn from British Rail's stock for the proposed journey. **The Queen's Saloon** comprises a formal entrance vestibule with double doors to the platform; a living area for the Queen—sitting room, bedroom and bathroom; a bedroom and bathroom for the Queen's dresser; and a second vestibule area. **The Duke of Edinburgh's Saloon** has an entrance vestibule; a sitting/dining room, bedroom and bathroom; accommodation for the Duke's valet; and a kitchen designed to provide meals for up to 10 people when the Saloon is being used on its own.

The furniture, furnishings and fittings were chosen by the Queen and Prince Philip, with the advice of Sir Hugh Casson. Ten other coaches include one for the Queen's Private Secretary and other members of the household; a staff dining car for members of the household; a dining saloon for the royal party as such; and a standard first class sleeping car.

Right: The private railway saloon built for Queen Victoria in 1869.

Below left: Queen Victoria and Prince Albert in a saloon of the royal train with King Louis Philippe of France.

Below: The Queen's saloon of the modern royal train. It is in a predominantly blue decor, following previous style.

ROYAL DIVERSIONS AND PASTIMES

Theatricals have been a favourite royal diversion, among various others.

Above: The Queen and Princess Margaret as girls pose with friends for a cast photo of their 1944 Christmas pantomine, 'Old Mother Red Riding Boots'.

Above centre: Prince Charles enjoyed undergraduate theatricals while at Cambridge.

Above right: For more than 50 years the Royal Family has patronized the 'Royal Variety Show', an entertainment event of international standing. Here the Queen Mother shakes hands with Sammy Davis Jr.

Centre right: Queen Elizabeth I's virginals.

Bottom right: Prince Edward, president of the National Youth Theatre, with Cliff Richard and Dame Kiri Te Kanawa at the charity 'It's a Knockout' organized by the Prince in 1987.

Left: The dining room from Queen Mary's Dolls' House.

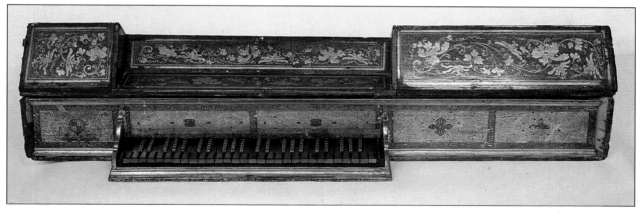

THE ROYAL CARS

In addition to the traditional equipages of royalty, the mews garages the Queen's five official state cars, all of them Rolls Royces and all converted for lead-free petrol. All of them are fully insured in accordance with the law, although none of them carries number plates—the sovereign being the only person in the kingdom to enjoy this privilege. The vehicles are as follows:

The Phantom VI, presented to the Queen by the Motor Industry in Britain to commemorate her Silver Jubilee of 1977. It is 19 ft 10 in (6.05 m) long; 6 ft 7 in (2.00 m) wide; by 6 ft 1 in (1.85 m) high. The transparent dome over the rear compartment of the car accounts for the unusual height; it has an elevating rear seat.

The **1960 Phantom V** and the **1961 Phantom V**: the roofs of both are fitted with glass centre Perspex side panels, which can be masked by folding metal exterior roof panels when required.

A **Phantom IV Landaulette** (i.e. a half open car) bought second-hand in 1954 with a coupé fold-down roof over the rear compartment. A closed **Phantom IV limousine**, a wedding present from the Royal Air Force to Princess Elizabeth and the Duke of Edinburgh.

All the vehicles, painted maroon, have fittings on the front of the roof to take a shield bearing the royal arms and also a small royal standard (the standard is never flown by itself). For state occasions the Queen uses her own mascot, a naked St George slaying the Dragon, in place of the Spirit of Ecstasy.

In addition there are two semi-official Austin Princess cars, one black and one maroon and black.

From the year 1900 when Edward [VII] Prince of Wales took delivery of a 6-horsepower Daimler (his first car) this marque was the royal car par excellence down to the 1950s. Queen Elizabeth the Queen Mother continued the association with the company into the 1970s. The first use of a car on official royal business was on 19 October 1904 when Edward VII was driven from Buckingham Palace for an inspection of the Garrison at Woolwich.

Left: One of the Queen's fleet of Rolls Royce cars bearing the royal arms and the royal standard.

Right: A plane of the Queen's Flight.

Right: A helicopter of the Queen's Flight.

THE QUEEN'S FLIGHT

Although it was his brother Bertie, later King as George VI, who was the first member of the family to get his wings, it was Edward VIII who, during his brief reign in 1936, founded the King's Flight. It is now a highly professional transport wing of five units, largely financed from Ministry of Defence funds and based at RAF Benson, Oxfordshire.

The Flight is at the immediate disposal of the Queen, the Queen Mother, the Duke of Edinburgh and Prince Charles. Other members of the family may have the use of one of the aircraft at the Queen's discretion.

The Flight comprises two British Aerospace 146 executive jets, a twin turbo-prop Hawker Siddeley Andover CC Mk 2 (said to be favoured by Prince Philip and Prince Charles if they are flying themselves because its slower speed allows them the chance to pile up flying hours) and two Westland Wessex HCC4 helicopters.

THE FIRM AT WORK

The present royals regard themselves very much as a working family and the Duke of Edinburgh is known to favour the coinage made by George VI who called his family 'The Firm'. In an age when image and 'perception' are considered a vital part of 'work' as conceived by politicians, when the worst failing of a government minister in the eyes of the Queen's chief minister is not the content of his policies but the success or otherwise with which they are presented to the public, it is perhaps not perverse to start a chapter on the royal firm with a look at its relations with the media. Whatever government may do, the royals certainly do useful work but for them as for the politicians, image is important. It was always thus.

Left: The Queen on Horseguards Parade at the Trooping the Colour ceremony, 1981. As head of state she is also commander in chief of the armed forces. Once the principal function of monarchy, it has now been reduced to a ceremonial but constitutionally important role.

Right: The Queen reading the Speech from the throne in the House of Lords, at the State Opening of Parliament, 1964. Today, the monarchy has a largely symbolic role to play in the nation's affairs. However, it is the Queen's formal assent which makes a Bill law and the constitution of Britain is that of a constitutional monarchy, governed by the Queen in Parliament.

Below: The Queen rides in a state coach for the State Opening of Parliament in 1986.

'DOING THE BOXES'

Doing the boxes, the phrase used by George V for the paperwork of monarchy, gives the Queen an important insight into the workings of government over the years. Every day the red leather dispatch cases of official communications from ministers of the crown arrive by special courier for the Queen's attention wherever she may be. The routine has been in force some 37 years and, we may be sure, will continue for many years to come.

King William IV began the routines of the modern constitutional monarchy. In the 1830s Chancellor Lord Brougham, familiar with the business style of three monarchs, made his assessment: 'King George III would ask too many questions and would not wait for answers; . . . George IV would ask no questions for fear of showing his ignorance; . . . whereas His Majesty King William asked as many as were necessary for him to let him fully understand.' Towards the end of his reign King George IV refused to sign any state papers. As a result, when he came to the throne, William IV 'patiently signed a backlog of 48 000 state papers. Every night he laboured through pile after pile, while Queen Adelaide stood patiently by with a bowl of warm water for him to bathe his cramped fingers'.

Today, no one has such a close, thorough and above all continuous knowledge of government procedures and decision making over such a period of time as the Queen. Victoria, who was conscientiously working on her papers up till within a week of her death, never allowed her son and successor Edward VII in on the secrets! Queen Elizabeth II is not so short-sighted. Prince Charles has long been permitted sight of some state documents. The corresponding documents from the Commonwealth countries, such as her ministers in those countries wish her to be informed of, go direct to the Queen without being filtered through Whitehall departments.

In addition to her large official post bag, the Queen of course receives thousands of letters every year from her subjects all over the world. This huge flow of paper is handled by her private secretaries. The mail is divided into three categories: routine to be dealt with by the secretaries themselves in the Queen's name; communications on which the Queen's instructions must be sought; and a third category, larger than many people might imagine, letters to be answered in the Queen's own hand. At the head of the considerable staff at the Palace stands the Queen's secretary.

Above: Queen Elizabeth II at her work table in Buckingham Palace.

Left: Henry VIII's writing box.

Right: King George VI at his desk in Buckingham Palace in 1940. Obviously a posed photograph, but the King's naval uniform, symbolic of his role as head of the armed forces, reflected an important part he played in boosting morale during World War II.

THE ROYAL HOUSEHOLD

The household officers of the monarchs were the earliest officers of state and many modern offices of state such as Secretary, Chancellor and Chamberlain reflect their origins. As the business of government increasingly became too complicated, so household and official business became increasingly separated. Nevertheless, personal service to the monarch remained a principal path to high office in the state for centuries. John Stuart, third Earl of Bute, familiar to history as Lord Bute and the first principal adviser to King George III, owed his brief importance almost certainly to the fact that he had been Groom of the Stole to George while he was still Prince of Wales. It was a literally necessary, though not what today might be considered very nice, appointment since the 'stole' in question was the King's close stool or commode, the cleaning of which and its 'maintenance' was, at some very remote date, the charge of the first lord of the King's bedchamber or Groom of the Stole. To this day the office survives, though fortunately for the office holder the function has long since ceased to be required. However, many of the officials who serve her Majesty today have almost equally quaint titles.

THE HOUSEHOLD TODAY

It is very much a hierarchy, at least in organization, though in style it is as democratic as can reasonably be expected in the precincts of a palace. There are three levels or grades, as they might be called in any other organization. The highest grade is that of the Members; this is followed by the Officials; below which come the Staff. Typical jobs are, for Members, Private Secretaries; for Officials, administrative and clerical appointments; and for Staff, domestic and other such employees. Among the longest-serving members of the Household are the senior Member, Lt-Col. Sir John Miller, the Crown Equerry, with the Queen for some 27 years; and the Queen's Dresser, Miss Margaret McDonald, known as Bobo and friend and adviser of Her Majesty for more than half a century.

There are three Great Officers of the household:

The Lord Steward, whose duties now are few and largely ceremonial. He supervises the lying in state of the previous monarch, attends the sovereign at state openings of Parliament and at the coronation. Technically he is the superior of the Master of the Queen's Household, who actually does the work. At state banquets the Lord Steward shares with the Lord Chamberlain the job of walking backwards in advance of the royal procession.

The Master of the Horse, who enjoys the privilege of riding immediately behind the sovereign on ceremonial occasions. Like the Lord Steward, he has larger titular authority than actual responsibility. In his case the work of running the stables and garages as head of the royal mews is done by the Crown Equerry.

The Lord Chamberlain, who is effective head of the Queen's Household, is in charge of all those numerous ceremonial duties no longer discharged by the Lord Steward. He has overall responsibility for royal garden parties, the maintenance and running of the Chapels Royal; state funerals; state visits by foreign heads of state and numerous other duties. Under him come such officials as the Master of the Queen's Music, the Marshal of the Diplomatic Corps and a range of other functionaries.

The day-to-day running of the household is in the charge of the

Master of the Household Since more than 600 meals are served in the Palace every day and there are some 80 functions held in Buckingham Palace alone each year, this is a post of considerable responsibility in terms of catering alone. Those functions of course include the Queen's official garden parties, each of

Right: Personal servants as well as business officers have always been an important part of the royal entourage. George III even had the court painter, Sir Godfrey Kneller, do this portrait of his Turkish servant and confidant Mehemet.

Below: Hafiz Abdul Karim, a favourite servant of Queen Victoria in her later years.

which can expect up to 8500 guests. To help in his work the Master has the Palace Steward; Page of the Chambers; Pages of the Presence; the Travelling Yeoman (who handles all the luggage arrangements when the Queen is on tour); the Yeomen of the Gold and Silver Pantries, of the Glass and China Pantry and of the Royal Cellar, whose titles are self-explanatory. Then there is the Flagman, who not only attends to the correct flying of the standard when the Queen is in residence and ensures that the right flags are available and flown when the Queen travels, but he is also in charge of security arrangements at the reception points of the post sent to the Palace.

The Queen rarely handles money and may never have signed a cheque in her life. Ladies in waiting generally attend to such matters, but the overall finances of the Royal Household are the responsibility of the

Keeper of the Privy Purse and Treasurer to the Queen Among his most important duties are the administration of the untaxed revenues from the Duchy of Lancaster, which includes properties not only in Lancashire and other northern counties but also the freehold of the site of the Savoy Hotel, centuries ago the site of the London palace of John of Gaunt, Duke of Lancaster.

PORTRAITS AND PORTRAITISTS

The venerable and patriotic Duke of Lancaster in Shakespeare's play on Gaunt's tragic nephew Richard II is hardly historical, great noblemen were interested in power. Like kings, they were also concerned about their public image.

Richard II (d. 1399), the first monarch whose physical likeness was captured by a court painter, began his reign as a brave boy confronting a rebellious peasantry at the Peasants' Revolt of 1381 and winning them over by his charm, courage and open-handedness, but ended his days deposed and murdered and a reputed tyrant. The court art promotes the image of a saint-like autocrat, rooted in the traditions of his people and devoted to justice. The Tudor court portraits of Henry VIII depict a man larger than life, and of almost monstrous vigour. Increasing in bulk almost before our eyes he seems to burst through the paint, a man of wild power and imperious will who would have his way whatever the cost. With this king one doubts whether the 'official line' could have been anything other than the truth.

After the death of his daughter Elizabeth, the official image changed once again. From the dazzling presence of the superhuman Gloriana we move to the ascetic, refined and saint-like but still superhuman qualities of Charles I. The cavalier saint of the pictures concealed the petulant autocrat of the council chamber. Weak

Above: King Richard II whose forced abdication was a thinly veiled deposition, sat for the first surviving life-like portrait of any medieval English king.

Left: King Charles I and Queen Henrietta Maria with two of their children, painted by Sir Anthony van Dyck, a master of the official portrait as well as a great artist. Notice, on the table, the old St Edward's Crown, sold during the Commonwealth period of the 1650s as an antiquated symbol of the overweening power of kings.

Above: Queen Victoria and Prince Albert and the Royal Family at the official opening of The Great Exhibition of industry and the arts in 1851. Inspired and promoted by Prince Albert, the Exhibition, in its magnificent prefabricated 'Crystal Palace' of glass and cast iron, was a monument not only to Britain's then industrial might but to the capacity for hard work of the Prince.

Left: The Royal Family at Sandringham in the summer of 1969. As the time approached for the investiture of Prince Charles as Prince of Wales in July of that year, the Palace released a series of pictures depicting the 'informal Prince'. Here

willed, Charles sacrificed his ministers to a Parliament he could only try to outwit and not until he came to die was he able to comport himself with the dignity and authority he supposed natural to a king. But Charles at least had an idea of monarchy. The restoration of the monarchy under his son Charles II brought in a kingship devoted, it seemed, solely to self-indulgence, curbed only by the ultimate priority, survival. The sensual images of the King and his courtiers convey the message effortlessly. With the Hanoverians royal portraiture became more formal, less lively and therefore less interesting, though the coronation portrait of George III presents us with a King conscious of the dignity of his office and determined to uphold it to the best of his ability. The flamboyant stylishness of his son, as portrayed by Sir Thomas Lawrence, remained the flattering official image of the reign, even though George actually looked more like the bloated glutton depicted by Rowlandson and his fellow cartoonists. William IV, a king who had no time for image making in any shape or form, is portrayed as real man, not over good looking nor especially intelligent but at least honest, 'a rare quality in kings', as a contemporary remarked.

With Victoria we come to the most familiar royal image in history, second only to the present Queen. Almost from the outset of her reign, thanks perhaps to the influence of her admired husband Albert, the Queen had herself portrayed as the ideal mother of the ideal bourgeois family. Even in later years as Queen-Empress, her artists seem to portray her as a kind of crowned grandmother. In fact she was a woman of immense influence. Was it the prevailing style of 'Victorian' painting or the preference of the sitter which

was more important in determining her appearance?

But if Victoria had little interest in elegance, her successors had. A dramatic society portrait of Queen Mary makes the point, and her granddaughter, the present Queen, followed the childhood fashions of her day.

From her first portrait as a little girl in a Kate Greenaway dress in 1933 up to February 1989, Her Majesty the Queen had been the subject of no fewer than 99 official portraits. Long before the 'making of the President' for President Richard Nixon's campaign, monarchs and popes had been engaging the services of professional image makers, known in those days as artists or portrait painters! A glance at some of the official portraits of Queen Elizabeth I will also indicate that these artists were working to a very explicit brief, no doubt supplied by the Queen herself or her advisers. The image is one of grandeur and power and a semi-mystical aura, physically expressed by 'haloes' of lace ruff and collars and clouds of jewels and precious stones, to imbue the monarchy with brilliancy and respect. Her successor, King James VI and I, and his son elaborated in writing and speeches the theory known as the 'Divine Right of Kings', but the cult of 'Gloriana' heavily promoted in the later decades of Elizabeth's reign, aimed to buttress and embellish the physical reality of an ageing and failing woman with the idea and presentation of a superhuman presence. The Second Elizabeth is perceived as a caring and duty-conscious woman, genuinely concerned with the well-being of all her subjects, throughout her Commonwealth of Nations and working, so far as lies within her powers as a modern constitutional monarch, to promote their interests. Above all, the Royal Family is presented as the model of family life.

we see the five-year-old Prince Edward and his father Prince Philip examining a magazine, Prince Andrew, immaculately groomed despite the bow and arrow and the Queen and Princess Anne in the background. Prince Charles himself appears to be planning his evening's TV viewing from the *Radio Times*.

Right: Today royalty cultivates a democratic image and photographers play a major role in promoting it. Here, the Queen is seen riding London's Tube at the opening of the new Victoria Line in March 1969.

A GALLERY OF ROYAL PORTRAITS

Above: King Charles II, after a painting by the English miniaturist Samuel Cooper.

Right: George III in his coronation robes and wearing the Order of the Garter. A potent image of the glory of monarchical authority painted (1760s) at a time when that authority was being continually challenged and overtaken by Parliament. By George's court painter, Allan Ramsay.

Left: George IV when Prince of Wales, the image of himself he loved to foster long after grotesque overweight made it an absurdity.

Below left: William IV. Typically of this bluff monarch with his hatred of flummery, the dress Garter Star, though worn as a proper reminder of his rank, is half obscured by the lapel of his every-day suit coat. Had William's reign been longer than it was (1830–37), today's British monarchy might have been nearer in style to the democratic Scandinavian families. As it was, that reign was a decisive period in the development of today's constitutional monarchy.

Below: A fine example of the society portrait. Queen Mary, wife of King George V painted in the 1910s—a time when the leadership of privileged high society was considered, at least by some, an important part of the aspect of the work of monarchy.

THE PRIVATE SECRETARY

The most important department in the Royal House-hold, the Private Secretary's Office, has been headed since April 1986 by the Australian Sir William Heseltine. Beginning his career at the Palace in the 1960s, he has worked in various capacities, including the Press Office. His numerous duties require him to accompany the Queen on her overseas tours; to super-vise the Queen's Archives held in the Round Tower at Windsor; to take final responsibility for the Queen's Flight, the assignment of aircraft and so forth, and for the Press Office. He is also in regular contact with the secretary to the Cabinet and it is through him that the Commonwealth prime ministers communicate with the sovereign. The staff of the Office comprises the Assistant Private Secretary, Deputy Private Secretary, Assistant Deputy Keeper of the Queen's Archives (the Queen's Librarian).

It has been said that the Queen's Private Secretary is one of the most influential people in the country. It was always so. The 'chancellor' of England's early medieval kings got his name from the fact that he had his work table behind a special screen or chancel (the Latin *cancellarium* means 'screen') in the great hall or possibly marquee in which the king's business was being carried on. A private office, even a private room, was undreamed of in the public and itinerant royal lifestyle. Court business was conducted amongst a crowd of petitioners, men at arms, officials, huntsmen, sheriffs' officers or any others who had business at court. The king himself might well be waiting impatiently for the day's hunting or be elsewhere altogether. In these conditions the man at the screen, responsible for the royal writs and charters, was the man to impress if one wanted one's business to reach the royal ear.

In the 12th century when Thomas à Becket was appointed chancellor by King Henry II, he was the most powerful of the King's servants and the chancery or royal secretariat would soon become a separate depart-ment of state. With the passage of time, royal govern-ment became increasingly departmentalized, though royal servants with the closest access to the king and regular contact with royal business naturally remained highly influential.

No doubt because they realized this, 18th-century politicians refused to recognize any king's secretary as the proper channel for official business. They feared such an official would cut them off from access to the monarch. In the early 1800s, however, George III's encroaching blindness obliged his ministers to deal through his secre-tary to a certain extent. With William IV, at the time of the constitutional crisis that led to the great Reform Bill of 1832, the King's private secretary, Sir Herbert Taylor, was accepted as intermediary by Lord Grey.

But the post had no recognized constitutional stand-ing and when the young Victoria came to the throne in 1837 she dispensed even with a personal secretary, rely-ing for advice on Baron Stockmar, the agent of her uncle King Leopold of the Belgians, and on Lord Mel-bourne, her prime minister. Within a year or so of their marriage, her beloved and admired husband Prince Albert had displaced all other advisers. At first she not only refused to allow him to see state papers, but even declined to discuss affairs of state. She was jealous of her own importance as Queen, no doubt, but she loved 'delightful and familiar' chat and dreaded clouding the idyll of her marriage with 'formal and stiff discussion upon political matters'.

And there was one more reason, as Albert came to realize. She did not really understand a lot of the com-plicated government business and rather than reveal her shortcomings would claim constitutional propriety or turn to small talk. Once she overcame all these inhi-bitions she came to rely on the Prince almost without question. Aided by his own private secretary, General Charles Grey, and with the increasingly enthusiastic participation of Victoria, he built up the Palace as an adjunct to government and effectively established the job description of private secretary to the sovereign. Hostility from the politicians changed to respect and gratitude at the way he kept the impetuous, somewhat limited but often stubborn intelligence of his spouse within the bounds of constitutional propriety and even sometimes saved her ministers from their own mis-takes. His rewording of Britain's provocative dispatch to the US Government over the Trent Affair in December 1861 very likely averted war. Late hours working on it, when he was already desperately ill with typhoid, hastened his death.

By this time, it has been said, Albert was king in all but name. In Victoria's opinion he had raised the monarchy 'to the *highest* pinnacle of *respect* and rendered it popular *beyond* what it *ever* was in this country'. Her retreat from the world, following his death, threatened to nullify his achievement. Yet she did continue to rely on the services of General Grey and with the appointment in 1870 of Sir Henry Ponsonby marked the beginning of the post of Private Secretary as an officially recognized part of government as such.

Sir Henry continued, as far as could be, the traditions of the Private Secretary's brief as anticipated by Prince Albert, combining absolute loyalty to the Queen and equally firm loyalty to the constitution, with tact. He did not even pass on to Archibald Philip Primrose, Earl of Rosebery, prime minister from 1894, the Queen's view that he was 'almost communistic'. Ponsonby had his own equally trenchant views, distrust of Disraeli being one of them, but suppressed these rather than invite open disagreement with the Queen. Lord Salisbury, who for a time combined the position of prime minister with that of foreign minister, classed the Queen as 'a third department of state, more exhausting than either of the other two'.

In 1895, Ponsonby suffered a severe stroke, being succeeded by Sir Arthur Bigge. The son of a Northumberland clergyman, he went into the army, and while still a young officer had to make a brief formal report to the Queen. She was so impressed that she appointed him a Groom-in-Waiting, later promoting him Assistant Secretary. He retained his post until Victoria's death when he was succeeded by Lord Knollys, who as Private Secretary to the Prince of Wales was retained when his master became King as Edward VII. Bigge joined the household of the Duke of York and remained as one of his two secretaries—Knollys being the other one—when he came to the throne as George

V in 1910. On the retirement of Knollys in 1913 Bigge, now ennobled as Lord Stamfordham, remained sole secretary until he in turn retired in 1931. It had been a distinguished career during which he had served three monarchs—according to George V, Stamfordham taught him how to be a king. His successor, Sir Clive Wigram, was a businesslike aide but in the crisis that led to the formation of the National Government, it seems King George acted on his own initiative after consulting Ramsay MacDonald, the prime minister, and the other political leaders.

The next Private Secretary, Sir Alexander Hardinge (later Baron Hardinge of Penshurst), had the unenviable job of go-between for his royal master Edward VIII and Prime Minister Baldwin. He it was who had to advise Edward that persisting in his desire to marry Mrs Simpson would provoke a cabinet crisis—partisans of the King would accuse Hardinge of jumping to Prime Minister Baldwin's tune, others no doubt marvelled that the King needed an adviser to tell him anything so obvious. Sir Alexander loyally remained at his post during the opening years of the new reign. He was succeeded by Sir Alan Lascelles, who in May 1944 faced the novel dilemma of how to deal with a 20th-century monarch wishing to lead his troops into battle. Or at least, the next best thing, for George VI was determined to accompany the D-Day landings on the Normandy coast if, as he was proposing to do, Winston Churchill did. In the event a truce was declared and neither king nor PM made the warlike gesture, no doubt to the great relief of everybody else concerned.

Under the regime of Sir Michael (later Lord) Adeane, the staff of the Private Secretary's Office comprised two assistant private secretaries, a press secretary and assistant, a chief clerk, a secretary to the Private Secretary and eight clerks. His successors were Sir Martin (now Lord Charteris) and Sir Philip Moore.

Left: Queen Elizabeth II seen at her desk during the filming in 1969 of the television documentary of the Royal Family.

Right: As head of state, it is one of the Queen's more important functions to receive visiting heads of state, to maintain good relations with allies and Britain's image in the world. Much behind-the-scenes work by the household staff goes into such meetings. When President Reagan visited Windsor Castle, the Queen's staff received phone calls complaining that the heads of state were not wearing hard hats!

THE QUEEN ABROAD

Left: At Benares during her tour of India in 1961, the Queen rode one of the state elephants of the maharaja of Benares.

Right: The Queen and Prince Philip on their state visit to Portugal.

Far right: The Queen attends a gala performance of Verdi's opera *Falstaff* at La Scala, Milan, during her state visit to Italy in 1961.

Right: The Queen and Prince Philip received by King Juan Carlos and Queen Sophia of Spain and their family, on their state visit of 1988.

Below left: The Queen seen with Mother Teresa.

Below centre: The Queen conferring a knighthood during her visit to New Zealand when she held a Commonwealth Investiture.

Below right: In audience with Pope John XXIII in 1961.

151

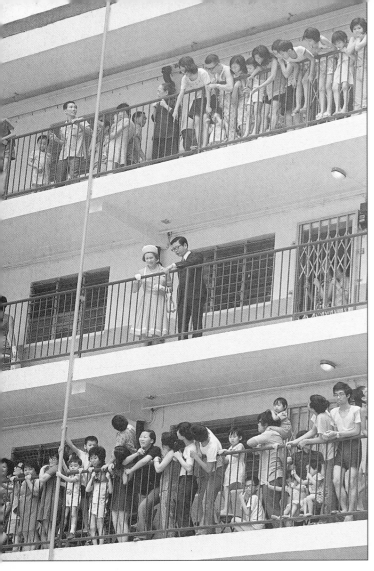

FOREIGN TOURS

Far left: The Queen during an official visit to Hong Kong, 1975.

Left: The Queen on her tour of the Gulf States, 1979.

Right: A famous picture of the young Duke of Windsor when on tour of Canada as Prince of Wales in 1919. It portrays him in the full regalia as 'Chief Morning Star', the title bestowed on him by the Storey Creek people of Alberta.

Left: The Queen talking to children during the tour she and the Duke of Edinburgh made of Australia in 1988.

Below left: On the Great Wall of China, 1986.

Below centre: The Queen and her Commonwealth Prime Ministers at the 1985 Commonwealth Conference in the Bahamas.

Below right: The Queen loves children and is popular with them wherever she goes, as here on one of her many Canadian tours.

YOUNG ROYALS OUT AND ABOUT

The continuing success of the Royal Family depends to a large extent on the younger members. Their public image is often one of glamour and sometimes controversial but all are willing patrons of numerous organizations, charities and institutions. These pages highlight the sort of public event and charitable work which is promoted by such patronage.

Left: Admired world wide for her work as President of Save the Children Fund, Princess Anne undertakes numerous overseas visits. Here she is seen with a group of children and workers in Somalia.

Right: The Princess of Wales leaving the Palace of the Sultan of Oman, during her 1986 visit to the Gulf State. Prince Charles can be seen in the background.

Right: Viscount Linley and his sister, Lady Sarah Armstrong Jones, Princess Margaret's children, on their visit to China's Forbidden City 1987.

Far right: The Duchess of York attends a charity auction at Sothebys, London, in aid of the Hospice movement, September 1987.

MODERN ROYALTY IN WARTIME

In both World Wars, Britain's royals played a vital role in raising morale.

Left: Edward, Prince of Wales (left), later King as Edward VIII, with his father King George V inspecting a gas bomb behind the lines in northern France during World War I. The Prince was bitterly frustrated by official insistence that as heir to the throne he should stay well clear of danger. 'What does it matter if I die?' he once remarked, 'I have four brothers'. As it was he had to content himself with privately-organized sorties behind the lines, inspecting positions and reporting on requirements, often much nearer the fighting than was officially approved. Senior officers were impressed by his thoroughness and close observation.

Above: King George VI and Queen Elizabeth touring London's docklands after a German bombing raid during World War II, April 1941. When a lone German bomber deposited a stick of bombs on Buckingham Palace, Queen Elizabeth felt she could 'look the East Enders in the face'.

Left: During World War II, the traditional royal Christmas broadcast, begun by his father King George V, was one of the important rallying gestures available to King George VI in maintaining British morale.

Right: The two Princesses in a wartime broadcast to the children of England. Elizabeth delivered the broadcast, Margaret signed off with a 'Goodnight children'.

THIS SPORTING LIFE

Today's royal family continues the traditional royal association with the horse but with an added, international dimension. Most years the Queen in her private capacity visits the great US stud farms in Kentucky or travels to Normandy. On official visits too, as on her visit to Jordan when she was guest of Princess Alia at the royal stud, she may take the time to widen her phenomenal expertise as horsewoman.

For more than 20 years the Duke of Edinburgh was president of the International Equestrian Federation, being succeeded in 1987 by the Princess Royal. But the Princess, as president of the British Olympic Association and a member of the International Olympic Committee, illustrates the breadth of the family's sporting interests.

Left: The Queen with Prince and Princess Michael of Kent at the 1988 Derby.

Bottom left: The Princess Royal, Chancellor of London University, at a boat-naming ceremony in the University's boathouse 1987.

Below: Persimmon wins the 1896 Derby for Edward VII, Prince of Wales.

Traditionally, the pastimes of royalty have been hunting and racing (both have extended treatment later in this chapter). But the modern royals enjoy the full range of sporting activities—always, of course, under the best available coaching. When young, Prince Charles and Princess Anne both took lessons in skating on Richmond ice rink and their coach was Betty Callaway, who was to bring Torvill and Dean to stardom. Queen Victoria's Prince Albert cut a dashing figure on the ice, according to contemporary prints, but his descendants have preferred the excitement of skiing—unknown as a sport in his day.

The Duke of Kent, with the Scots Greys in Germany, captained their team in the British Army of the Rhine skiing championships while the Duchess of Kent, herself very proficient on the slopes, has given her name to a cup competed for at St Moritz. Prince Michael of Kent is another devotee of winter sports, bobsleighing with an army team and for Britain in the 1960s, while the Duke of Gloucester has a penchant for adventure on the slopes to match that of his cousin Prince Charles. In fact, skiing most fully reveals the Prince of Wales's need for challenge and danger. Since 1978, he has made an annual visit to Klosters in the Swiss Alps and the annual photo call with the royals became something of a tradition. Then, in January 1988, tragedy struck. Skiing off piste, the royal party was caught in an avalanche. Major Hugh Lindsay, the Prince's Equerry, was killed; Prince Charles barely escaped with his life and his friend Patty Palmer Thomkinson was badly hurt. In January 1989 the Duke and Duchess of York returned to Klosters to a chorus of press comment and in March Prince Charles also returned to his favourite resort in the mountains.

Left: Her Majesty Queen Elizabeth the Queen Mother, on tour in New Zealand in 1966, spent almost every free moment fishing. Here she is seen on the Waikato River, near Wairakei, where she had hooked a fine two-pound rainbow trout. Her Majesty first explored the fine trout fishing in New Zealand some 40 years earlier when on tour with her husband the then Duke of York (later King as George VI).

Right: King George VI when Duke of York in play in the men's doubles at Wimbledon, 1926. He and his partner Commander Greig, although winners in the RAF championships, were knocked out in the first round by two Wimbledon veterans in their late fifties.

Far right: The 16th-century 'real' tennis court at Scotland's royal Falkland Palace.

TENNIS

Ball games have never characteristically been royal pursuits, although the Duke of Edinburgh enjoys a decent game of cricket. Captain of his school's First XI, he had a useful offspin and was a hard-hitting batsman. For years his team played the Duke of Norfolk's XI at Arundel to raise funds for the National Playing Fields Association while the Duke was President of MCC in 1949–50 and 1974–5. Various members of the family have also played golf—a favourite with Edward VIII—for relaxation. Fittingly, among the earliest known performers on the links were the Scottish royals, among them Mary Queen of Scots. However, royal participation has been prominent in tennis. In 1926, Prince Albert, Duke of York (King as George VI), partnered by Wing Commander Louis Greig, played in the men's

doubles at Wimbledon. The two men had won an RAF championship in the 1920s, but even then Wimbledon was too high standard for all but the most dedicated players and the Duke and his partner were knocked out in the first round. Today, Prince Edward has brought royalty once more into the world of tennis, but the 'real' rather than the lawn variety.

Real tennis (the name derives from the medieval French word for 'royal') originated in France, probably in the 14th century. The great English devotee was Henry VIII who, as a young man, delighted spectators with his athleticism, 'his fair skin glowing through a shirt of the finest texture'. He had courts at his palaces of Richmond and Greenwich, and built facilities at St James's, Westminster and Whitehall Palaces and at Hampton Court Palace. His on-court gear was positively fetching, the shirt of long lawn sleeves and embroidered at collar and wrists with blue silk. But he was also a competent player. In those days the game involved heavy betting and Henry took his servant marker with him wherever he went.

Although no tennis player himself, James I 'commended bodily exercise and games' and ordered repairs to the 'great tennis court in the brake at Whitehall'. He also had a small building added to the facilities there for the Prince of Wales 'to make himself ready for to play tennis there'. The Prince, James's first son Henry, died in his teens, some thought as a result of his unwise devotion to the game. In November 1612, it is recorded, 'the Prince played at a great match of tennis clad only in his shirt, despite the cold weather, and on going to bed complained of lassitude and a headache'. He died, apparently of a chill, some days later. Henry's brother Charles I was an ardent player while his son Charles II made major improvements to the court at Hampton Court where Prince Edward still plays.

YACHTING

The sea has always provided a characteristic profession for the sons of the English royal family, since the days of Prince William (later to be king as William IV) in the late 18th century. In our own generation both Prince Charles, as commander in the minesweeper *Brondesbury*, and Prince Andrew, as a full-time officer RN, have done their turn. Yet it seems that only Prince Philip, another professional sailor, has taken up boating as a hobby. Catching the sea fever while a boy at Gordonstoun, he was finally hooked, sailing the little Dragon Class *Bluebottle* presented to himself and his wife as a wedding present by the Island Sailing Club of Cowes. Since those fairly distant days, the Duke has sailed many boats, introducing the younger members of the family to the delights of sail. Prince Charles and Princess Anne both crewed on *Bloodhound*, a 63-foot (19 m) yawl dating from the 1930s and sold by Prince Philip in 1969. Possibly more exciting was the Flying Fifteen class *Cowslip* which Philip used to race with the renowned yachtsman Uffa Fox. Thanks to his enthusiasm, the present Royal Family continues a sporting tradition at sea which has deep roots.

The association with Cowes has been traced back to the time of Elizabeth I, who had a pleasure boat, the *Rat*, built at the mouth of the Medina River at the village of Shamford, later renamed Cowes. Early in the next century, Phineas Pett, mastershipwright and commissioner of the navy, built a pleasure boat for Henry, Prince of Wales. The distinction between pleasure boat and official royal yacht was not always clearly marked. Both Charles I's *Sovereign of the Seas* and the *Charles*, built for his son after the Restoration, were as much sporting as official vessels. It seems also that the very word 'yacht'—from the Dutch *jachtschip*, a pursuit vessel—came into the language with Charles II. But it is certain that such a vessel brought him back from Breda to Dover while the *Mary*, presented to him by the burgomaster of Amsterdam, was the first of many pleasure boats in which he and his brother James loved to race.

In fact, the King commissioned a copy of that boat for James called the *Anne*, no doubt after his love for Anne Hyde, and a second boat for himself called the *Catherine*, no doubt for his own wife Catherine of

Braganza. To commemorate the marriage of James II's daughter Mary to William of Orange (later joint monarchs as William and Mary) the Dutch built a yacht called the *Mary* in 1677. This boat seems to have served as the official royal yacht up to the reign of George I in the 1710s. The Hanoverians replaced her with the royal yacht *Caroline*. Later, King George III's brother Henry, Duke of Cumberland sponsored the first organized yacht race. Then, in 1815, a group of gentlemen formed themselves into the Yacht Club, meeting regularly in the thatched tavern at St James's. The Prince Regent was elected member of the club which became the Royal Yacht Club; in 1833 it was renamed the Royal Yacht Squadron. Prince Albert duly became its patron, Queen Victoria already being patroness of the Royal Thames Yacht Club. In 1865, Edward [VII] on becoming patron, bought his first yacht, the 37-ton cutter *Dagmar*. She was succeeded by two steam yachts, the *Princess* and *Zenobia*, all used simply for cruising. He began serious racing in 1876 with the schooner *Hildegarde*, winning the Queen's Cup at Cowes. In 1892, he commissioned the first *Britannia*, launched in 1892, a luxury racing yacht so well found that when sailing the French riviera Edward stayed aboard in pref-

erence to using the hotels ashore. When the German Emperor's team at Cowes won most of the trophies, Edward lost interest in yachting for a time but *Britannia* had won 33 prize flags out of 43 starts before he sold her (later bought back). It was Edward's son George V who was the Royal Family's true yachtsman. He refitted *Britannia* after the war so that she could win handicap races. She was soon outclassed by massive new boats of the 1920s and 1930s. But *Britannia* remained the King's first and only love of the sea. During his Silver Jubilee year he reviewed the fleet in the Solent from her decks and in the same year he declined the offer of a new racing yacht from the yachtsmen of England. 'As long as I live I will never own any yacht other than *Britannia*.' One July night in 1936, some months after the King's death, pursuant to George V's instructions, *Britannia* was towed out into the Channel at midnight, a garland of wild flowers round her stem head, and scuttled.

Left: King George V at the helm of his beloved yacht *Britannia*.

Below: The Duke of Edinburgh, Cowes, 1987.

THE ROYALS AND THE WORLD OF THE HORSE

THE QUEEN

Though she hunted regularly as a young woman, the Queen's passion is for horses and racing. She once said: 'If it were not for my Archbishop at Canterbury, I should be off to Longchamps [the Paris racecourse] every Sunday.' Expert in all the details of breeding and the race game, as well as an outstanding horsewoman, she is respected throughout the international horse world.

Her first winner, in 1949, was Astrakhan, given her by the Aga Khan. Three years later her father died and the Queen inherited the studs at Sandringham and Hampton Court (with nearly 20 brood mares) and nine horses in training at Newmarket. Her first success as an owner was thanks to a horse called Aureole which, in 1954, won £40 000 in stake money and was an outstanding success at stud. Her first classic was in 1957, when Lester Piggott won the Oaks on Carozza. That year she had also 20 other home-bred winners—among them Almeira and Mulberry Harbour (voted respectively first and third fillies of the year). In 1958 came her first home-bred classic winner, with Pall Mall in the Two Thousand Guineas.

The victory of her filly Highclere, ridden by Joe Mercer in the 1974 One Thousand Guineas, marked the beginning of a marvellous season during which Her Majesty's horses won prize money totalling £140 000 in 11 races, making her one of the leading owners of the

Horses are very much a part of the public and private life of Queen Elizabeth II.
Above: She is seen at the 1974 Royal Windsor Horse Show.
Left: The Queen inspects horses at the private stables of an American owner, Kentucky.

year. Her Silver Jubilee year (1977) ended with the Queen at the top of the English winning breeders' list, having opened with Dunfermline ridden by Willie Carson wining the Oaks as a prelude to the official national celebrations (he followed this by taking the St Leger from Lester Piggot on Alleged)—another great season.

THE QUEEN MOTHER

By the end of the 1987–8 season, the Queen Mother had been an owner 35 years and won some 400 races. Thanks to her interest in steeplechasing, both the quality and standing of the sport with the public had grown. When she celebrated her first 25 years in racing in 1974, the Clarence House ball for her racing staff—from racing manager to stable lads—had long been a regular fixture in her calendar but that year the Jockey Club hosted a dinner at the Savoy in her honour.

The famous royal racing double act of the two Elizabeths began in July 1949 with their joint ownership of an Irish horse called Monaveen which she owned with her daughter, the then Princess Elizabeth. The most famous event to date in the Queen Mother's career as an owner—and one of the most famous events in the history of racing—was the 'belly flop' collapse of her horse Devon Loch in the 1956 Grand National when it was leading the field a clear winner with only 30 yd (27 m) to go. Dick Francis the jockey launched a distinguished writing career with a mystery-thriller *Dead Cert* which offered an ingenious explanation of just such a dramatic reversal of fortune and in several subsequent novels depicted heroes with crippling handicaps, whether literal or metaphorical.

THE PRINCE OF WALES

Prince Charles's first venture 'over the sticks' was under the tuition of his sister at Gatcombe Park, his first ride to hounds with the Beaufort. He hunted subsequently with many packs all over the country on a variety of mounts, greatly to the advantage of his riding, as he admitted. He wears the old Windsor uniform designed by George III in the field. His debut as a steeplechase jockey was at Sandown in 1980 after such training as his crammed business schedule would permit and wasting down to the weight—all, unfortunately, to no avail. The following year he had a headline-grabbing fall in the Grand Military Cup on the same course. Like his great-uncle, the Duke of Windsor, Charles showed courage, but he found himself the butt of ribald comment in the press and, at the same time, sermons on the dangers of racing; four days later, he was 'on the floor' once more, this time at the Cheltenham National Hunt Festival. His brief career as jockey had not much longer to run; it remained his modest ambition to win a race.

Meanwhile he accepted the offer to become patron of the Amateur Jockeys Association. In eventing he prefers the less formal team cross-country event and has given two of his titles to the renamed Earl of Chester's Chasers and the Duke of Cornwall's Chasers.

Encouraged by his father as a polo player, he made his debut in 1964 and captained his first side while at school at Geelong, Victoria, New South Wales, where his ponies were supplied by a local pony club, during the summer of 1966. In 1967, in a team captained by his father, he played for Windsor Great Park to beat the team captained by Major Ronald Ferguson. Charles gained his Half Blue playing for Cambridge and captained the highly successful Royal Navy team. By this time Major Ferguson was effectively the Prince's polo manager; in 1980 his handicap was raised to four and in 1981 he played for the winning England team against Spain (scoring one of the goals, although playing in defence) in a match three days before his wedding. The following year he captained England II against USA. He has said of polo: 'I love the game. I love the ponies . . . It's the one team game I can play.' He has also said of the game: '. . . sometimes I feel sheer terror', but Charles's emotional need for danger is an unexpected trait of his complex character.

THE PRINCESS ROYAL

Although she has occasionally hunted with the Beaufort from Gatcombe Park, Princess Anne is better known as a horsewoman on the eventing course. On 23 April 1985 she made her debut in the racing saddle over Epsom's Derby course, to raise funds for Riding for the Disabled of which she had been President since 1970. She rode her first winner in spring 1986 at Redcar in Cleveland, offering to continue to have a go 'so long as owners are prepared to allow idiots like me to ride'. But three-day eventing had long been her real passion, and her first great partnership was with Doublet (bred in the royal stable) at Badminton in 1971.

Leaving school, she was encouraged by Sir John Miller the crown equerry in her riding career. She had advantages—excellent hands and balance—but above all the Princess is courageous. In 1969 she won the Windsor Horse Trials on Royal Ocean, closely followed by a young cavalry officer called Mark Phillips. She went on to win the European three-day event championship at the Burghley Horse Trials, being presented with the cup by the Queen and winning popular acclaim as BBC Sports Personality of the Year and Sportswoman of the Year. Two years later, she represented Great Britain in the European championship at Kiev, where, unfortunately, she had a severe fall. To her considerable pride, the Princess has represented Britain at Olympic level.

Top, left to right: Queen Victoria and Prime Minister, Lord Melbourne, arrive at Windsor, 1839.
The Duchess of York wins her pilot's licence, 1987.
Princess Anne and family in the French Alps, 1986.

Below, left to right: Billiards table at Osborne, designed by Prince Albert.
Princess Anne rides for a charity Funday Sunday, 1987.
Prince Charles on the polo field and (right) Prince Edward playing rugby at Cambridge.

THE JOYS OF THE CHASE

For centuries hunting, whether with hawk or hound, was *the* royal pastime. That hard-working and thoughtful ruler King Alfred the Great had his sons trained in the 'arts' of riding and hunting from childhood and St Edward the Confessor was also an addict of the chase.

The Norman Conquest meant the introduction of the French hunting code. It also meant the introduction of a bloodthirsty legal code, designed to protect the animals and thus the royal sport against poaching. William the Conqueror was said 'to love the tall deer as if he were their father'. Henry II (1154–89) extended the area of forest and established the Royal Buckhounds, not finally disbanded until the early 1800s. Henry ruled England from the saddle; if he was not riding to hounds he was riding to do justice or put down rebellion in some part of his vast domains or another. His son Richard I spent most of his time abroad whether on Crusade or campaigning against the French king. Like his father, he was a passionate huntsman and once, it is said, hunted a stag more than a hundred miles, from Sherwood in Nottinghamshire to Barnsdale in Yorkshire. John took hunting and even quarry animals to France to ensure good sport when going on campaign in 1204—he lost Normandy the same year. Edward III was accompanied by 300 couple of hounds and a hundred hunting falcons on his rather more successful Crécy campaign of 1346.

Henry VIII, considered a first-rate horseman, had horses staged across the country he intended to hunt and regularly tired eight or nine mounts in a day. He was equally addicted to falconry or 'birding'. Henry established the 'Privy' or 'Household Pack' and enclosed large tracts plundered from the Church at the dissolution of the monasteries in and about London to give him new hunting nearer home. This provided the basis for the modern Royal Parks of London, for example Hyde Park and St James's Park.

Neither Henry's son, Edward VI, nor his eldest daughter, Queen Mary, were devotees—the great Elizabeth I was an addict. She both rode to hounds and shot in the *battue*, which her father had taken to when his obesity made riding impossible—a form of hunting long known to the Persian and Mogul rulers of India, organized in large enclosed parks. Dogs and huntsmen-beaters drove the game down wide fenced rides, past specially designed pavilions where the huntsman or woman stood, armed with a crossbow. Elizabeth was reckoned a crack shot. She equally relished a day in the saddle and was still riding to hounds in her mid-sixties.

When he rode south to take the throne as her successor, James VI of Scotland came with a cavalcade of horsemen and, it is said, hunted all the way. James despised the *battue* and also the continental vogue for guns. He spent months at a time at his hunting box at Newmarket, preferring fox to stag hunting because it was faster. His son, Charles I, built up a stable of 20 fine thoroughbred hunters. With the ending of the monarchy in 1649, the harsh laws of the forest were abated and men hunted freely. On his restoration in 1660, Charles II imposed a five-year ban while the game was restocked, though his real passion was racing. His brother, James [II], Duke of York, loved the chase, once making a run of 75 miles (120 km). His daughter, Anne, verged on the obsessive. She kennelled the royal buck hounds near her racecourse at Ascot and when the gout and obesity made it impossible for her any longer to follow them on horseback, she commissioned a special two-wheeled chariot, its wheels of such a diameter that the carriage would ride clear of full-grown corn and she had wide rides cut through Windsor forest and bogs drained. She would drive furiously for vast distances, her ladies following on horseback.

George I hated hunting English-style, much preferring the gun. George II extended the duties of the master of the Royal Buck Hounds to feeding the King's turkeys at Bushy Park and his tiger in the menagerie in Hyde Park. But with George III, who prided himself as a true English gentleman, the gun was banished and the master of the hounds put to his proper work. The King designed a special dress for his favourite sport, the 'old Windsor' (worn by Prince Charles) of a dark blue coat with scarlet collar and cuffs with royal livery buttons. By contrast to his ancestor, James I, he preferred stag to fox hunting as the chase lasted longer. As the King's health went into decline, the Royal Buck Hounds, without exercise, followed suit and were sold by his successor, George IV (though he did re-establish them later at Ascot). Prince Albert often hunted stag with the royal pack in Windsor Great Park or hare with his own pack of harriers on the Isle of Wight and at Balmoral.

Edward VII was a mediocre horseman. Though he hunted frequently enough to satisfy social conventions, shooting was his passion, especially vast *battues* at Sandringham. His son, George V, rode much better but rarely appeared in the field. During his university days at Oxford, Edward [VIII] followed the drag hounds and hunted with the university beagles. His horsemanship was notoriously poor, his falls being a constant theme of delighted comment in the American press. His young brother, the Duke of York and future George VI, was a much more proficient horseman and loved hunting. When, in the depression years of the 1930s, the Royal Family decided to make economies as a gesture of solidarity with the sufferings of their poorer subjects, 'Bertie' gave up hunting and sold his horses; 'the parting with them will be terrible', he wrote.

RACING WITH THE ROYALS AT ASCOT

It was George IV who instituted the carriage drive on the course, one of the best-loved institutions of Britain's racing year. The Queen has a house party at Windsor, with up to 30 relatives and guests, during the meeting. Lunch tends to be early to allow time for the racing. The party is driven by car to Duke's Lane where they change into the familiar Ascot landaus drawn by Windsor greys. The Queen and Prince Philip are accompanied by the Master of the Horse in the first carriage. Her Majesty Queen Elizabeth the Queen Mother, Princess Margaret, the Prince of Wales and the Princess Royal generally share the remaining landaus with guests. The owner of the winning horse of the day's major event may find him or herself invited for afternoon tea in the royal box. The day for the house party ends with dinner in the state dining room, followed by a film show in the throne room or a dance in the crimson drawing room.

FOUR CENTURIES OF ROYAL RACING

Horse racing in England has been associated with royalty at least since the time of Henry VIII, who imported bloodstock from Italy, Spain, Flanders, Turkey and Scotland and Ireland. Newmarket, home of British racing, began life as a royal hunting box established by James I, who discovered excellent game in the area. But James was also a devotee of the racecourse and addicted to gambling although, like others, he found that 'with the riding of running horses there was much cheating in that kind'. He contributed to the improvement of British bloodstock with the importation of mares and stallions from Italy; but the Markham Arabian (1616) failed to establish a breeding line.

The history of the royal stud really begins fittingly, one might say, with Charles II. He acquired a number of Arab mares and encouraged the importation of stallions, among them the Byerly Turk. It was Charles of course who transformed Newmarket into a racing centre with the Newmarket Town Plate complete with its own rule book—whenever there, he loved to watch the training gallops, often from the saddle of his hack Old Rowley. He revelled in the talk of professional jockeys and trainers, and himself raced with reasonable success.

Less colourful, but equally important in the history of English racing, William III continued royal interest in bloodstock, being associated with the import of the Darley Arabian, and the racecourse at Hampton Court. His trainer, William Tregonwell 'Governor' Frampton, managed the royal racing stable at Newmarket and was inherited by Queen Anne. She died on 31 July 1714, having had a winner at York the day before. But Anne is honoured above all as the founder of the Ascot meeting where the first race is still, to this day, the Queen Anne Stakes. It all began in the Queen's passion for hunting and a particularly memorable day, probably in 1710, with the Royal Buck Hounds in the country around Swinley. Shortly after, she ordered the establishment of a racecourse there on Ascot Heath. At the first race in August 1711 the best horses competed for the Queen's plate worth £100.

George I, who appears to have spent the whole of his reign wishing he was in Hanover, went only once to a race meeting at Newmarket but he did keep on 'Governor' Frampton at the royal training stables with three boys to keep eight running horses. By this time there were various 'royal plates', races run in the King's name

The Queen makes the traditional drive along the course at Royal Ascot at the start of the meeting, 1983.

for silver cups, and George II converted these into cash prizes of £100 each.

Probably the most influential royal in the history of British racing was George III's brother Henry, Duke of Cumberland. A founder member of the Jockey Club, he helped inaugurate a definitive set of rules for the sport and the registration of colours, the Duke's, described simply as purple, heading the list. Since every jockey then wore a black cap, purple and black remain the basic royal racing colours. The Duke's stud was at Cranbourne Lodge in Windsor Park and his stud manager Smith gave the name to Smith's Lawn. In the eclipse year, 1764, his horse Herod won all of its 18 races while a colt foaled the same year at Cranbourne and called Eclipse had a still more notable career, though unfortunately the Duke died before the horse ran. Herod and Eclipse are reckoned to be two of the three most important sires from which today's best thoroughbreds descended. George himself went only occasionally to Epsom and never to Newmarket, disapproving of the gambling fraternity there. Ascot he did enjoy and had a road cut from Windsor to the course.

George [IV], Prince of Wales had the luck to win the ninth running of the Derby in 1788, but three years later his jockey Sam Chifney was accused of pulling a race. The Prince refused to run his horses at Epsom for some 10 years rather than follow a Jockey Club ruling and dismiss Chifney. The first royal-bred Derby winner was Moses in 1822 owned by the Duke of York. Although no great racing enthusiast, William IV did maintain the royal stud; Victoria disbanded it but in 1850 Albert re-established it.

Edward [VII], much to his mother's disgust, revelled in everything to do with racing, the people, the gambling, the two royal studs at Sandringham and Wolferton and what he called 'the glorious uncertainty of the turf'. After a run of bad luck as owner-trainer, his horse Perdita II produced three great horses—Florizell II, Persimmon and Diamond Jubilee—all at the Sandringham stud and all to the Prince's stallion St Simon. Persimmon won the 1896 Derby by a neck—he also won the St Leger and the Eclipse Stakes—and his statue stands outside the royal stud at Sandringham. In 1900, Diamond Jubilee won the Two Thousand Guineas, the Derby and the Eclipse Stakes, the Newmarket Stakes and the St Leger. In 1900 the King also won the Grand National with Ambush. His horse Minoru won the Two Thousand Guineas and the Derby in 1909. On the day he died, 6 May 1910, his horse Witch Of The Air won at Kempton.

No royal owner has had success to compare with Edward's. His son George V knew little about the race game but earned a tragic notoriety in the 1913 Derby when the heroic suffragette Emily Wilding Davidson threw herself to her death in front of his horse Anmer (horse and rider were virtually unscathed). Of George's sons, Edward [VIII] did not patronize the turf but, though a poor if courageous horseman, he did ride point to point, while George [VI] was a much better rider and had some luck as an owner, winning the 1942 Two Thousand Guineas with Big Game, the One Thousand Guineas with Sun Chariot, the Oaks with Sun Chariot and the St Leger with Big Game. The leading owner that year, he never equalled this success.

Above: The Princess of Wales and Duchess of York entering the Ascot Royal Enclosure.

Left: The Hon. Angus Ogilvy and the Princess of Wales arriving at Ascot with the Queen Mother, June 1987.

Right: Her Majesty at the 1985 Derby.

POLO, PRINCES AND FOUR-IN-HAND

If what we are told is true, very little of the foregoing will have been of interest to the Duke of Edinburgh who is said to be bored by racing and everything to do with it, preferring to watch cricket on the television in the royal box if obliged to attend Ascot. Apart from the sons of George III, almost numerous enough to make up a team of their own on the lawns of Kew Palace, cricket has attracted few royals. Prince Philip, however, is said to be a useful player and is an enthusiastic supporter of the Lord's Taverners. As we shall see, he is also a keen yachtsman; as a horseman, his preference was for polo, having caught the bug from his uncle 'Dickie' Mountbatten.

Polo, its roots deep in the history of Persia and the Mogul emperors of India, came to Britain with returning young cavalry officers of the Indian army in the late 19th century. As Duke of York, George [V] was an enthusiast for the game; his eldest son Edward [VIII] found the game a revelation on his tour of India in the 1920s and had a third train added to his retinue to accommodate the 30 polo ponies given him by the Indian princes and maharajahs. His cousin Mountbatten accompanying him on the tour, a mediocre horseman but a born competitor, took the game up with enthusiasm and founded the Royal Naval Polo Association, recruiting King George as its first patron.

Prince Philip—a founder member of the Household Brigade Polo Club at Smith's Lawn, Windsor Great Park, in 1952—had a distinguished career on the polo field and achieved a handicap of five goals at the peak of his game. He held it at four when, in 1974, plagued with increasing arthritis in the hands, he reluctantly decided to retire. As President of the International Equestrian Federation since 1964, he cast about for some new equestrian sport. His attention was drawn to carriage driving, the first international championships having just been held at Budapest. Advised by the crown equerry, Sir John Miller, he began his own career in the sport with training sessions at Windsor in 1972 and made his driving debut in the spring of 1973 with a quaintly old-fashioned vehicle called the Balmoral dogcart. In 1975 he represented Great Britain in the international driving trials in Poland; he drove in the 1976 and 1978 world championships, and came second in the 1977 International Grand Prix held in Windsor Great Park. In 1980 he was a member of the gold medal British team in the world championships held in Windsor Great Park and has enjoyed various successes since. Prince Philip has also written a book on the sport, *Competition Carriage Driving*. He has in fact brought royal patronage back to an old royal diversion. George III is said to have enjoyed driving his two-horse phaeton around Windsor Great Park at speeds which terrified his daughters. His son George [IV] had a 'passion for the ribbons', once driving the 56 miles (90 km) from Brighton to his London home of Carlton House in 4 hr 30 min—an average of over 12 miles (20 km) an hour—an achievement over the roads of the time.

The Duke of Edinburgh at the Brighton four-in-hand Driving Trials.

SHOOTING

One of the duties of King George V's private detective was to keep a record of the number of birds shot when the King went hunting.

Prince Philip is also considered an excellent shot, and a skilled organizer in the sport. The changes he introduced at Sandringham included the reduction of pheasant and partridge in part to reduce the damage to neighbours' crops. The fortnight after Christmas has been the traditional time for shooting at Sandringham. As president of the World Wildlife Fund (World Wide Fund for Nature) since 1982, the Prince has learned to live with criticism of his activities with the sporting gun. Prince Charles has long been a devotee of the sport. His younger brothers have also shown considerable skill; Prince Edward—a school rugby player, sailing enthusiast and devotee of real tennis played at Hampton Court—was also captain of the Gordonstoun School clay pigeon shooting team, and continues to keep his eye in. The Duke of York, another rugby player, has also proved a regular mainstay of the royals' charity clay pigeon shooting team. This takes part in a match organized by Jackie Stewart for the Save the Children Fund with Mark Phillips, the Duke of Kent and ex-King Constantine of Greece.

Shooting has been a royal sport at least since the time of Henry VIII, recognized by his arch-rival Francis I of France as 'a marvellous good archer and a strong and right pleasant to behold'. A generous comment at any time but especially so at the Field of the Cloth of Gold, Europe's premier diplomatic encounter of the early 16th century. King James I, however, considered shooting unsportsmanlike; he also introduced the first game laws regulating the sport.

Shooting as a sport came to England properly with George I, who hated riding to hounds and organized occasional shoots in Windsor Great Park. In the 1780s, Holkham Hall in Norfolk became renowned for its shooting under Lord Leicester. Prince Albert revived the royal interest in the sport, organizing great shoots at Balmoral. Possibly the fine shooting terrain around Sandringham prompted his advice to his son Edward [VII] to buy the estate. New covers were laid out with the advice of the Earl of Leicester. At Sandringham a single day's bag could amount to over 3000 birds. The shooting at Windsor was reserved for visiting royalty. Whilst Edward was an average to good shot, probably the best shot the royal family has ever produced was Edward's son Prince George [V], rated in the country's top six in 1903. He had a distinctive straight arm action and is reported to have practised his swing and stance at any time of the day—or night.

George VI, a good shot, kept a meticulous record of his kills in his gamebook. When as Duke of York he was courting the Lady Elizabeth Bowes Lyon (the present Queen Mother), among the additional charms of Glamis Castle, her family home, was his discovery of the fine rough shooting there. As king he established the grouse moor at Balmoral. Like his father, George VI was a fine shot and loved the sport. On 5 February 1952, a dry, cold and sunny day, he distinguished himself in the annual hare shoot at Sandringham. That evening, in excellent spirits, he sent a special message of thanks to all the keepers, and settled down to plan the next day's sport. He died in his sleep.

STALKING

That other aspect of the sporting gun features importantly in the royal lifestyle. Prince Edward is a noted exponent of the art. As a young woman, the Queen was skilled at stalking, shooting her first stag aged 16, while the Duke of Edinburgh's name features frequently in the Balmoral stag book. The Prince and Princess of Wales even went on a stalk during their honeymoon.

PIGEON RACING

Edward [VII], Prince of Wales received a gift of six pair of pigeons which spurred the interest of his son Prince George [V]. A loft was built at Sandringham and in the 1890s pigeons were raced for the Wales family by the Prince's friend J. Walter Jones in his own name. When, in 1899, they won the sport's Grand National and also took third and fourth places, their true ownership was disclosed. During World War I the denizens of the royal loft were lent as messenger birds to the Admiralty. George [V] continued his interest in the sport, particularly in breeding; as king, the royal loft winning at four classics; his son George VI won three classics. During World War II, the birds were seconded to the RAF. The royal loft, now at King's Lynn, continues in competition.

GREYHOUND RACING

King John early in the 13th century maintained a pack of some 250 hunting greyhounds. London's Isle of Dogs district derives its name from the fact that Queen Elizabeth I's greyhounds were kennelled there. Today, the royal fancy has been the racing variety. The winner of the 1968 Greyhound Derby was Camira Flash, given to Prince Philip only a year or two previously to be run in his name for the National Playing Fields Association. The Prince was also happy to lend his name to The Duke of Edinburgh Trophy at Haringey stadium.

HAZARDS OF ROYALTY

In earlier times, monarchs often went in fear of their lives (though Henry VII was the first to feel the need for a special bodyguard). Today, the security surrounding the Queen and other members of the Royal Family is probably more intense than anything known in the past but, despite this, in July 1982 an intruder was able to climb through a window in Buckingham Palace and make his way to the Queen's bedroom. This section traces some of the hazards faced by monarchs in the past, from incompetent doctors to fanatical assassins and also shows how on more than one occasion, pressures of politics could lead to the loss of a crown. In the late 20th century, when the British monarchy seems as secure as an institution as at any time in its history, it is as well to remember that kings and queens, like common mortals, are subject to the chances and hazards of life and death.

Right: King Charles I.

Left: Richard II being marched into the Tower of London to await news of his fate at the hands of his cousin Henry Bolingbroke, later king as Henry IV.

Below: James I of Scotland.

ILLNESS, DEATH AND DOCTORS

EFFECTS IN HISTORY

While death comes to all men, illness can hasten its onset and when the talk is of kings this can be important. In the squally days of October 1216 King John, campaigning against a rebellious baronage, was hospitably entertained by the townsmen of Lynn, celebrating a handsome contract to supply the royal garrisons. Runnymede and the humiliating terms of Magna Carta were last year's news. The pope had ruled it null and with half the baronage loyal, John seemed set for eventual victory. The desserts brought on at the end of the banquet included his favourite, peaches in wine. John gorged himself and drank hugely of cider. He died a few days later of dysentery. His realm was in turmoil but his death meant the monarchy was too weak to cancel Magna Carta, which survived to become England's Great Charter of Liberties.

Six centuries later that other great killer, typhoid, claimed the life of Victoria's Prince Consort, Albert the Good, on 13 December 1861. Prime Minister Palmerston described the death as 'an overwhelming calamity'. The Prince's illness had been caused partly by the appalling drains at Windsor, partly by exhaustion brought on by overwork and partly by worry over his eldest son's youthful irresponsibilities. Ironically when, 10 years later, that son himself very nearly died of typhoid, the surge of sympathy for the Queen as mother submerged the growing criticism of her absurdly exaggerated mourning.

DISEASE AND DIAGNOSIS

One difficulty in writing about the health problems of past monarchs is that doctors often did not know what the illness was or used different terminology from ours. The medieval use of the term 'leprosy' is particularly hard to pin down. It seems to have comprised not only the disease as we understand it today but various other disfiguring skin complaints and possibly forms of venereal disease. According to his biographer, the Welsh churchman Asser, Alfred the Great suffered throughout his life from a mysterious disease which plagued him almost daily with pain or the fear of an attack.

In 1688 James II allowed a heavy nosebleed to sap his resolve for a crucial two days in November during the long-drawn-out confrontation between his army and the advancing troops of William of Orange. His army was based in Salisbury under its commander, but James could not rally the enthusiasm of his men. Churchill (later the Duke of Marlborough) deserted to the Dutchman and James eventually ordered a withdrawal to London. It may well have been the decision that lost him his crown. Thirty-seven years later, when James's son, the Old Pretender, James III, landed in Scotland to rally his already lost cause, he was listless and uninspiring with a streaming cold.

There were numerous diseases which today we tend to regard as comparatively unimportant but were once killers. The childhood ailments of Edward I were a constant worry to his loving parents, Henry III and Queen

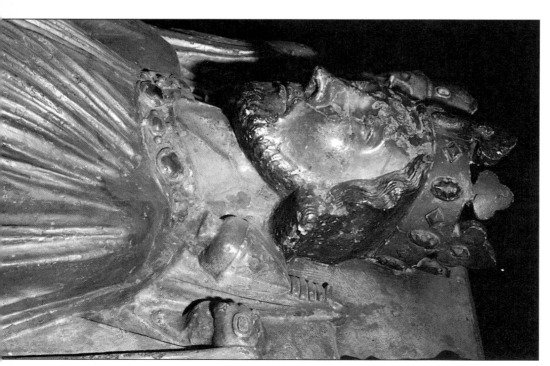

Left: King John, buried in Worcester Cathedral, died, so tradition has it, of dysentery brought on by overeating. He died on campaign against rebels in 1216, after a rich meal topped off with his favourite pudding—peaches stewed in wine, washed down with lashings of cider.

Right: The wooden funeral effigy of King Edward III (d. 1377), probably taken from the King's death mask.

Eleanor (four of his brothers had died in infancy). When the Prince was just seven, the royal family made a visit to Beaulieu for the consecration of the new abbey. Edward fell dangerously ill, probably of measles. He sickened for three weeks and, with regal disregard for monastic conventions and to the consternation of the newly inaugurated abbot, Queen Eleanor stayed on in the abbey guest house until her son was fit to leave.

Although he lived to his 68th year, Edward suffered periodic bouts of illness, among them a painful and lingering skin disease. Not leprosy in his case, though his enemy, Scotland's hero Robert I the Bruce, was said to have died of the disease and so may the unloved Henry IV of England.

Probably the most mystifying royal death was that of James V of Scotland (father of Mary Queen of Scots) who, after humiliating defeat by the English at Solway Moss in 1542, though quite unscathed, took to his bed in Falkland Castle some three weeks later and on 14 December died of pure melancholy. Certainly no sign of illness was observed on the King.

The case of his contemporary Edward VI of England who, it used to be said, died of syphilis inherited from his father, was very different. The diagnoses now range from measles and smallpox to acute tuberculosis or a combination of all three. Between January and July 1553 his physicians watched powerless as he 'steadily pined away' wracked by a cough that brought up a 'livid, black, fetid sputum' and unable to sleep 'except he be stuffed with drugs'. Small wonder that his prayer in those final months was 'Lord God, deliver me out of this miserable wretched life'.

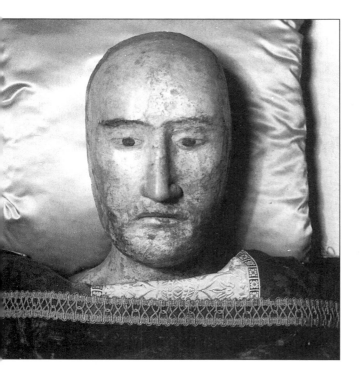

His half sister Mary I's great tragedy was her childlessness compounded by a false pregnancy during the last year of her life which may have been some form of dropsical swelling in the region of the womb. She was probably killed by some form of influenza. Her life had been as miserable as her half brother's but her ending at least seems to have been happier, for she told her waiting women of dreams where 'many little children like angels' played before her.

Illness did not become a major issue in British politics for another century until October 1788 when George III suffered his first bout of madness. While the Prince of Wales looked eagerly forward to the Regency and his brothers joked callously about the old man's condition, George battled with a disease whose symptoms undoubtedly suggested madness.

The story of the treatments inflicted on George make harrowing reading. Restraint by straitjacket and special chair to which the protesting monarch was strapped, his objections silenced by a gag, was supposed to torment not the patient but the evil spirits in possession of him and so drive them out. This may have been the theory but the blows and insults with which the doctors' assistants discharged their duties were both insolent and sadistic. Yet they had the full support not only of the Princes but also the terrified Queen, for his illness not only made the King hysterically garrulous but also at times violent.

It is now believed that at this point George was not mentally ill but victim of a rare disease called porphyria, a malfunction of the body mechanism which produces the red dye of the blood. An excess of the pigment sabotages the body's metabolism and in severe attacks the pain and other effects can produce forms of delirium chronicled in the King's case histories. But the really telltale sign, apparently, is the colour of the urine which can fluctuate, in the course of a day, from pink to dark purple—hence the name of the disease. It is said the illness can be traced to George's Stuart ancestor James VI. In 1810 a recurrence of the condition, advancing age (73) and his fear of madness combined to precipitate him into insanity and violence. He lived his last years a bearded, babbling recluse while his son George [IV] held the regency.

Convalescing in 1788, George had taken a course of sea bathing at Weymouth. As the bathing machine was wheeled to the water's edge and the King descended the steps to take his constitutional dip, the town wind band struck up the loyal strains of the national anthem. Sea bathing was something of a novelty and threatened to displace the spas such as Cheltenham, another of the King's favourite resorts. George's statue may still be seen on the front at Weymouth, while his son established the fortunes of Brighton. Belief in the recuperative virtues of sea air and ozone continued and in the

Left: Queen Mary I 'touching for the King's Evil'. In the early 11th century, as part of a cult of divine monarchy, it came to be believed that the royal touch could cure scrofula and other painful and unsightly skin complaints. In England the first such miracle cures were claimed for St Edward the Confessor. The ritual required the monarch to stroke his or her hands over the sores. King Charles II was very conscientious in discharging this part of his royal duty. The last monarch to touch for the 'Evil' was Queen Anne (d. 1714).

Right: Queen Charlotte in later life. Queen to King George III, she was at first terrified and then deeply saddened by the King's attacks of violent madness in the last years of his life. The portrait is by Sir William Beechey.

1930s the ageing King George V, following doctor's advice, stayed at Bognor (now Bognor Regis) in Sussex, though it seems his chief delight there was the visits of his granddaughter 'Lilibet', the present Queen.

Her mother, Queen Elizabeth the Queen Mother, gave birth both to the Queen and to Princess Margaret by Caesarian section and in the 1960s had serious surgery both for an appendectomy and for a colostomy. Her husband George VI had a poor medical history. Terrorized as a baby by his nurse, he was afflicted by bouts of indigestion into early manhood; his legs were considered weak and were clamped in calipers; attempts were made to 'correct' his left-handedness. By his teens a childhood stutter had become a serious speech handicap. He dreaded public appearances. But he did not shirk them, and the occasion of his speech at the closing ceremony of the Wembley Empire Exhibi-

tion proved his salvation. In the audience was a young Australian speech therapist named Lionel Logue who had won renown at home with dramatic results in treating shell-shocked victims of World War I. His treatment began even before he met his patients—he never went to see them but insisted that they, no matter how privileged, make the decision to visit him. Prince George eventually went to Logue's consulting rooms. The treatment, based on a combination of breathing exercises and the building of self-esteem, began to work results almost at once. Logue refused to accompany the Yorks when they made their state visit to his native Australia in 1927, insisting, as always, that his patients must learn to stand alone. Returning, Prince George wrote, 'I have so much confidence in myself now. I am sure it comes from my being able to speak properly at last'.

Late in 1948, the King's physicians discovered the beginnings of arteriosclerosis and for a time his right leg seemed in danger. However, an operation in March the following year eased the situation. It had been suggested that he go into hospital. 'I never heard of a king going into a hospital before', he observed drily and a fully equipped operating theatre was set up in Buckingham Palace. In the autumn of 1951 tests revealed the presence of a malignant growth on his left lung. It was removed but now there were fears for his life. Elizabeth and Philip were scheduled for a visit to Canada and it was agreed, under urging from Philip, that they might fly. Official pronouncements that the King was recovering led, early in December 1951, to a day of national thanksgiving. On 5 February he was planning the next day's shooting at Sandringham. The following morning his valet found him dead. King George had died, apparently in his sleep, of a coronary thrombosis.

Most mystifying to us today in the history of George VI's illness is the apparent indifference displayed by his physician to the King's heavy smoking. But it was all part and parcel of the attitude of the time. There was still something stylish about tobacco. The views of that great royal anti-smoking publicist James I were considered quaintly Jacobean, just as Queen Victoria's detestation of the habit was, of course, merely Victorian. Smoking was forbidden in all the Queen's palaces and residences so that one foreign royal, afflicted by the tedium of life at Balmoral under the ageing Queen, was reduced to smoking in his bedroom lying on his back, his head resting on a pillow in the unlit fire grate, blowing the smoke of his cigar up the chimney.

MEDICINES AND DOCTORS

One contributory factor to Prince Albert's death had been the appalling state of the drains at Windsor; but at least there were drains. In 1298, Edward I slipped away from London to avoid awkward demands from Parliament, on the quite plausible pretext that the air was so foul from uncleared night soil round Westminster Palace that his health was in danger. Some 150 years later, Henry VI actually suspended the sittings so that members might leave town for the same reason.

Medicine was expensive. A canon at Hexham Abbey, attending on the ailing Edward I during his last campaign, was paid the sum of 20 shillings, sufficient to keep a small company of infantry in the field for a week and more. One can well believe it. One prescription favoured by the King was an electuary (a paste to be taken orally), made up from amber, jacinth (a form of zyrcon), musk, pearls, gold and silver. On crusade in Syria, Edward came into contact with Jewish and Arab medicine, then superior to European remedies, and this may explain the entries in the royal accounts for Damascus rose water and tonic wine made from pomegranates—while sugar, that other eastern rarity, was also prized for its supposedly medicinal qualities.

Sir Theodore Mayern, physician to James I, noted his master's opinion that the art of medicine was supported by mere conjecture. Yet, over 100 years later, the 1789 celebrations for George III's recovery to fitness were patriotically scheduled for St George's Day, 23 April. However, the Archbishop of Canterbury expressed concern that the service in St Paul's might prove dangerously tiring. 'Sir,' replied the King, 'I have twice read the evidence of the physicians in my case and if I can stand that I can stand anything.' He would surely have envied Edward I, at least one of whose doctors was actually useful. The surgeon accompanying Edward on his last campaign into Scotland took charge of the approach assaults at the siege of Loch Doon castle.

Of all the British kings it was probably George who suffered most at the hands of the doctors and few men have had better reason to distrust their claims. When Dr Francis Willis, a churchman turned doctor, was presented as his new physician, George, observing his clerical style of dress, asked if he was a clergyman. Willis, explaining that he had given up preaching for medicine, unctuously submitted that Christ himself had gone about healing the sick. 'Yes, yes,' came the testy response, 'but He had not £700 a year for it.' With James I, he might have 'laughed at medicine and declared physicians of very little use', a view which for centuries represented common sense. The favour shown by Prince Charles and other members of the present Royal Family for various types of alternative medicine continues a long-established theme of scepticism of the claims of conventional therapists.

ROYAL PRISONERS

In civil war or at times of a *coup d'état*, the prison cell or house arrest was usually but a preliminary to assassination. Capture in war meant the prospect of crippling ransom either in money or policy concessions—a risk considered possible even in the 20th century.

Although serving on the Western Front during World War I, Edward [VIII], Prince of Wales was kept well behind the lines, to his own intense frustration. 'What does it matter if I get killed?' he would complain; 'I have four brothers.' No one ever doubted his courage. What haunted government thinking in the first months of the war, before there was a settled front line, was the prospect of his being captured by the Germans.

During the Middle Ages two English and three Scottish kings had to be ransomed from prison, while the overweight Welsh prince Gruffydd ap Llywelyn suffered the embarrassment of killing himself when his rope of sheets broke as he attempted an escape from the Tower of London (1244).

REASONS OF RANSOM

Feudal custom laid various obligations on the liegemen of a lord or king, most of them rated according to tradition. But there were exceptional levies which tradition could not govern but which had to be paid nevertheless—chief among them was the ransom of the lord's person.

King Richard I of England, known to Europe as 'the Lionheart', sailed from Palestine in October 1192. He had recovered much territory for the Christian kingdom of Jerusalem but, thanks to the Muslim hero Saladin, the Holy City itself remained to Islam. Richard was anxious to return to Europe where the French king was manoeuvring to oust him from his family possessions in France and his own brother John seemed intent on taking over the kingdom of England.

With winter approaching, the long sea trip to England seemed a hazardous undertaking but overland the route lay through either France or the hardly more friendly territories of the German empire. Richard opted for the German route, making his way through the Alpine passes apparently disguised as a monk. But the party of monks, one immensely tall and deferred to by his companions like some great lord, alerted a Tyrolean tavern keeper. The man sent word to Archduke Leopold of Austria, himself a returned crusader, who held a bitter personal grudge against Richard and seized him.

At the siege of Acre, Leopold had set up his standard on a section of the wall, only for Richard as the senior commander present to have it hurled into the moat, to the anger of Leopold and all the German crusaders.

The Archduke soon sold his royal prisoner to Emperor Henry VI, who set the ransom at 150 000 silver marks. The first massive instalment was found and Queen Eleanor, in her sixties but beautiful still, went with the bullion convoy to Cologne and returned to London with her royal son. The German knights who provided the honour escort, astounded by the wealth of the city, swore that had they been better informed the King would have had to pay more for his freedom.

Some 20 years earlier, William I the Lion had become the first Scottish king to fall captive to the English. Captured while besieging Alnwick Castle in 1174, he was taken to King Henry II at Northampton, his feet roped together under the belly of a horse. Henry sent him on his way to confinement in the castle of Falaise in Normandy and meanwhile dispatched an avenging army to Edinburgh.

At the Treaty of Falaise in July 1174, William knelt in homage to the English King as a vassal for his own kingdom of Scotland. In addition he was bound to a payment of 10 000 marks of silver. The treaty held until 1189 when Richard I, looking for money to finance his crusade, sold William back his oath for a further 10 000 marks.

In October 1346 David II of Scotland, son of Robert the Bruce, came prisoner to England. He had taken advantage of King Edward III's absence on campaign in France to lead a marauding army south. Instead at

Neville's Cross, near Durham, David's army was routed and its leader captured by northern English forces led by nobility and churchmen. King David was sent into house arrest at the Tower of London—it was the time of the Black Death and David's enforced quarantine may have saved his life.

He was released in 1357 on promise of a 100 000 marks ransom, which was to be paid in 10 yearly instalments. Five years later, hoping to be spared the remaining payments, David offered to make Edward his heir to the Scottish crown should he die childless. But the Scots considered he had been corrupted by his long imprisonment and refused to have anything to do with the proposal. In 1371 David was succeeded by his nephew Robert II, son of Walter the Steward and first of the house of Stuart.

In 1406, the 12-year-old James [I] Stuart of Scotland, grandson of Robert II, was making his way to France 'for his education' but in fact to avoid the ambitions of the scheming Duke of Albany (his uncle, Prince Robert, the Regent) when he was waylaid by English coasters off Flamborough Head. He was brought to London before King Henry IV who, uncharacteristically jovial, quipped that the boy need go no further since he could teach him French. On hearing the news of the capture, James's father, the ineffectual King Robert III, died—of grief, it was said. The Scottish parliament recognized James as king, but Albany was confirmed governor of the realm in his absence. For 18 years James lived in England, under comfortable house arrest. In November 1412 we find him issuing Scottish land confirmations at Croydon, Surrey, in letters 'wrate with our propre hand'. Seven years later he was paraded through Normandy, as a friend of Henry V, in the hope that the Scottish brigades supporting the French in the Hundred Years War might decide to return home rather than fight against their liege lord.

He may indeed have been Henry's friend, since in 1420 he also attended the coronation of Henry's queen Catherine at Westminster Abbey and was afterwards knighted at Windsor. It was perhaps at Windsor that James made his debut as royal author with *The Kingis Quair*, which celebrates his love for Joan Beaufort, cousin of King Henry V. In December 1423 James signed the Treaty of London by which he agreed to pay a ransom of £40 000 in four annual instalments and to ensure that no more Scottish soldiers go to France. In February 1423 he and Joan were married in the church of St Mary Overy, now Southwark Cathedral, going to Scotland for their coronation at Scone in May of that year.

REASONS OF POLICY

Henry VIII sentenced his first wife Catherine of Aragon to house arrest once he had convinced himself that their marriage had been unlawful. Her confinement became increasingly arduous and her daughter, the future Mary I, was denied visiting rights. Then in 1534

Left: The tomb of Richard I, the Lionheart, at the abbey of Fontevraud, France. The mausoleum church of the Angevin family, it also holds the tombs of Richard's mother, Queen Eleanor of Aquitaine (here on his left) and his father King Henry II.

Right: The execution of King Charles I.

the ex-Queen was sent away from London to virtual imprisonment in the medieval fortified manor of Kimbolton Castle in Huntingdonshire. Here she spent the remaining two years of her life. For the most part Henry simply neglected her but when he heard of her approaching death he reaffirmed the prohibition on Mary's seeing her when she lay dying in January 1536. Indeed, the Princess was forbidden even to receive the furs which her mother had bequeathed in her tragically modest will. Later that year, Catherine's old rival Anne Boleyn had a miscarriage. It was her own death warrant. Charged with adultery and even incest, she was confined in the Tower of London while witnesses were put to the torture. Henry's Anne of a Thousand Days met her death on Tower Green with composure, thanks, it was said, to the ministrations of Archbishop Cranmer.

It is hardly to be wondered that the fourth wife, the vivacious but foolish Catherine Howard, was less phlegmatic. Only 17 years old when she was placed under arrest at Hampton Court, Catherine made desperate attempts to see the ageing King, convinced she would be able to cajole him to grant her mercy. The King, it seems, was of the same opinion for he gave orders she should be denied access. It is said that the gallery behind the King's pew in the Chapel Royal, where she was dragged away by the soldiers, is still haunted by her ghost. She was subsequently executed on Tower Green.

With Mary Queen of Scots, the Queen without a throne, we come to one of the most celebrated of all royal prisoners. When Mary crossed into England in May 1568, she was escaping some 10 months of imprisonment at the hands of her own Scottish nobles in the island castle of Loch Leven, Kinross, where she had signed her kingdom away to her baby son James VI. Disingenuously, she came as one woman to another asking for asylum. In a century when religion was the principal cause of war and rebellion, Elizabeth of England was faced by the question of what to do with the woman who in happier times had once boasted herself true Queen of England. To the credit of Elizabeth, her rival survived a further 19 years, despite constant petitions from Parliament and demands from her ministers. Where Mary had condoned the murder of the husband she herself had had proclaimed King, Elizabeth resisted for as long as she could the judicial murder of a Queen deposed by her own people and rejected by her own son.

Although strictly guarded by Sir Amyas Paulet at Fotheringhay castle in Northamptonshire, Mary was focus of various more or less ill-conceived Catholic conspiracies against Elizabeth's life and throne. In 1586 she fell in with the Babington conspiracy, provoked, it is said, by Elizabeth's devious secret service chief Sir Francis Walsingham, and in February 1587 was beheaded at Fotheringhay on a warrant signed at long last by her cousin.

In May 1646 Charles I, his army crushingly defeated at Naseby the year before by Cromwell's New Model Army, gave himself up to the Scots, hoping for their indulgence and support to their Scottish monarch. At Newcastle, in January 1647, they surrendered him to the representatives of Parliament who, after years of bloody civil war provoked, as they saw it, by this same Charles Stuart, in due course put him on trial for his life.

But first he was escorted in triumphant arrest to Holdenby House, Northamptonshire. He spent the next few months trying to play Parliament off against the army until, in June, Cornet Joyce arrived to take him under guard to the army's HQ at Newark. When the King asked to see the commission of arrest, the young soldier simply turned in the saddle and gestured to the troopers behind him. Charles smiled thinly with the words: 'It is a fair commission and as well written as I have seen a commission written in my life.'

From Newark he was sent to Hampton Court where he lived in semi-regal confinement. In November he made a dramatic escape to Carisbrooke Castle on the Isle of Wight where he opened secret negotiations with the Scots and prompted the second Civil War. In April 1647 an army meeting at Windsor resolved that should God 'ever bring us back in peace', they would 'call Charles Stuart, that man of blood, to an account for the blood he had shed, and mischief he had done to his utmost'. Parliament's victory over the Scots at Preston in August opened the final act for the royal prisoner. In December the triumphant army ordered Parliament to set up a High Court of Justice with powers to try the king.

On Christmas Day 1648 Charles I rode into his old home of Windsor, this time under armed escort while preparations for his trial went forward in London. He was treated with respect and for the first four days his meals continued to be served to the sound of trumpets, the dishes presented to the King by gentlemen on bended knee. When these rather incongruous privileges were withdrawn, he decided to dine alone rather than 'to diminish his dignity'. To his last gaoler, Captain Matthew Thomlinson, who had come to admire the King as a friend, Charles gave as a keepsake from his few remaining personal possessions, his gold toothpick. Having recognized that the game was over, Charles had spent the final months of his imprisonment preparing the great last scene of life, his death. For the public men of his day, liable to the reverses of fortune and in the last resort the executioner's block, making a good death was an important art. When he walked out on to the scaffold in Whitehall from the great banqueting room on 30 January 1649, every detail was perfect.

ABDICATIONS AND DEPOSITIONS

EDWARD VIII, DECEMBER 1936

'I have found it impossible to carry the heavy burden of responsibility and to discharge my duties as King as I would wish to do without the help and support of the woman I love.' Ex-King Edward VIII, abdication broadcast, Friday 11 December 1936.

The most dramatic event in the history of the royal family this century was the abdication of King Edward VIII so that he could marry Wallis Warfield Simpson. He first met Wallis and her second husband Mr Ernest Simpson in 1930; from the summer of 1934 she was his almost constant companion, and in the autumn, to the dismay of King George V and Queen Mary, he presented her at court. For the next two years London society kept the secret that the heir to the throne was infatuated with an American divorcee. With the death of King George in January 1936 there were those who foresaw that society gossip could balloon into constitutional crisis. In August, Edward invited Wallis to Balmoral and later that month chartered the yacht *Nahlin* for a cruise in the eastern Mediterranean.

The King of England's holiday with his married lady friend gave the world's press a field day, but London's newspaper barons barely reported the story. The self-censorship continued for months—even when Wallis was granted her decree nisi, then the essential first stage in any divorce proceedings, at Ipswich on 26 October. On 3 November, the King opened Parliament. But 10 days later his Private Secretary, Major Alexander Hardinge, warned him that the media would not hold their silence much longer and urged him to send Mrs Simpson abroad. On 16 November Edward informed Prime Minister Baldwin that he would abdicate rather than give up the woman he loved. 'His face at times wore such a look of beauty as might have lighted the face of a young knight who had caught a glimpse of the Holy Grail,' the PM told his family, following this interview with the 42-year-old monarch.

There have been numerous conspiracy theories to explain the remarkable sequence of events that followed, but the King's proposed marriage was sufficient cause in itself. In the words of the society diarist Sir Henry 'Chips' Channon (father of 1980s cabinet minister Paul Channon), 'The country . . . would not accept Queen Wallis with two live husbands scattered about.' At this moment the country was still ignorant that any such option was in the offing. Not only were the English papers censoring their reports, foreign magazines referring to the scandal had the offending stories cut out.

As the pressure mounted, a devious friend suggested the King go to his coronation and try to resolve the marriage question later (i.e., marry the lady when he was safely crowned). Honourably, King Edward refused

Above: The Queen and Prince Charles visit the Duchess of Windsor in Paris.

Left: The Abdication produced ill feeling between the ex-King Edward VIII and the new Palace establishment under his brother King George VI. It was not until 1967 that the Duke and Duchess of Windsor visited Britain as the guests of Her Majesty Queen Elizabeth II.

such a line of action. Next, the idea of a morganatic marriage was floated. Under this arrangement, Mrs Simpson would marry the King but would not become queen nor could any children she might have inherit the throne. Such marriages between people of widely different social rank were found in Europe but unknown to English law, under which a woman automatically assumes her husband's rank.

Baldwin proposed that before any decision be taken the opinion of the Dominion governments be sought and Edward agreed. With this decision he lost his case before it began. Having asked for his ministers' advice he was in constitutional terms bound to accept it. The issue was no longer in doubt. In due course, the prime ministers of Australia, Canada, South Africa and New Zealand refused to contemplate the morganatic proposal, while De Valera of Catholic Ireland responded that Edward would not be recognized as king by Dublin if he married a divorcee, whatever her social rank.

On 2 December the news finally broke on a stunned British public. The following day Mrs Simpson did leave England for the south of France, the 'hounds of the press' in hot pursuit. Edward's friends, among them Winston Churchill, urged the formation of a King's Party to appeal to the country over the heads of his ministers. Edward refused to have anything to do with the idea. It was in any case becoming obvious that the country in general was not willing to let their former 'Prince Charming' have his way. For Edward had not merely breached the conventional morality of his church and his times, he had deserted one lover, the nation, for another. On the afternoon of Monday 7 December Churchill tried one more appeal to the House of Commons on the King's behalf: he was shouted down. The same evening Wallis, in one of her innumerable and interminable phone calls from Cannes, announced her willingness to 'withdraw from a situation that was both unhappy and untenable'. But, in the words of one of his friends, 'the King was besotted'.

On Thursday 10 December 1936, King Edward VIII signed the instrument of his Abdication; the next day the Bill of Abdication received the royal assent to become law. That evening His Royal Highness Prince Edward made his farewell broadcast from Windsor Castle. After the broadcast, now entitled Duke of Windsor, he returned to Royal Lodge Windsor to say goodbye to his family. Late that night he left by road for Portsmouth where HMS *Fury* was standing by.

From Boulogne the Duke travelled to Ensesfeld in Austria, a castle of his friend Baron Eugène de Rothschild. He and Mrs Simpson had to live apart while the decree absolute for her divorce was pending to avoid all suggestion of collusion. The Duke and Mrs Simpson were finally married on 3 June 1937 at the

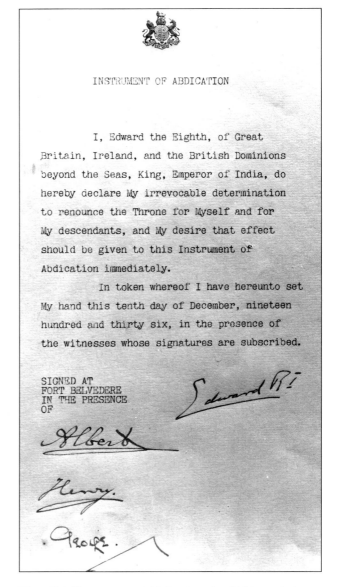

The official Instrument of Abdication, dated 'this tenth day December, nineteen hundred and thirty six . . .' whereby King Edward irrevocably renounced the throne for himself and his descendants. Signed 'Edward R.I.' (i.e. rex imperator, 'king emperor') it was witnessed by his brothers Albert (the Duke of York), Henry, the Duke of Gloucester and George, the Duke of Kent. The formalities complete, Albert became king with the regnal title of 'George VI'.

Château de Candé, loaned for the occasion by the French-born American industrialist Charles Bedaux. Bedaux had wide contacts among German industrialists and at his suggestion the Windsors toured Germany so that the Duke could 'investigate labour conditions'. In fact he and the Duchess were received by Hitler and other Nazi leaders so that in October 1937 the *New York Times* was led to comment: 'The

King Edward VIII photographed on a visit to a broadcasting studio early in his brief reign. After the abdication, he made a famous farewell broadcast to his people.

Duke's gestures and remarks during the last two weeks have demonstrated that the Abdication robbed Germany of a firm friend on the British throne.' Of more concern to the Duke then and for years to come seems to have been the denial of the title and style HRH to his wife in letters patent issued by King George VI just before the wedding. This extraordinary ruling seemed after all to force a morganatic union on the Windsors; its legality has since been questioned.

EARLIER ABDICATIONS AND DEPOSITIONS

Voluntary abdication, well known for example in the modern Dutch royal family, is virtually unknown in Britain. A few of the old Saxon kings had resigned their thrones to go on the pilgrimage to Rome or to dedicate themselves to the life of religion, but since the Conquest abdication had been effectively synonymous with deposition. In Scotland, while many early monarchs were deposed, Mary Queen of Scots was the only one in modern times to abdicate. Married first to Francis I (d. 1561), she was briefly Queen of France; she had a good hereditary claim to the English throne. Nevertheless, she spent 19 years as a private citizen under house arrest.

Mary Queen of Scots (born 6/7 December; acceded 14 December 1542; abdicated July 1568; executed Fotheringhay, 1587), lived the first 19 years of her life at the French court, Mary landed in Scotland in August 1561, shortly after the death of her mother who, as Regent, had attempted unsuccessfully to establish Catholicism. Six years of increasingly contentious policy and passion, then her marriage to James Hepburn, 4th Earl of Bothwell, the suspected murderer of her second husband, sparked insurgency amongst opposition lords 'of the Congregation'. As the Queen's forces melted from her, Bothwell fled to Denmark (where, 11 years later, he died as a madman) and Mary was taken prisoner to Edinburgh. Here she was forced to abdicate in favour of her one-year-old son James VI (later I of England) with the Earl of Moray as Regent. The ex-Queen was confined in the island castle of Lochleven. In May 1568, helped by a romantic youth, she escaped, but her attempt to regain her throne ended in defeat at Langside on 13 May 1568 and she rode south to England to become once more a prisoner.

In 688 Caedwalla, King of Wessex despite his Celtic name, abdicated and made the pilgrimage to Rome, where he died just 10 days after his baptism. His successor King Ine, noted for his extensive and influential law code, also resigned his throne to journey to Rome, where he died the same year, 726. Æthelred of Mercia, son of the pagan king Penda, abdicated in 704 to become a monk—he died in 716. In 825 Baldred, last King of Kent, was deposed and expelled by King Egbert of Wessex; in the 870s Burgred of Mercia was deposed by the Danish invaders and went to Rome, where he died shortly afterwards. In the later 10th century, new waves of Danes repeatedly harassed the prosperous kingdom of Wessex and were as regularly bought off by King Æthelred II Unraed of England. After a reign of 35 years he was deposed and exiled by King Swegn of Denmark in 1013. Even so, Æthelred returned for a brief second reign from February 1014 to his death in April 1016.

Æthelred's defeat by foreign invaders did not raise constitutional problems—conquest broke all patterns. The tragedy of King Edward II some 300 years later was a different matter. In 1326 he was defeated and imprisoned by his own wife and her lover with the intention that he should surrender the crown. By the early 14th century the overthrow of a crowned and anointed king was an awesome procedure for which there were no precedents and no machinery. The King had been charged with various heinous and tyrannical acts but there was no legal way to remove him if he was not willing to go. The opposition moved with care.

In October 1326 his son Prince Edward was proclaimed 'Keeper of the Realm' and in January the Archbishop of Canterbury preached on the text 'vox populi, vox dei' ('the voice of the people is the voice of God') and announced that all the estates in Parliament had decided that Edward should succeed his father. Parliament swore an oath of confederacy and sent a deputation to the castle of Kenilworth, where King Edward II was being held. It demanded his abdication on blackmail terms—if he refused, Parliament would appoint a king from outside the royal line. The King, we are told, consented and his steward broke his wand of office to symbolize the dissolution of the royal household.

Next, the handsome but humbled monarch affirmed his character failings—his voluntary surrender of the crown in words that must have carried all the conviction of a Moscow show trial of the 1930s. On 2 February the 14-year-old Edward III, having publicly affirmed that his father had taken his decision 'of his own good will and by the common consent of the prelates . . . nobles . . . and community of the realm', was crowned and duly succeeded under the dangerous regency of his mother and her paramour. In September his father's life was horribly ended in the dungeons of Berkeley Castle, Gloucestershire.

The transfer of power, achieved by armed insurgency, had been 'sold' as the resignation of the King authorized by the community of the realm was represented in Parliament. A contemporary manuscript illustration, an early example of propaganda art, shows a king seated on a cushioned throne, reaching his hand to the crown on his head while looking at a boyish figure standing in front of the throne with a crown in hand as if in the act of receiving it.

In 1399 Richard II suffered the fate of his great-grandfather. Once again the deposition of a king was presented as his voluntary abdication, but this time there was no son to succeed him. The King was challenged by his cousin Henry Bolingbroke who claimed the throne as Henry IV by the acclamation of his peers and the need to replace the misgovernment of Richard. Following his public humiliation, the ex-King was sent to confinement in Pontefract castle, where he shortly 'died'.

Henry IV's Lancastrian dynasty lasted until his grandson Henry VI (40) was displaced in March 1461 by the 19-year-old Yorkist, Edward IV. Once more Parliament was the forum in validating the transfer of power. With King Henry a fugitive in Scotland and the Yorkists supreme, in November Parliament ruled that Edward had 'right and title to the realm of England', having 'removed Henry, later called Henry Sixth . . . from the occupation, usurpation, intrusion, reign and governance of the said realm'. In December they passed an act of attainder against the ex-King. Ten years later, Henry was briefly restored but when Edward returned victorious once more, the Lancastrians' figurehead found himself trapped in London and handed over to the triumphant Edward. At their meeting Henry opened his arms as if to give an embrace of welcome with the words 'My cousin of York, you are very welcome. I know that in your hands my life will not be in danger'.

In the circumstances it amounted to an act of abdication. Henry was the last king of England to make such a gesture. Within a month he was dead, probably on Edward's orders. Defeated in battle, Charles I was tried as a traitor to the Commonwealth and people of England while his son James II, although frightened out of his kingdom by William III, never renounced his title as king.

ASSASSINATION AND OTHER HAZARDS

AN ENGLISH KING AND THE ORIGIN OF ASSASSINS

One hot June evening in 1272 an attendant in the crusading entourage of King Edward I of England entered the King's room at his Acre headquarters in Israel and thrust at him with a dagger. An athletic 33-year-old, the King, showing impressive reflexes, wrestled the man to the ground and killed him. At his squire's suggestion that the weapon might be poisoned, Queen Eleanor, it is said, sucked the wound, hoping to clear the infection. Some said the would-be killer was in the pay of the emir of Ramlah, others said he was an Assassin.

The word Assassin came from a Muslim sect created some two centuries earlier as a kind of Murder Inc., for the elimination of Muslim rulers disapproved of by the sect's founder, possibly the world's first dedicated terrorist, 'The Old Man of the Mountain'. In Edward's time the sect's headquarters was a mountain retreat in the Lebanon. The name derived from the fact that the first Old Man of the Mountain fired his fanatical followers to kamikaze devotion by feeding them the drug hashish. When they were 'high' they were taken to a garden attended by beautiful girls to induce visions of the Muslim paradise which he promised to be their immediate reward if they died on mission. The 'Hashshashin' became a byword of terror in the Middle East, while in the West their name became the synonym for ideological or political killings. It remains so to this day.

MODERN OFFENCES AGAINST MONARCHY

On the morning of Friday 9 July 1982, Queen Elizabeth II was awoken by an intruder. He had climbed through a Palace window and found his way into the Queen's bedroom around 7 a.m. As the Palace staff went about their morning routine Her Majesty found herself trapped in surreal conversation with a simple-minded stranger called Michael Fagan who, he said, had domestic problems.

Sitting on her bed, Fagan spilled out his troubles. The Queen responded, calmly taking up the dialogue and pressing her night emergency bell. It did not work. She then tried the one for the corridor outside but her footman and maid were busy elsewhere. Next the Queen used the telephone, but the operator thought she sounded too casual for an emergency. Eventually, the intruder asked if he might have a cigarette, which gave Her Majesty reason for going to another room. Once outside her bedroom she was able to summon help. The man was charged with burglary—technically he had not broken into the Palace—but this corner of the law is such an ill-defined area, he was acquitted. (He was sent to a mental hospital and discharged in January 1983.)

The incident was followed by an outcry in the press, a vigorous passing of the buck among the higher echelons of the responsible departments and the scapegoat disciplining of a junior. Conventionally reassuring as the official reaction was, the event had been a security nightmare. In an age of terrorist killings and kidnappings, the British public had for a moment glimpsed the potential vulnerability of the Queen in her own official residence and they were appalled. The situation was the worse since it was the second time in two years that her life had seemed in jeopardy.

On 13 June 1981, as the familiar figure riding side-saddle at the head of the Guards to the Trooping the Colour Birthday Parade turned on to Horse Guards Parade, a shot rang out. The Queen had been shot at by a 17-year-old youth who had loaded six blanks into a starting pistol that morning. Burmese, Her Majesty's famous black mare, skittered dangerously for a moment but immediately responded to the Queen's cool touch of control. In no time at all the incident was over as police and detectives moved in to overpower the offender. He was sentenced to five years in prison under the Treason Act 1842, without leave to appeal.

ANNALS OF CRIME

Such incidents are shocking not only because of the hazard to Her Majesty but also because of the lapse in what the public hopes are foolproof security measures. In earlier times monarchs had less protection. More than one of England's pre-Conquest kings fell victim to murder. Among the most notable were Cynewulf of Wessex, killed at Merton in 786; and the mighty Æthelbald of Mercia, victor over the Northumbrians, the West Saxons and the Welsh, self-styled 'King of Britain', who was murdered in 757 at Seckington near his great hall at Tamworth.

Perhaps the most famous was St Edward the Martyr. Eldest son of the great King Edgar, he succeeded in 975

The martyrdom of St Edmund, king of East Anglia, as imagined by a 19th-century illustrator of a popular history.

at the age of 13 against the opposition of the supporters of his brother, the six-year-old Æthelred [II]. At that time the law of succession was not fixed and a joint kingship might have been arranged. But Edward's opponents could not bear that he should rule. On 18 March 978, the young King rode down to Corfe in Dorset to visit his brother. As the royal party approached, the retainers of Æthelred crowded round the King's horse in welcome, but once he was separated from his companions they stabbed him to death and carted the mangled corpse to hurried burial nearby. A year later the bones were solemnly reinterred in the church of the ancient hilltop town of Shaftesbury where, it was said, they worked miraculous cures.

A good case has been made out for believing that William II Rufus, who died in the New Forest in August 1100, was killed by a hired assassin. If not, wrote the historian Christopher Brooke, 'The most we can say is this: . . . Henry I [his brother] was an exceptionally lucky man'.

There was no doubt at all about the fate of Edward II, overthrown by his wife and her lover in 1327 and confined to the dank, rat-infested oubliettes of Berkeley Castle. When weeks in the foetid ordure of his own excretions had failed to kill him, he was finished off by the introduction of a red-hot 'brooch in the place posterial'. The idea, apparently, was that no mark should be left on his body. His tomb in Gloucester Cathedral became the focus of a cult and 60 years after his death his great-grandson, King Richard II, petitioned the pope, without success, for his canonization.

Richard, it seemed, tempted the evil eye, for he himself was deposed and surely murdered in Pontefract Castle by order of his cousin Henry IV. The sorry tale continued through Henry's grandson Henry VI, secretly done away with in the Tower of London on the orders of his rival Edward IV, and the mysterious deaths of Edward's sons, the Princes in the Tower, who were killed, said his enemies, by their uncle Richard III.

Compared with these skulking crimes, the Scottish procedure has an almost melodramatic splendour. After a catalogue of Dark Ages dynastic murders to match those of the English, with Kenneth II (971–95) we come to something of a novelty. He died victim of a crime of passion. A lady love sent him the present of a bronze image which proffered a golden apple in its hand. When the King took the apple, a spring mechanism was triggered that released a dart piercing his heart. Constantine III (995–7) was killed by his successor Kenneth III and Duncan II (May–Nov 1094), on the orders of his half brother Edmund (reigned 1097–1107).

The death of James III of Scotland (1460–88) is still something of a mystery. Fleeing the field after his defeat at the Battle of Sauchieburn, the King was thrown

heavily from his horse. Desperately hurt, he dragged himself to a crofter's cottage and called for a priest. The unknown man who came, instead of giving absolution, drew a knife from his cassock and murdered the King. Neither the motive nor the identity of the killer has ever been discovered.

On 20 February 1437 James I, who after 13 years of strong and often ruthless rule had antagonized many of the nobility, was staying at Perth. At about midnight, the castle was filled with the clatter and savage cries of armed men who had crossed the moat on planks laid by co-conspirators in the King's household. Wakened by the commotion, James shifted the floorboards of a ground-floor room and, being a man of 'excessive corpulence', lowered himself into the vaulted culvert that fed the drains beyond the castle wall only to find the exit had been blocked off. Hoping to find another escape route, he levered himself up through the hole, only to be caught by the assassins making one last search. The deed was done but the follow-through was bungled. James's son was crowned within weeks and the murderers and the masterminds behind the plot were hunted down in their turn. Their fate was grisly— one was crowned with a glowing circlet of red-hot iron.

The most extraordinary assassination in the annals of British royalty was that of Henry Stuart, Lord Darnley, proclaimed king by the royal heralds in the chapel of Holyrood at his marriage to Mary Queen of Scots, on 29 July 1565. Both marriage and consort were deeply unpopular, only his father among the assembled nobles responding to the proclamation with a loyal 'God save his Grace!' Darnley began his reign as king consort with many enemies.

Left: 'The Murder of King James I of Scotland' by a 19th-century history painter.

Right: An artist's impression of the attempt on the life of George III by Margaret Nicholson on 2 August 1786.

At two o'clock on the morning of Monday 10 February 1567 Kirk o'Field, an old collegiate house just outside the city wall of Edinburgh, blew apart with a roar that awakened the whole city. The explosion was followed by a furnace of flame and within hours the building was a blackened stump of a ruin. At the time of the explosion, Kirk o'Field had been empty, except for the presence of the King and his valet. It would seem they had been 'blawn up wi' pooder', as a contemporary account had it, yet in fact the two bodies were found half naked and strangled, their clothes nearby, beneath a pear tree in the garden some way from the ruins.

The Queen was at a wedding masque ball in the Palace of Holyroodhouse with the Earl of Bothwell and other nobles. Her husband was on his sickbed with a foul disease, possibly smallpox, and the party-goers had been with him only a few hours before, attempting to cheer him. The fact that Queen Mary and Bothwell were lovers and married shortly after the event and that witnesses reported having seen the Earl's men storing gunpowder beneath the house, inevitably led to accusations that he was responsible for the deaths, probably with her connivance. It has never been proved.

If Mary was implicated, she suffered a just fate both for that and the plot against the life of her cousin Elizabeth that she lent her name to, being executed—judicially murdered, say her devotees—at Fotheringhay Castle. Her grandson Charles I died on a scaffold in Whitehall and his grandson, the Duke of Monmouth, was also executed for treason before the killings in the luckless line of Stuart came to an end.

Their successors, the Hanoverians, did not raise such fatal passions. Nevertheless, there were at least three attempts, bungled though they may have been, on the life of George III.

On 2 August 1786, he was getting out of his carriage at the garden entrance to St James's Palace, when Margaret Nicholson, daughter of a barber from Stockton-on-Tees who believed the crown was hers by right, pushed her way out of the crowd and thrust out a paper at the King. As he bent forward to look, she produced a knife and tried to stab him to death. In fact the blade was so flimsy that it bent on the King's waistcoat. Onlookers overpowered her and for a moment it seemed she would be torn limb from limb. But George, genuinely interested as well as concerned, interposed with the words: 'The poor creature is mad; do not hurt her; she has not hurt me.' She was duly put up for trial and made her claim to the throne. If she were not made queen, England would be deluged in blood for a thousand years. Asked as to how she knew this, Nicholson replied: 'It is a mystery.' She was judged insane.

In 1795 George III was riding in his state coach to the opening of Parliament when the crowd surged forward with cries of 'Bread, bread, bread, peace, no King!' A shot was fired through the window of the coach as it passed into Old Palace Yard. On the way back rocks were hurled into the coach, several of which hit the King. The crowd forced the coach to a halt and George had to be rescued by the Horse Guards. A few months later, the Queen was hit in the face by a stone as she was leaving Drury Lane Theatre. It is not surprising that George told Lord Eldon that he would probably be the last King of England.

On 15 May 1800, George was at a military review in Hyde Park when a shot rang out and one of his atten-

In November 1605 the government of King James I uncovered a plot, laid by a number of Catholic gentlemen, chief among them Guy Fawkes, to blow up parliament and the King. History's most sensational assassination attempt may have been connived at by government agent provocateurs. Before each State Opening of Parliament the cellars of the Houses of Parliament are ceremoniously searched by the Yeomen of the Guard.

dants collapsed with a leg wound. The culprit was not traced, and the event was dismissed as an accident. London, however, was soon abuzz with rumour. When George appeared in the royal box at Drury Lane that evening for a comedy starring Mrs Jordan (his brother William [IV]'s mistress), the audience gave him a loyal standing ovation.

The box was flanked by Yeomen of the Guard, their halberds conscientiously at the ready. But these proved inadequate to their purpose when James Hadfield rose from his place in the pit, mounted the bench, levelled a pistol at the King and fired. Missing by inches, the bullet embedded itself in the woodwork of the box. After recoiling with surprise George, to his courtiers' dismay, calmly returned to the front of the box to survey the theatre, now in turmoil, through his opera glasses. The would-be assassin was overpowered by the guards and George ordered the play to continue after Mrs Jordan had led a fervent rendering of 'God Save the King'. The play, apparently, did not grip the King's attention as he fell asleep during the interval. At his trial it emerged that Hadfield was a former soldier who had received severe head wounds on active service. The verdict was guilty but insane.

Three years later another attempt was planned by a Colonel Despard. He and six others plotted to fire on the state coach carrying the King to the 1803 opening of Parliament with one of the captured French cannons on show in St James' Park. The madcap scheme was discovered in time and, although Despard had a gallant war record, he and his accomplices were hanged.

The attempts on the life of Victoria, George's grand-daughter, were equally feckless but none the less frightening for that. Between 1840 and 1842 no fewer than three assailants, working alone for a confused mix of real or imagined political grievances, attacked the Queen in the streets of London. The first of these occurred as the Queen and Prince Albert were being driven up Constitution Hill in an open landau, when a young man fired twice without effect. Making no attempt to resist arrest the youth was hauled off while the Queen, after being driven to her mother's house to set her mind at rest, continued on her way. All the 'equestrians formed themselves into an escort, and attended her back to the palace, cheering vehemently'.

In May 1849 an unemployed Irish labourer called John Hamilton levelled a pistol at Queen Victoria as she rode in her carriage in the park, while the following year a deranged ex-officer of the Hussars was able to approach closely enough to strike the Queen a severe blow to the head with his stick. Although a little concussed, Victoria pluckily kept her engagement at the opera that evening and was given a standing ovation from an affectionate audience. When so much is made of today's carefully policed royal walkabouts, it is interesting to see how dangerously accessible Victoria was to her subjects.

As the 19th century advanced, European monarchs had reason to go in fear of their lives. The Empress Elizabeth was shot down in Geneva, of all places, while the Russian Tsar Alexander II was killed in his own capital of St Petersburg by a bomb thrown at his carriage by an anarchist. Even Edward [VII] found himself initiated into the full status of a European autocrat when an anarchist called Sipido took a pot shot at him as his train pulled out of a Brussels station. He was bound for Copenhagen, where he was to celebrate Easter. Since that time until 1981 when the shots rang out over Horse Guards in London, no attempt is known to have been made on the life of a British sovereign.

INDEX

To avoid a long list of single-name page entries, numerous lesser figures, mostly early kings and princes, have been omitted from this index. However, many have brief mentions in the lists and short outlines for the early Anglo-Saxon kingdoms, pages 32–4; Ireland, 18–19; Scotland, 20–1; and Wales, 22–4. Many of the principal monarchs will also be found in the genealogical tree (p. 52–3 and 84–5) specially designed by the author of the *Guinness Book of British Royalty*. Readers are also recommended to study the magnificent series of coats of arms in the frontispiece (caption on p. 4) specially drawn for this book by the heraldic artist, Charles Heath-Saunders.

Page numbers in italics indicate illustrations.